Happiness, Morality, and Freedom

Studies in Moral Philosophy

The titles published in this series are listed at *brill.com/simp*

Happiness, Morality, and Freedom

By

Arthur Melnick

BRILL

LEIDEN | BOSTON

Library of Congress Cataloging-in-Publication Data

Melnick, Arthur.
  Happiness, morality, and freedom / by Arthur Melnick.
    pages cm. -- (Studies in moral philosophy, ISSN 2211-2014 ; VOLUME 8)
  Includes bibliographical references and index.
  ISBN 978-90-04-28320-6 (hardback : alk. paper) -- ISBN 978-90-04-28321-3 (e-book)
  1. Happiness. 2. Ethics. 3. Liberty. I. Title.

BJ1481.M47 2014
170--dc23

2014029511

This publication has been typeset in the multilingual "Brill" typeface. With over 5,100 characters covering Latin, IPA, Greek, and Cyrillic, this typeface is especially suitable for use in the humanities. For more information, please see www.brill.com/brill-typeface.

ISSN 2211-2014
ISBN 978-90-04-28320-6 (hardback)
ISBN 978-90-04-28321-3 (e-book)

This book is printed on acid-free paper.

Printed by Printforce, the Netherlands

For John Senters

∴

Contents

Introduction

The central place of morality in our lives is threatened on the one hand by the pursuit of happiness and on the other by a lack of freedom according to which we can be held morally responsible. If a person's pursuit of happiness is promoted by doing what is morally wrong on occasion then it is unclear why he should act against his happiness by avoiding wrong doing. What is the motivation for a person to go against his own happiness? Even if it can be shown that there is good reason to avoid wrong doing morality would have no significant place in our lives if we lack the freedom to avoid wrong doing. Morality would be an inert ideal capable perhaps of stirring feelings of regret when it is violated but otherwise incapable of guiding our lives and governing our relation to one another.

One could try to settle the issue of the place of morality in our lives directly by considering in its own right what value morality has. Unless however morality is the ground or source of all value this would leave it open that what else has value has a claim against morality. Without settling what is at the bottom of anything's having value no consideration of values that morality realizes will secure its predominant place over all other values. But now following Aristotle it is happiness that is our final good and our final end. Happiness, whatever else, lies at the bottom of all that we value for our lives and all that we aim for in our lives. Just as truth is the final good and the final end of our theoretical endeavors, happiness is the final good and the final end of our practical endeavors. The surest way then to secure the place of morality in our lives is to find a conception of happiness by which it is the ground of all value and then show that morality is essential to happiness so conceived. The task of Part One is to set out a conception of what it is to be happy that in this way secures the place of morality in our lives.

Being completely self-fulfilled by how our lives are going would seem to be at the bottom of our values and aims. Something is valuable to us all things considered if its realization in our lives contributes to complete self-fulfillment since there is nothing but ourselves for value to be responsible to. Likewise something is to be aimed for all things considered if what it aims for is valuable to us all things considered. Part of being self-fulfilled is being fulfilled in our emotional nature. Only if we are predominantly content or serene or buoyant or blissful in our lives are we emotionally fulfilled in how our lives are going. We are more than emotional creatures however. When we think of our lives certain aspects of how our lives are going may or may not appeal to us even if we are emotionally content. That contentment can seem worthless, insignificant and unfounded. A person may be content or joyous for the most part and yet find his life to lack meaning when he thinks about it. Such thinking then estranges him from the contentment he feels. When a person finds himself thus estranged from his contentment he fails to be self-fulfilled. Self-fulfillment requires not just emotional contentment but the endorsement of how one's life is going when one evaluates it. To be happy then requires that one be satisfied with how one's life is going not just emotionally, but also in the conception of it. It requires that one's life is going according to a standard the person has for what constitutes a way for it to be going that is appealing in the thought of it. Self-fulfillment requires besides fulfillment of our nature as emotional beings, fulfillment of our nature as valuing beings.

We are also reasoning beings. If our standard of satisfaction is not in turn appealing to our reasoning nature – if we find certain ways in which life can go to be appealing but the appeal makes no sense to us when we consider grounds or reasons for it – then we are not completely self-fulfilled by how our lives are going. Our values would be estranged from our nature as reasoning beings. But now grounds or reasons themselves fulfill us as reasoning beings only in so far as they in turn conform to a norm of what makes for good reasons. It is in giving ourselves over to such a norm of reason that we are fulfilled as reasoning beings. Ultimately then only if a person's standard for being satisfied with how his life is going conforms to a norm of having good reasons for that standard is the person fulfilled in his entire nature in regard to how his life is going.

Overall a person is happy with how his life is going if he is satisfied both emotionally and in conception with how it is going according to a standard for being satisfied that he can claim or own as a reasoning being. Only so is the person in all his aspects fulfilled in regard to how his life is going. It is because being happy is identified with complete self-fulfillment that happiness is the final good and the final end of our practical being. There is nothing about us, so to speak, in regard to feelings, values, aims, and reasons, that is left out to "challenge" happiness as the point or focus of our practical existence.

If it is supposed that there is no conclusive, definitive proof of what the standard is for being satisfied with how our lives are going, then the norm of reason regarding standards is to be open to whatever reasons there may be for or against standards. To pursue happiness is to consider reasons for adopting a standard and reconsider the standard in the light of how things pan out. The original reasons are prospective and may or may not hold up in the face of reasons that one hasn't anticipated as one considers the standard in retrospect. But then it is in others' pursuit of happiness that reasons for and against standards of satisfaction are to be found. To fail to have regard for others' pursuit of happiness is to fail to have regard for prospective and retrospective reasons for standards of satisfaction. It follows that only if I have regard for others' pursuit of happiness do I give myself over to the norm of reason appropriate to the open, non-conclusive nature of standards of satisfaction. If I am to pursue happiness then my pursuits in life must be consistent with what it is to be happy. Since that involves being self-fulfilled as a reasoning being which in turn involves regard for others' pursuit of happiness, it follows that my pursuit of happiness, and whatever happiness I may achieve thereby, entails regard for the pursuit of happiness of others.

To have regard for others' pursuit of happiness is to respect and care enough for it. If I interfere with another's pursuit I interfere with, block, or distort their prospective and retrospective reasons. If I fail to promote another's pursuit I diminish or keep prospective and retrospective reasons from arising. In either case I fail to give myself over to the norm of having regard for whatever reasons there may be for or against my own standard of satisfaction. Hence it goes against what it is for me to be happy if I fail to respect and care enough for others' pursuit of happiness.

If we define an act to be wrong just in case it fails to respect or care enough for others' pursuit of happiness then it follows that doing wrong always, no matter what, goes against my own happiness. In this way the threat against the central place of morality in our lives from supposed competing claims of happiness is removed. There are no *competing* claims.

This definition of an act being wrong implies that the fundamental principle of morality is to respect and care enough for the pursuit of happiness of others. In Part Two the content of this principle is clarified. What does caring enough mean? How does respecting relate to caring enough when these seem to conflict with one another? What does the principle come to in relation to future generations, animals, and the environment? Also in Part Two the principle is clarified and defended by contrasting it with competing accounts of morality – both those which put forth other fundamental principles (utilitarianism, contractualism, principles of rational agency and autonomy) and those which demote the importance of fundamental principles altogether (virtue theory). The claim is that as regards both content and comparison to other accounts the fundamental principle of morality of respect and care for others' pursuit of happiness provides a cogent account of morality. Hence the justification of the principle as integral to what it is to be happy is indeed a justification of morality.

If moral failings go against one's own pursuit of happiness, and if being held responsible for such failings is a way of restoring that pursuit, then to be held responsible is for one's own good. Hence to deserve to be held responsible requires only that one be capable upon being held responsible of restoring one's pursuit of happiness. Only someone who has the capacity to pursue happiness has the capacity to restore themselves to this pursuit when they fail to exercise their capacity by doing something wrong. The freedom that is required for being held responsible is just that freedom that constitutes the capacity to pursue happiness. Persons with such freedom then deserve (for their own good) to be held responsible for moral failings. Part Three sets out what conception of freedom constitutes the capacity to pursue happiness. This conception first involves that one's actions be subject to determination in accord with the norm of reason for standards of satisfaction, even on occasions when in fact one's actions fail to accord with that norm. This much is a version of a classical compatibilist conception of freedom. However unless it is the self or the agent that determines actions to be in accord or not with the norm of reason, it isn't the self or the agent that gives itself over to the norm—in which case there is no *self*-fulfillment as a reasoning being. Once it is realized that it is the presence of the self or the agent in consciousness that has to be what determines actions and that this is not the presence of an entity but of a dynamic condition from which control of action emerges, then determination of action by an agent is not a case of problematic entity causation at all. Nor, however, is it a case of sub-personal processes going on in the agent. Finally, the capacity to pursue happiness entails a kind of ultimacy in the determination of actions to be in accord or not with the norm of reason. It turns out that unless the agent is the ultimate source of this determination the person is estranged from his giving himself over to the norm of reason and so is not after all completely self-fulfilled. This ultimacy however is not an ontological causal ultimacy, but an ultimacy of the person's place in relation to himself and others in the pursuit of happiness. Freedom, so understood as involving ultimate determination by the conscious agent, is claimed to be something un-problematically real. Since this is the freedom constitutive of the capacity to pursue happiness and so the freedom required for being held morally responsible, the threat against the central place of morality in our lives from a supposed lack of freedom by which we deserve to be held morally responsible is removed.

PART 1

Happiness

∵

CHAPTER 1

Happiness as Endorsed Contentment

(i)

Being happy with how one's life is going involves not just endorsing it as going well or as proceeding in a way that is worthwhile, but also being emotionally content or positive. Van Gogh might endorse his life as a painter as worthwhile and valuable, but his emotional distress and lack of emotional contentment implies that he fails to be happy with how his life is going. Conversely a person might be emotionally content and serene, but find this contentment insufficient for endorsing how his life is going. He might have everything he wants in his life, but still hold it to be lacking for failing to be worthwhile or valuable. A person needn't be malcontent, anxious, or despondent in order to find his life lacks the meaning or significance that is needed for him to be fulfilled or happy. Only when emotional satisfaction harmonizes with one's life going in a way that one can endorse and appreciate is one happy both in heart and mind.

The emotional component of happiness is rich and varied, but a few aspects seem to be universal and inherent to the emotional condition. One cannot be happy with what is happening while being basically depressed about it. One cannot be happy with one's circumstances and yet basically troubled by them. One cannot be happy with one's lot and be in a continual state of anxiety about it. On the other hand one can be happy with one's friend even though disturbed at what they just said to you, and one can be happy in, even though presently struggling with, furthering one's endeavors. Happiness is consistent with the existence of negative emotional component so long as one's overall basic emotional condition is positive.

There are different varieties of positive affect. One can be blissfully happy or ecstatically happy, but one can also be serenely happy. In each of these cases one is emotionally content. One's being thus content is incompatible with one's predominant or overall state being one of anxiety or depression or cold indifference. Anxiety opposes contentment in that it is an unsettled, troubled state-not a state within which one can rest content. On the other hand depression is a state that we can rest in. It isn't per se an unsettled state of turmoil. Although we can be resigned to our depression, we cannot be content in being depressed. In a state of melancholy sadness is encompassed within a wider emotional state of contentment (it is bitter sweet), but predominant sadness

© KONINKLIJKE BRILL NV, LEIDEN, 2014 | DOI 10.1163/9789004283213_002

that is not so encompassed, although it is not necessarily a troubled state, is not a state of contentment.

The positive affect of contentment has at least two components of being an overall settled state, versus anxiety or turmoil, and being an overall "expansive" state. In depression one is withdrawn, contracted inward, even tightened or strained. In cold indifference or boredom one is neither outward and expansive nor inward and strained. In being blissful or serene on the other hand, one's state is settled in an overall relaxed way even if the relaxation is intense as in bliss. These various emotional conditions are holistic states of the body. It is my body as a whole that is settled into an expansive relaxed condition. It is my body as a whole that is settled into a contracted and strained condition in curling up on itself as in depression. Likewise my body as a whole is unsettled by alternately tending to contract and withdraw, to be braced on the one hand while struggling to open up as with anxiety. It is as overall bodily conditions that these emotional states are incompatible with each other.

Moods have the character of being overall emotional states. If one is in a despondent mood all of one's particular feelings are tempered by and infused with the despondency. One may feel cheerful at the smile of a child, but this feeling is engulfed and tempered by one's despondency, whereas the despondency is not in the same way engulfed and tempered by the cheer. The despondency suffuses any cheerful feeling, which feeling seems to float as foreign within one's emotional condition. Although I feel cheer I am not overall cheered by the child's smile, nor am I filled with or immersed in the cheer.

One's overall state is not a mere balance or summation of two feelings of despondency and cheer, but a certain organization that asymmetrically structures the feelings. This is one way that hedonism which calculates individual feelings and their intensity to arrive at an overall sum is mistaken as to the emotional component of happiness. We don't aim to obtain pleasurable feelings; we aim to be in an overall mood of contentment, serenity, or bliss. Even if one's despondency is not intense while one's pleasure at the child's smile is, it is still the case that one is taken up with the despondency, not the pleasure. Similarly one's contentment need not be intense to be predominant and encompassing. When one's mood is stable over time it can evolve into a familiar non-intense (almost diaphanous) state that nevertheless remains the predominant coloring pervading one's condition. Consider someone watching a fearful movie and having intense feelings of fear. Despite the intensity the fear doesn't grip them because their overall mood is one of being calm in a safe movie theatre. A mountain climber may be content and even ecstatic despite having feelings of fear and anxiety. The deeper, wider, more inclusive component of an emotional state needn't be the one that is most intense.

As Haybron (2008;319) notes the condition of contentment is not an experience at all and so a fortiori not a pleasurable experience. It doesn't follow from this that it is not a pleasurable condition. Clearly conditions of despondency or anxiety which are opposed to contentment are unpleasant conditions to be in. If so then contentment even when mild or serene would seem to be a pleasurable condition to be in. The positive emotional moods are outgoing, extroverted or engaging. In such a mood one's body is open and at ease for active engagement. Because of this one's attention in such a condition is likely to be outwardly focused on what one is engaging with rather than focused on the mood itself. It is for this reason that the condition of contentment can seem almost diaphanous. It isn't that it isn't a pleasurable condition to be in, but rather that we barely focus on its pleasurable character. Still when we enter into a state of contentment from one of anxiety or despondency we can and do focus on it and it becomes something experienced as pleasurable.

One may momentarily settle into a state of contentment. If, for example one has been in great danger and the danger has now passed, one may temporarily settle into a calm serene mood. In this mood any annoyances which might in other circumstances be deeply troubling may still trouble one, but the troubling feelings don't grip one or take one over. They are there somewhat at a distance. In such a case we can say that for the moment at least we are happy. However what we aim for in life are not momentary pockets of contentment but stable lasting contentment. We aim to be in and remain in a condition of basic contentment. As long as someone is in such an enduring condition he is happy in his life. The aim is that the contentment be the condition of emotional stable equilibrium. One may temporarily get dislodged from the condition, but not easily dislodged from it, and when dislodged there is a tendency to snap back into it. Haybron (2008;135) calls this a condition of emotional resilience.

The emotional component of being happy in one's life is not a mere disposition to be in a content mood. Rather it is being in such a mood which actually remains stable. Being disposed to be content is a matter of temperament. An organism may be naturally disposed to be content but circumstances in its life make it a nervous, anxious, or depressed individual. If it has a sunny or calm temperament then so long as circumstances are not too unfortunate it will be and remain content and so happy in its life. Such a temperament is not being happy, but only being disposed to be happy. An organism with a nervous or sullen temperament might yet be happy in its life if circumstances are favorable enough for its predominant mood to be calm or serene. Stable mood is a resultant of temperament and fortune. Such temperaments are particularly clear in dogs. Some dogs are naturally joyful and calm, while others are naturally nervous. The naturally joyful temperament of a dog can be beaten down by repeated cruelty so that it becomes an anxious and depressed dog. It doesn't just become anxious and depressed in a way that allows it to snap back into its original sunny nature. There has been a change not just in the predominant mood in its life, but a change in temperament. It is hard for the dog to be content even if circumstances improve. Being happy in one's life is sensitive to circumstances or fortune, while temperament is a gage of the extent to which happiness is thus sensitive. Pain, sickness, hunger, isolation will preclude even an organism with the most sunny disposition from being happy in its life. An extremely nervous, fearful or sullen temperament will preclude the organism from being happy even in the best of circumstances.

One can be in a stable condition of emotional contentment and so happy within one's life without having any conception at all of how one's life is going, let alone a conception of how it is going that one endorses. This seems to be the case with animals. Human beings emotionally content in their lives, however, may yet not be satisfied with how their lives are going in that they do not value or endorse how their lives are. This may be so even though the lack of endorsement doesn't particularly dislodge their contentment. It needn't make them anxious or depressed. Still, such persons cannot claim their contentment as fully their own. Although they are content within their lives, still their lives, including their contentment within, are not fulfilling to them because some part of them, the part that assesses how their lives are going, is not fulfilled. They are emotionally positive, but not fully positive in regard to their lives. Their contentment, though real and even intense, may seem shallow to them and something foreign to them when they think about what their lives come to. They do not completely, if at all, identify with their contentment not because they prefer anxiety or despondency, but because the contentment seems unfounded in their own eyes.

To say that happiness is what we seek entails that we also seek to avoid or correct unhappiness. Suppose that our emotional contentment is not sensitive to our failing to endorse how our lives are going. The failure of endorsement, that is, leaves our purely emotional state of contentment intact. Since the failure to endorse doesn't unsettle us emotionally, we would not be motivated to find a new direction for our lives that would make our lives something we can endorse. The failure of endorsement would be no more than a thoughtful apprehension of our lives as falling short, juxtaposed with no emotional push to alter it. We would be stuck then in the unhappy condition of a contentment we cannot identify with. The failure of endorsement has to lead to enough emotional mal-content to set us off onto a change in our lives if we are to avoid being stuck in unhappiness. Equivalently, one's contentment must be sensitive to the failure to identify with it. Since in seeking happiness we seek to avoid unhappiness, it follows that we do not seek a juxtaposition of emotional contentment and dispassionate positive endorsement, but an emotional contentment that is sensitive to, or tracks positive endorsement. On the other hand we do not seek mere positive endorsement, but endorsement that carries with it emotional contentment. Van Gogh may endorse a life of painting for himself. To his mind no other kind of life is worthwhile. Clearly in his case that endorsement is not effective in making him emotionally content. Just as clearly he was not happy despite living the life he endorsed. To endorse something is to find it appealing in thought or to be content in the idea of it. This contentment attaches to or suffuses, so to speak, just the thinking and considering aspect of the person. Since the whole body is not specifically involved in thinking, and emotional contentment is a full body condition, there is the possibility of a discrepancy between finding one's life appealing and being emotionally content.

To be happy with how one's life is going is for one's contentment to be in part directed by one's idea that it is going well. This involves having a conception of how it is going, a conception that one approves of or stands behind. Animals have lives and their lives go certain ways, but apparently they do not have conceptions of having lives or conceptions of their lives over long stretches going certain ways. Therefore they cannot endorse how their lives are going. To endorse is to positively evaluate and what is up for evaluation is my conception or understanding of how my life is going. This is not to say that how an animal's life is going doesn't influence whether they are content or not. A dog subject to repeated cruel treatment is hardly likely to be content. The lack of contentment in the dog however is not directed toward how its life is going – it is only an upshot of it. Because of the lack of conception the animal may be happy (content) *in* the course of its life, but cannot be happy *with* (in regard to) the course of its life.

Suppose a person endorses his life simply in that his basic animal needs are met. Having enough water and food, not being sick or in pain, etc. is sufficient for the person's endorsement. The conditions that make for an animal being happy *in* how its life is are pretty much the same as make the person happy *with how his life is going*. Such a person may be fully happy as a human being or happy in leading a human life, although the life he leads is pretty much the same as an animal happy in its life. The person's contentment is directed toward how his life is going. The person, that is, has his life as an object of conception (Scheler 1962). Whether those same circumstances make him happy depends on his endorsement of that conception, not just on being in those circumstances. A person who does not endorse such a conception will not be happy under those same circumstances of having his animal needs met. At least to some extent the circumstances that make for a person's being happy depend upon what they endorse. As far as human happiness is concerned circumstances are filtered through what conception of life a person endorses. In this sense we in part determine what circumstances are fortunate and what counts as a misfortune. Endorsement is not a perfect filter. Even circumstances that conform to endorsement may not be enough for happiness if they overwhelm the sensitivity of contentment to endorsement breaking the bond between them. A person emotionally beaten down by others or by poverty may endorse how his life is going as an artist, while yet circumstances extrinsic to that endorsement leave him unhappy.

To the extent that a person's contentment is sensitive to his endorsement, circumstances that might emotionally grip an animal as troubling might not grip the person as troubling. The mountain climber may feel fear at his dangerous circumstances but his fear is encompassed emotionally by an exuberant contentment sensitive to a conception of living that he endorses. A dog in such a circumstance is gripped by fear. A person may fast for religious reasons and be content with his hunger, whereas for an animal there is no contentment in its hunger. Our primitive emotional reactions are similar to animals. Danger calls up anxiety or fear; hunger calls up unpleasant unsettledness. Emotional sensitivity to endorsement in humans enables these reactions to be emotionally encompassed within and tempered by contentment. Humans then can be emotionally content (happy in their lives) in ways that are more complex than animals and in ways quite different than animals in regard to circumstances and fortune. Sensitivity to endorsement is thus a two edged sword. On the one hand we may fail to be happy or content with what makes an animal happy due to lack of endorsement, but on the other hand we may succeed in being happy where an animal fails due to the filtering of circumstances through endorsement.

(ii)

What we aim for in our lives is a continuing and resilient condition of endorsed contentment. What we aim at is a continuing ongoing happiness with how our lives are going. Despite the inclusion of an emotional component this may still seem to be an artificially over-intellectualized understanding of happiness. People don't often seem to have a fully worked-out explicit conception of how their lives are going to either endorse or fail to endorse. Further, even to the extent that they have a conception of how their lives are going they aren't often endorsing it or failing to endorse it. In spite of this we don't deny that people can be happy with how their lives are going. The question is how to understand the role of endorsing a conception of how one's life is going in regard to happiness, when we so seldom seem to do that while yet being happy. The problem is that it seems to be habits or skills of facility in living that drive contentment and with it constitute happiness rather than abstract conceptions that are endorsed.

The response is that a person can be happy with how their lives are going without explicit endorsement, so long as endorsement is a standing condition of the person. A person can have a standing intention to behave a certain way in certain circumstances which remains in force and evolves over long periods of time without his explicitly reformulating it. Similarly a person can have a standing endorsed conception of how his life is going in force over long periods of his life without explicitly reformulating the endorsement. A standing intention will show up as a sense of behaving appropriately and a sense of owning behavior that is in accord with it; a sense that a person without the standing intention will not have. Similarly a standing endorsed contentment will show up through the person's life as a sense that things are going smoothly and felicitously; a sense that things are going as they should and that the felicity in the way our life is going belongs to us. Even when the person's condition is no more *explicitly* intellectual or conception-driven than an animal whose life is proceeding felicitously, the person though not the animal has a sense of owning the felicity of it. Engaged as we are in the skill of living we need not and often do not attend to what the source is of our sense that our lives are running smoothly (which source is the standing endorsement). When we start to feel deep and wide malcontent or when circumstances fail us or when our endorsements fail to stand up to what we learn about that kind of life by living it, the sense of our lives going well is disturbed or comes apart and we may revert explicitly to the issue of what to endorse.

A second related objection of over-intellectualizing is that we have no determinate conception of how our lives are going to serve as the object of endorsement. Whereas the first objection is that endorsed conceptions aren't explicitly involved in periods when we are happy with our lives, the second objection is that there are no determinate conceptions to be had at all as the content of even a standing endorsement. According to this objection the sense of how our lives are going is basically practical – a matter of developed habits and skills, not a matter of even implicit conceptual recognition. As an analogy consider an organism's condition of being familiar with a certain environment. Experience, practice in getting around in it, manipulating aspects of it, etc. is the basis of its familiarity, far outstripping any concepts or intellectual grasp of its surroundings. No determinate conceptions are adequate as the basis of its gained sense of familiarity and so felicity in getting around. It isn't just a matter of a conceptual grasp not being explicitly employed. It is a matter of there being no such conception to employ. Similarly, so the objection goes, for our familiarity with how our lives are going A sense of smoothness and felicity with how our lives are going is due to a practical grasp or familiarity with it—not to any conception of it which may or may not be endorsed.

When a person conceptually grasps what it is about an environment that is familiar, even if the grasp is only partial and indeterminate, he can indicate it and explain it to others and to himself without having to engage it in its familiarity. The conceptual grasp is not a substitute for practical familiarity, but a way of communicating it to those without practical familiarity of that environment. They thereby gain some practical sense of how to deal with that environment without having to engage it. If it is a dangerous environment that the other has no sense of it is important that they be able to gain this sense without having to engage the environment. Similarly a conceptual grasp of how my life is going may be partial and indeterminate in that it is far outstripped by experience and practice in getting on with my life that way. The point is that endorsement of my life going on that way doesn't have to await this further practical specification and enrichment of how that will be. By endorsing it as a somewhat favorable way of my life continuing on I am led to or directed to enter into this future, while evaluating it in an unfavorable way leads me to avoid that future without having to engage it. Once I endorse my life going on a certain way the further engagement with it (living of it) gives me a deeper practical sense or comprehension of such a way of going on. When I am led to the further practical engagement (living that way) by an anticipatory conception that is endorsed there will also be a sense that how my life is going belongs to me, that it is owned by me, and that it is directed by me. This further sense is an essential component of a person's being happy with how their lives are going, and does not require the anticipatory conceptual grasp to be as determinate and detailed as what we get from living that way.

(iii)

The view that being happy with how our lives are going is a matter of endorsed contentment with it is basically equivalent to the view Sumner (1996;143) holds-

> It seems roughly right to say that we are happy when we have a (preponderantly) affirmative attitude toward the conditions of our lives.

This affirmative attitude for Sumner includes cognitive aspects or judgment, as well as an affective component of feeling satisfied or fulfilled. This feeling must be emotionally wide and deep constituting an overall emotionally positive condition of contentment. If the satisfaction is purely intellectual, failing to pervade our emotional condition, it would allow that Van Gogh in all his ongoing emotional distress was happy with his life for his affirmative attitude toward a life of painting. Roger Crisp (2006;116–117) contends that if appreciation (the satisfaction that comes from endorsement) can contribute to welfare (happiness) alongside enjoyment, it should be able to contribute to it on its own. Van Gogh's appreciation of his painting could have contributed to his happiness, but it didn't, and it didn't because it was not "alongside" enjoyment or contentment. The positive affect that comes from endorsement has to be adequate to emotional contentment if it is to contribute to happiness. On its own, without the emotional contentment, it is tantamount to the way our lives are going having value or meaning by our own lights, but not to our being happy with how our lives are going.

The view of happiness as endorsed contentment requiring a positive attitude both cognitively and emotionally is what Haybron (2008;99) calls a hybrid understanding of the life satisfaction view of happiness. As the van Gogh case makes clear a "pure" view of life satisfaction as sheer cognitive satisfaction is inadequate. The life satisfaction view then is to be understood in the hybrid way. Since emotional contentment is clearly necessary, the defense of the life satisfaction view turns on whether emotional contentment alone is sufficient for happiness. For Haybron (2008;304) happiness consists totally in what he calls psychic flourishing. His understanding of such flourishing in terms of stable and resilient deep positive moods is basically the account of emotional contentment set out at the beginning of this chapter. Indeed much of that account was borrowed from Haybron. For Haybron this emotional component is all that is required. He holds (2008;84) that a person can be dissatisfied with his life (fail to endorse how it is going) and yet still be happy if he is for the most part untroubled and in good spirits. In a similar vein Feldman (2010;107) says,

> ...it is possible for a person to be very happy even though he never makes any judgment about the extent to which his life measures up to his ideals...there very well might be some who are in fact happy, but who would make negative judgments about their lives if they were called upon to make such judgments.

For Haybron and Feldman happiness is consistent with failing to endorse one's life at all and even with negative endorsement.

Haybron holds that the hybrid view conflates two notions which should be kept distinct-happiness (emotional contentment) and life having value by the subject's own lights (endorsement). I contend it is Haybron who is conflating being happy *in* one's life as an animal can be, with being happy *with* one's life as only a person can be. The latter does involve two components (endorsed contentment) and so is a hybrid, but humans, unlike animals, are hybrid creatures. We aim at being happy with our lives. Even if what a particular person aims at is sheer emotional flourishing, to say he aims at it implies that he endorses it. To that particular person being happy in his life is all that matters to his being happy with his life. Haybron (2008;147) says that happiness on his view

> most fundamentally concerns an individual's emotional or psychic stance toward her life

But to have a stance towards one's life, as opposed to an emotional orientation within one's life, is to endorse one's life.

Haybron convincingly argues against hedonism that a pleasurable experience does not contribute to happiness unless it is emotionally deep. Even a depressed person can go from pleasure to pleasure, being driven by their depression to attain more pleasurable experiences than they ever did before they became depressed. This preponderance of pleasurable experiences Haybron would say is not emotionally deep enough for happiness. It doesn't grip our emotional psyche as a whole. Equivalently it is not emotionally fulfilling. But now human beings don't just have an emotional nature—they are also beings that consider and evaluate. Haybron's conception of happiness is too shallow and superficial for a human psyche that seeks to be satisfied in thought with their emotional condition. A person who is not depressed, sad, emotionally anxious or struggling, but yet finds his life as he considers it strangely unsatisfying, meaningless, etc. would find his emotional contentment not to be deeply fulfilling, but rather shallow, superficial, and something he can't own as a thinking being. Once again a hybrid view is appropriate because we are hybrid creatures. The two components of contentment and endorsement are not a conflation of two notions that need to be kept apart; they are two components that need to be integrated into a life one can be happy with.

Haybron (2008;193) allows for what he calls narrative-self-fulfillment, but contends it is something distinct from happiness. He calls it well-being at least by the subject's own lights. His idea seems to be that satisfaction of the narrative self goes on separately from emotional contentment. He says (2008;86) we typically seem not to have broad feelings of satisfaction or dissatisfaction with our lives to any degree,

and that such feelings arise only when we are reflective and so are short lived. If this were true then since happiness is supposedly a lasting ongoing condition it would follow that narrative endorsement would indeed be peripheral to happiness. I have already claimed that standing endorsement gives rise to a broad and persistent sense that one's life has a direction (one we are aiming to keep), and gives rise to a persistent sense that one's contentment belongs to one as opposed to a contentment that proceeds in a way that is independent from and foreign to oneself.

Haybron contends that life-satisfaction even as involving emotional contentment cannot be necessary for happiness because something like gratitude can be the source of a person's satisfaction rather than his life going well even by his own lights. But if gratitude is indeed sufficient for my endorsed contentment with how my life is going, then my life is going well by my own lights. This doesn't mean that things couldn't go better. It is no part of the endorsed contentment view that things for a person are going as well even by his own lights as they possibly could. A person can be happy though their foot hurts which is neither something that they care about or endorse. For the grateful person not having other things they endorse in their lives doesn't destroy their happiness. For them, though on a broader scale, it is like having a foot that hurts. This doesn't imply that gratitude is merely a way of lowering expectations (just be happy with what you have). The grateful person may endorse the vigorous pursuit of other things they consider important for their lives. It is just that the grateful person is content with his life as he aims vigorously to make it better by his own lights. One can be happy in pursuing important things one doesn't yet have. When gratitude functions as a source of endorsed contentment, it does track one's life going well, where part of one's life going well is that one is content to be pursuing other things one doesn't yet have. A person can be happy without being as happy as they can possibly be. Otherwise, for most of us at least we would never be happy. Similar considerations apply to Haybron's own view of happiness. Gratitude might be the source of a person's stable psychic flourishing (his overall deep positive emotional condition) even if by his own lights his life leaves much to be desired. Haybron is correct to hold that happiness should "track" subjective well-being, well-being by the subject's own lights. Where Haybron is mistaken is in thinking that subjective well-being is equivalent to having everything you care to have.

The gratitude objection to the life = satisfaction view is that one's standard for life-satisfaction may be too low in regard to one's subjective well-being.

A similar sort of objection may be made in regard to one's welfare. A person who is sick with a terminal disease may be more satisfied with how their lives are going than when they were healthy. A person who is paralyzed in an accident may be more satisfied than before the accident. There is no question that in each of these cases there has been a significant loss of welfare. By this I mean a loss in what options for happiness the person has. In this regard the person's capacity for happiness, by living such and such ways, has been diminished. This is different than the gratitude case because not yet having everything you can endorse for yourself is not a diminishment of the capacity to pursue things. Nothing the sick or injured person can endorse or feel changes the fact that he has suffered this loss in capacity, whereas in the gratitude case, his endorsing and being content with pursuing what he doesn't have determines whether he can be happy as things are. Happiness, however, is not the same thing as the capacity for happiness. Prior to the tragic loss the person might have had a greater capacity and not have exercised it well (his exercise of the capacity just didn't pan out) and so he was unhappy. After the loss the person manages to use his diminished capacity well. He gains perspective, appreciates what is really important and so is happier than he was before. This is not to say that he endorses his tragedy, but only to say that a person can be happier after such a tragedy. Nobody would aim for a terrible sickness or injury, in which case we seem to be left saying that happiness after those events is not what we aim for. However what we aim for is to be as happy through our lives as our condition allows. Otherwise we would have to say that since it is no part of a capability for happiness that we can flap our arms and fly around (as wonderful as that would be) that therefore we cannot be happy, but can only resigned to a second-grade level of endorsed contentment.

Haybron (2008;291) objects to the life-satisfaction view that judgments about how our lives are going are perspectival. Someone can judge himself satisfied in relation to others whose lives are going worse, while judging himself unsatisfied in relation to others whose lives seem to be going better. The issue here is not so much what judgments one is prepared to make on the spot. If I stab my toe or fail an exam I may judge that I hate my life or that life is terrible, but then I get a call from a friend I haven't seen in a while and judge that life is good. This kind of relativity of judgments is not an objection to the life-satisfaction view, for such judgments are poorly made. They are made in opposition to what one's stable condition of endorsed contentment is. Suppose then that a person's stable condition is one of only endorsing how their life is going in relation to how he thinks others are going. What such a person is flat-out endorsing is doing better than others. This is not an objection to the life-satisfaction view. Rather it is a kind of stable, resilient endorsed contentment one is not likely at all to achieve.

Haybron's last objection (2008;296) is that life satisfaction is unable to answer what the practical interests are in being happy. By this he means that it doesn't promote or lead to well-being even by the subject's own lights. It is somewhat odd to bring up an issue of the practical interest in happiness since happiness apparently is the basic aim of all our practical interests. Haybron's point can be recast as follows – If happiness is a condition that doesn't psychologically promote further engagement toward further well-being, then it is a self-defeating end or aim. Happiness, that is, has to be a condition that makes us practically good at sustaining it. It is true that a flourishing psyche or a deep positive emotional condition, as against depression or anxiety, will lead us to get on with engaging with life and so promote whatever well-being that engagement brings. But emotional flourishing is not enough for such getting on. We also have to have a conception of what way or ways to get on. On a more minor scale a person may be emotionally upbeat, optimistic and so ready to face the day. Without some conception of what the day is supposed to be, they are left just sitting there waiting for something to face, and thus not promoting a well-lived day. The life-satisfaction view incorporates what I endorse as well as emotional contentment. This gives me a direction of sustaining and further developing what I endorse about my life or what I find satisfying. Without this a positive emotional condition is inert. Of course happiness may not last; neither continued endorsement nor continued contentment is guaranteed. At least however the satisfaction view gives both direction and emotional aptness to further promotion of well-being.

Haybron raises significant issues in regard to the epistemology of happiness. How well do we know whether we are happy? How clear are we about our happiness? How stable is our knowledge of it? These are issues that will arise for any account of happiness. To think life-satisfaction accounts are specifically prone to any problems in these matters is to confuse issues about reflective judgments made at particular times with the underlying standing condition of happiness these judgments are about. All views of happiness will have issues regarding reflective judgments about whether we are happy. Only by thinking the life-satisfaction view makes such judgments constitutive of happiness will one think there are special problems with the view.

In sum, Haybron's account of happiness as emotional flourishing is at best an account of being happy in or during one's life rather than being happy with or in regard to one's life, which latter requires the contentment to align with endorsement. It is an account of happiness as deep emotional fulfillment, but unless that fulfillment is endorsed it is not an account of deep self-fulfillment for selves such as we are who require our thoughts of what is valuable and meaningful to be realized in order to be fulfilled. Further, emotional flourishing by itself is not tied to subjective well-being. At best, as with animals, it is tied to being carried along without direction by what comes up in life.

(iv)

The elements missing from the sheer emotional contentment view of happiness are missing as well from hedonistic accounts according to which happiness is a preponderance of pleasure in one's life. At best these are accounts of being happy in one's life, not with one's life, since they do not hold that the pleasure has to be endorsed. Further, they are not convincing even as accounts of being happy in one's life. A dog with an extremely nervous unsettled temperament may experience a great preponderance of pleasure in the circumstances of its life, while yet its continuing underlying deep and basic emotional condition is not at all a happy one. As noted, a depressed person may seek and attain a great preponderance of pleasurable experiences to cover up or flee from their depression and yet remain basically in a depressed condition. The hedonistic summing of individual pleasures and pains ignores the depth of "pleasure" that constitutes emotional contentment (Haybron:2001;525). Mill considers quality as well as quantity and intensity of pleasure. He seems to have in mind some distinction between higher pleasures (in art, love) and lower pleasures (food, sex). This distinction seems to concern how one's higher capacities are exercised in attaining the pleasure. A person is happy if there is a preponderance of pleasure in their lives weighted toward those pleasures that involve the exercise and perfecting of our intellectual and imaginative capacities. This would allow humans to be happy in a way that animals cannot be since pleasure is weighted toward specifically human (versions of) capacities. So understood, Mill's view would be a kind of perfectionist account of happiness according to which happiness consists in taking pleasure in what exercises and perfects our capacities. Such pleasure, however, is not necessarily sufficient for emotional contentment. Van Gogh's anxiousness and emotional unsettledness remains despite the fact that he seems to come out high on the scale of weighted pleasures. Further a person might persist in an underlying condition of cold detachment from any pleasures derived from activities that exercise his higher capacities, finding them divorced from what he can endorse in regard to how his life is going. A person might endorse and be content with his life in that it includes a preponderance of pleasure in Bentham's sense while another might endorse his life for including a preponderance of pleasure in Mill's sense. The preponderance in either case is what about their lives makes them happy – not what happiness per se is. None of this is to deny that pleasurable experience is intrinsically good; i.e., good when considered just according to its own nature as experientially felt. However, there are other intrinsic goods (endorsement, deep emotional contentment self-fulfillment) that pleasurable experience must measure up to in order to contribute to happiness.

Feldman's attitudinal hedonism is subject to similar objections. The fundamental "atoms" of Feldman's theory are not sensations or experiences of pleasure, but rather positive attitudes of being pleased with so-and-so or taking pleasure in such-and-such. Despite the significant advantage of Feldman's view of pleasure over sensory hedonism, the objections against hedonism remain. A person with a preponderance of positive attitudes towards things going on in his life may still be in an underlying emotionally troubled condition. Further he may still find all that he takes pleasure in to be lacking in meaning and substance. As such he may fail to endorse how his life is going, remaining detached from what he takes pleasure in. A non-atomistic version of Feldman's view would be that a person is happy with how their lives are going if they have a positive attitude toward how it is going or are pleased in that it is going that way. This positive attitude has to be understood as encompassing both deep emotional contentment and endorsement. If we understand being pleased with how one's life is going as simply favoring its going that way (its being pleasing to one's thought of it), then van Gogh could be said to have such an overall positive attitude toward his life of painting, while yet not being happy. In this sense having a positive attitude is basically equivalent to endorsing without contentment. On the other hand if we understand being pleased with how one's life is going as finding oneself taking (deep emotional) pleasure in how it is going, then a person who disavows the pleasure he takes and so finds it unfulfilling would have a positive attitude toward his life while yet not being happy with how it is going.

According to Kant happiness is the maximal satisfaction of our desires. Griffin (1986) at one time likewise held that the fulfillment of desires is what happiness is. Sumner (1996;129) objects that desires are always for future states of affairs which in being realized can be disappointing. Clearly a person who is disappointed with the fulfillment of his desires is not thereby happy. Sumner notes that the possibility of disappointment is not avoided by Griffin's later addition that the desires be informed. Even a well-informed desire may disappoint in the realization. At one point Griffin (1986:18) considers enjoying or liking. To avoid the problem of disappointment we could vary his account by saying that happiness is the pleasant or enjoyed fulfillment of our desires. If a desire for something in being fulfilled does not disappoint, we will still want to have that fulfillment even if we can no longer be said to desire it. Hence the varied account is that happiness is having all that one wants. But now one can have all that one wants or have all his desires pleasantly fulfilled and still not be happy. A person may have the family he wants, the career he wants and yet be anxious or depressed. Even if not anxious or depressed it may seem that there is something missing in his life, that his life is not fulfilling, etc. Both of these are possible even if there are no further particular desires the person has that are not fulfilled. He can't put his finger on what would relieve the anxiety or what would fulfill him. Of course he still may have the unfulfilled desire to be emotionally content or to be able to endorse his life. But then it seems that it is this desire being fulfilled that matters for happiness – which returns us to the life-satisfaction view.

Further it seems that one can be happy even if he doesn't have all that he wants and some of what he wanted and has is disappointing. Disappointment in certain areas of one' life is not inconsistent with happiness If not having some of what one wants is neither emotionally troubling nor important enough to be in the way of the person's endorsing how his life is going, then he can still be happy. This might seem to divorce happiness from subjective well-being (life's going well by the subject's own lights), and Griffin's later view is that the desire account is an account of well-being rather than happiness. It seems to me however that my subjective well-being is not the same thing as things going as best they can by my own lights. Rather it is things going well enough in order to endorse and be content with things. Things going as best they can may be an idealized version of subjective well-being which with endorsed contentment would equal something like ideal or perfect happiness. This is a different notion, however, than flat-out subjective well-being or happiness. There may be some people for whom only ideal happiness brings endorsement and emotional contentment (happiness), but this is just what would make those people happy—not what it is to be happy per se.

CHAPTER 2

The Final Good and the Final End

(i)

A person's happiness can be defective in various ways. Even if his contentment is sensitive to his endorsement, the endorsement may be faulty. For example it may be based on false information or it may be unfounded in the values that are endorsed. Non-defective happiness is the topic of the next chapter. Through the course of the present chapter it is supposed that happiness signifies non-defective happiness. If happiness at all is to be the final good and the final end, it is surely as being non-defective that it is such. The burden of Part Two is to establish that morality is an absolutely necessary condition of happiness. Even so this would not establish the pre-eminent status of morality if happiness were not the final good and the final end. If there were things that were good or valuable apart from happiness, then even if moral values were essential to happiness they might not trump these other things. Morality however is not one value among others but a condition of all goodness or value. Similarly if there were ends or aims outside of or apart from happiness, then even if morality were essential to our aims as far as happiness is concerned it would not be essential for all our aims. Morality would then have only a limited standing governing our conduct only to some extent. Morality however should be in force as governing all our aims.

To say that happiness is the final good is to say it is the basis of all value; that there is nothing to be valued that stands out of all relation to happiness. That some values at least are related to happiness is clear from the fact that happiness involves endorsing how one's life is going. To endorse in part is to positively evaluate. It is to think one's life is going well or good, in a way that one approves of or can stand behind. One's more particular values elaborate what it is about one's life that makes for such endorsement. One's values contribute to the positive evaluation of one's life by being endorsed components or aspects of the how one's life is going. We endorse our lives when they are infused with what we value. When various dimensions of our lives fit or measure up to our system of values, we thereby endorse or positively evaluate how our lives are going.

We need some idea of what dimensions of life there are that are up for evaluation. What is there about life or living to evaluate? Consider the life of a dog and of many other mammals during a day. It will at times work to satisfy its

© KONINKLIJKE BRILL NV, LEIDEN, 2014 | DOI 10.1163/9789004283213_003

needs for food, warmth, etc. Even a house pet will work to get treats, remind its master it needs to go out, etc. At other times during the day it will amuse itself at play. Then it might explore its environment to see what is and isn't new. It may then rest in the grass contemplating the wind blowing across its face and the birds chirping, where to contemplate means to be in a receptive mode for experience that has no specific connection to interests or needs. At other times it will engage in social interactions which may include elements of friendship as well as "political" elements pertaining to its place in the hierarchy (which dog gets to sit where). This seems to be pretty much what there is to a dog's life. Work, play, exploration, contemplation, social and political interactions are the basic modes or dimensions of a person's life as well. Of course the person's work projects may cover years in what they are working for, whereas the dog works only to meet its needs. A person may explore over long periods of time to find how the universe works, and a person can contemplate in an intellectually sensitive way the stars or the Mona Lisa. People have projects, ways of amusing themselves, things to find out about, things to contemplate and ways to engage with others which go beyond the dog in scope and complexity, but are still dimensions that parallel those of the dog. Unlike the dog some of a person's life is taken up with self-improvement; developing into what kind of person he wants to be. The dimensions of a person's life or of a dog's life for that matter are not mutually exclusive. A dog can work with other dogs in hunting for food, thus combining the dimension of work with the dimension of social relations. It can contemplate flowers in a garden that it is exploring. If the dimensions of living are modes of being (the work-mode, play-mode, etc.) then much of our lives involve mixed or combined modes.

The realization of the dimension of work for a dog is achievement of food, shelter, and so on; that of play is amusement. Knowledge is the realization of exploration and appreciation that of contemplation. Bonds of friendship, social standing, etc. are part of the realization of the dimension of social relations. The usual list of things thought of as valuable are things that are valuable for or in relation to dimensions of life. They are thus valuable by having certain characteristics making them suitable in regard to those dimensions. Scientific knowledge has value for attaining by exploration because of the kind of knowledge it is. To say that it has value in regard to exploration is to say that it is to be endorsed in regard to this dimension. It is valuable as knowledge if exploring for it, achieving it, elaborating it, etc. is to be endorsed. Equivalently, its value as knowledge is in its being a suitable candidate for endorsement in regard to exploration. It is because the character of scientific knowledge makes finding it or achieving it endorsable that such knowledge is valuable. Similarly the value of art is what about it makes contemplating it or producing it for contemplation worthwhile. It is valuable by its being something one can endorse contemplating. Knowledge that is not endorsable by anyone for attaining has no value no matter what its internal characteristics. Art that is not endorsable by anyone for contemplating or producing has no value. Even if it should be that exploration for any knowledge whatsoever can be endorsed, it is still the fact that it can be endorsed that makes it valuable, or that gives it any value. There is no value apart from what can potentially be valued. One might object that a bogus or defective endorsement cannot give anything value. If the only basis of the endorsement, say, is ignorance or illusion or misrepresentation of the object, then the object has no value, or at least no true value. The issue of true value, what is really valuable, is taken up in the next chapter. For purposes of this chapter it is simply presumed that the endorsement is non-defective.

The value of knowledge *just as knowledge* is independent of anything other than its being worthwhile to explore and attain. That scientific knowledge can lead to technological advances may give it value for other dimensions of life. What can be endorsed in relation to productive work may be broadened and enriched by such knowledge, but that forms no part of what can be called the intrinsic value of knowledge. Intrinsic in this sense doesn't mean value that belongs to it apart from what makes it endorsable as something to be explored. Rather it means value that belongs to it just in relation to the dimension in which it enters life. The intrinsic value of knowledge or art is independent of whether it contributes to anyone's happiness. Even if art failed to contribute to happiness it would retain its intrinsic value; its value in regard to the specific dimension in which it enters life. The same is true of the relation of intrinsic value to morality. The cinematic art of Nazi film makers retains its intrinsic value even if it should be the case that no one can endorse contemplating it when they also consider its role as Nazi propaganda. This failure to endorse contemplating it is a failure to endorse contemplating it in regard to the moral dimension of our lives; it is not a failure in regard to the contemplative dimension. I cannot all out endorse contemplating it even though I can endorse contemplating it so far as contemplation alone is at issue. Oppenheimer couldn't all out endorse the knowledge achieved in building a bomb, even though he could endorse it simply as knowledge.

Something has flat-out value if it can be flat out endorsed—not merely endorsed in relation to a specific dimension of life, but flat out endorsed as belonging to one's life. If endorsing contemplating art in our lives precludes other things in our lives that we endorse more strongly, then no matter what the intrinsic value of art for contemplating is, it cannot be flat out endorsed as belonging to our lives. Something that cannot be flat out endorsed by anyone has no flat-out value at all no matter what characteristics belong to it internally. Only if it can be endorsed as belonging to our lives does something which has intrinsic value also have flat out value. But now to endorse something as belonging in our lives is to endorse it in the way that is involved in being happy with how our lives are going. If so, then something has flat out value by contributing to that endorsement pertaining to being happy with how our lives are going.

It is complexes of values that are the basic candidates for flat-out endorsement, and so basically have flat out value. The individual values within the complex get their flat out value by being part of a complex whose flat out endorsement exactly constitutes endorsing how our lives are going. What can be endorsed and so has value in regard to a specific dimension of life may fail to be part of a complex of values constituting an endorsement of how life is going in two ways. It may be inconsistent with or excluded from that complex or there may be no complex. It may that is fail to contribute to my overall endorsement because it is excluded from my life by that endorsement or it may fail to contribute because even with it being valuable and included in that dimension of my life, I do not overall endorse how my life is going. If I find contemplating art to be valuable but find I cannot endorse it as being contained in my life for going against my endorsement of my life, then it is intrinsically valuable but not flat out valuable. If I find contemplating art to be valuable but find I cannot endorse how my life is going even though I endorse that contemplation being in my life, then contemplating art is at best provisionally valuable—not flat out valuable since its value in my life is provisional upon what I may come to endorse for my life as a whole.

There are two kinds of complexes or systems of values. The first is a sheer complex without any further integration or systematic character beyond the component values not interfering with or nullifying each other. This is consistent with the individual values mixing with and enriching each other, since the dimensions of life are not usually isolated. Valuable work projects can involve exploring (knowledge) and social interaction, and valuable friendship can involve knowledge of the other, contemplation of the other, etc. As far as overall endorsement is concerned one does not have to balance such friendship and such contemplation since the latter is part of the value of friendship. On the other hand there can be a kind of contemplation that precludes friendship because its value requires dedication that leaves no room for friendship. The complex of values needn't include all dimensions of life to be flat out endorsable. Variety as opposed to single-minded dedication may or may not characterize the completely endorsable complex.

In a sheer complex any overall characteristics such as variety or single-mindedness derive simply from the adjudication of various intrinsic values in relation to one another. The complex contains no further value beyond the various component values fitting together. Though it isn't simply an additive conjoining of values, any systematic character it has derives simply from how the values align with and modify each other. Such a sheer complex can be a candidate for flat out endorsement. In a sense it is the minimal kind of candidate. Minimal doesn't mean less valuable, but rather it means adding or needing no further value beyond the components of the complex.

Contrast this with a person who values variety per se in their lives. Variety doesn't just fall out of a complex of values they otherwise endorse, but is a value in addition to or beyond the adjudication of individual values. It may allow the substitution of various individual values for others without loss of overall endorsement, so that in this sense it is a basic or driving value. It doesn't just integrate individual values; it integrates them according to a theme of variety. Such a complex of values can be called a thematic system. All complexes of values are structured, but only thematic complexes involve specifically structural values. A thematic system will involve the basic or minimal kind of adjudication. One cannot endorse sheer variety that includes no endorsable components. This would be to find no value in anything going on in one's life but yet endorse it for its variety. A variety of disappointing, boring and annoying activity is hardly endorsable for its variety. Although thematic systems add themes as further values, while mere complexes do not, this doesn't make them more valuable than complexes. Complete flat out endorsement is not a maximizing notion (the more values, structural or not, the better). A person who fully endorses how his life is going without endorsing any specifically thematic values doesn't thereby have a defective or lesser grade of endorsement than a person who specifically endorses certain themes.

Thematic values include values of simplicity, complexity, novelty, variety, developmental unity, and so on. The last of these in particular allows that standing endorsements during a period of one's life of how one's life is going during that period may depend on how other periods of one's life have been endorsed. What would otherwise be endorsed during a particular period of one's life may not be endorsed for its lacking some sort of developmental unity with how one's life went on before. The issue then of how much of one's life is involved in being happy with (endorsing) how it is going is sensitive to such values of developmental unity (Velleman 1991). For people without such a value, however other parts of their lives may not be very important for endorsing how their lives are going during a particular period.

On one understanding of the term perfectionism is a thematic value. One may endorse only what one thinks one is good at or can become good at. The system of values one can endorse is restricted by what one can exhibit excellence in. Samuel Freeman (2006;68–69) says that there are or may be a plurality of objective goods, but which of these goods to pursue depends on a person's capacities, skills, and so on. If we take him to mean that which values to endorse depends on our skills and capacities this seems to be true only for a perfectionist theme. One might however endorse bumbling along on the piano throughout one's life without much if any skill.

Thematic valuing need not encompass all one's complex of values—it can be partial. The various dimensions of life can be thematically valued in different ways. One may value simplicity or novelty in one's work, while yet valuing complexity and variety in the contemplative dimension. One may value narrative developmental unity in one's social relations, but not in one's play or sport. The more specific such themes are to particular dimensions of life the less clear the line is between these themes being values of the system versus part of the intrinsic value of the components.

Nicholas White (2006;166) allows that happiness involves

> the right viewpoint from which to combine and organize and sometimes reconcile the various things that...we think worthwhile

What has to be emphasized in his eyes however is that this viewpoint is amorphous, vague and indeterminate. However true this often is, it is this viewpoint from which the various things thought worthwhile are flat-out worthwhile. If it is an amorphous viewpoint, then flat out value is amorphous to the very same extent. This still leaves all flat out value being value that is in relation to flat out endorsement of how our lives are going, since only what can be flat out endorsed has value that is not limited in and to certain respects.

(ii)

The value of something is that which attracts us to it, that which attaches us to it. To endorse something is to be attracted to it in thought. But to be fully attracted to something is more than to be attracted to it even fully in thought. It is to be emotionally attracted or attached as well. For something to have flat out value versus only having value in respect of thought, it must potentially be fully attractive. If no one can be fully attracted to something, then even if it can be flat out endorsed its value is limited to being only in respect to thought or conception and so is not full flat out value. It is something that can pull us toward it in thought, but cannot fully pull us toward it. If something cannot but leave everyone whatsoever indifferent or unsettled it has only superficial value.

It doesn't deeply matter to anyone. No one deeply cares about it. There may be some sort of conceptual inclination toward it, but there wouldn't be such a thing as being fully inclined toward it. What is beyond all emotional mattering and caring and has value only in relation to thought of it is valuable at best in an attenuated sense.

Scheffler (2011;32) distinguishes believing X is valuable from valuing it. The latter involves in addition to the former what Scheffler calls emotional vulnerability – a susceptibility to a range of emotions both positive and negative. His idea of emotional vulnerability is basically the idea of its emotionally mattering to me. Scheffler further holds that valuing involves a disposition to experience these emotions as merited. This condition is tantamount to emotional attraction being endorsable. Fully valuing for Scheffler then coincides with full attraction emotionally as well as in thought. The only point I would emphasize is that value itself exists only as what can be thus fully valued. Kagan (1989;354) makes this point as follows:

> An adequate theory of objective value, I take it, can recognize that the ultimate source of value of many goods (and maybe even all of them) lies in the fact that people care about these things, that it matters to people.

Parfit (1987;502) holds that there is no value in things such as knowledge, rational activity, love, or awareness of beauty if they are entirely devoid of pleasure Parfit's way of putting it seems to suggest that so long as there is pleasure in things they can be valuable. As Haybron has pointed out however not all pleasure runs very deep. If a pleasure is emotionally shallow and certain objects or activities are emotionally attractive only in giving shallow pleasure then they are clearly not deeply valued. For something to be a deep value is for it to be capable of being deeply emotionally attractive. Following Haybron again, the deep positive emotions are those that are involved in being happy—contentment, serenity, enthusiasm, jubilance, etc.

Just as flat out endorsement pertains to a system of values, deep emotional contentment may pertain to a system. Oppenheimer may have a deep emotional affiliation toward the knowledge involved in building the bomb, but it may not be deep enough for contentment given how even more troubling it is for him emotionally in regard to weaponry that can wreak devastation. In this manner the emotional value of the knowledge, though deep in its own right, is also deeply mitigated so that overall there is no emotional contentment in building the bomb. In the Oppenheimer case the failure of endorsement of the system of values works to override the emotional value of an individual component of the system. The reverse is also true. A system can provide for emotional embracing of components, even though they would not be embraced individually. Thus someone may be emotionally attached to their work (not just endorse it) just because it contributes to what they can flat out endorse (being an overall responsible parent), and this flat out endorsement is strongly emotionally embraced in a way that encompasses the work. Their overall emotional attraction is deep enough to make the work emotionally attractive even if it wouldn't be attractive but boring or emotionally indifferent on its own. In this case the work has flat out un-attenuated value. It is flat out endorsed and emotionally embraced.

In sum, something has flat out un-attenuated value as opposed to mere intrinsic value and as opposed to flat out value only in regard to thought if it can be a component of flat out endorsement in regard to the various dimensions of one's life all together that can be emotionally embraced in all its components. But this latter is just the endorsed contentment that is equivalent to full heart and mind satisfaction with how one's life is going, which in turn is what it is to be happy with how one's life is going. It follows then that something has flat-out un-attenuated value only if it can contribute to someone's being happy with how his life is going. If something cannot be part of anyone's being happy with how his life is going then it cannot have any flat out un-attenuated value. Since intrinsic value is incomplete and attenuated value is diminished relative to flat out un-attenuated value, it follows that only incomplete or diminished value can exist apart from the possibility of happiness with it. Happiness then is the final good in the sense that it is that in terms of which anything else is a flat out un-attenuated good. If then it can be shown that morality is required for the possibility of anyone to be happy, then moral values (valuing morality) would trump all values such as knowledge, art, friendship, etc. in that incorporating moral values would be a condition of any of these being a flat out and un-attenuated good.

(iii)

The identification of happiness with the final good is a relation between happiness and value which will not seem plausible if the relation is not understood in the right way or if either of the terms of the relation (happiness and value) are not understood in the right way. Each of these failures of understanding needs to be addressed.

Happiness is not the final good in a sense that it is a value separate from all other values, to which all other values are merely a means and hence merely instrumentally valuable. Understood this way art as art for example would have no value for contemplation, but only value for how one's life is, and knowledge as knowledge would have no value for exploration but only value for how one's life is. This may be the case for a person who endorses a thematic value such as wide variety. He doesn't endorse art for what is valuable in contemplating it, but rather just for adding contemplation to his life. This merely instrumental value of art is not entailed by happiness being the final good, but obtains only because the value of variety happens to be this person's happiness. For this person variety is not instrumentally valuable as a means to their happiness; it is valuable as thought of and embraced in its own right (intrinsically valuable) and also sufficient for flat out endorsement. The latter isn't what makes it valuable, but what makes it flat-out valuable. Happiness is not a value separate from and beyond all others, but rather that in terms of which other values have flat out un-attenuated value. Happiness gives or determines the flat-out un-attenuated character of all other values; it does not give value to other values as what these values are instrumental for. Happiness with how one's life is going is not the final good in the sense that some global, thematic, or narrative value is a value distinct from and dominant over the coherence of local values. This may be the case for someone whose endorsement of variety leads them to abandon some of the value of art or knowledge for its not fitting in with variety. However, it is not variety which is the final good, but rather how it contributes to flat out un-attenuated endorsement. To say happiness is the final good is not to say any thematic global value is per se the final good.

To say that happiness is the final good is not to say that no value is embraceable unless one is happy. If Van Gogh, perhaps hypothetically, not only endorses his art, but is emotionally content with it when he is doing it then he fully and flat out embraces his art despite the fact that he is not happy with how his life is going. For it to be flat out valuable, however, he cannot think that it is his art which is the source of his not being happy with how his life is going. If he thought there was something about art itself despite its being attractive to both thought and emotion that precluded him from happiness, then he cannot flat-out endorse it or embrace it with all his mind and heart. It is because he thinks his art in its own right is a candidate for his being happy that he can flat out endorse it despite his not being happy. The connection between happiness and value is that something is flat out valuable if it can contribute to happiness— not if it does. Even for van Gogh art is a component of what would make him happy, if only other components of happiness were not missing. Happiness is the final good then in the sense that only something that can potentially contribute to happiness can be flat out good.

That happiness is the final good does not mean there cannot be a conflict between value and happiness, so long as this conflict is understood as a conflict "within" happiness. I may endorse certain values even if I cannot emotionally embrace them, even if I cannot be content having them in my life, while yet being unable to endorse abandoning them because their value as thought by me is too great to be abandoned. This is a conflict between what I hold to be valuable and emotional contentment. It is not a conflict between value and happiness, but a conflict within the components of happiness between endorsed value and contentment. One may object that there can be a conflict between moral value and happiness which is not a conflict within happiness but a conflict to happiness. The burden of Part Two is to show there cannot be such a conflict by showing that moral value is an essential component of any possible happiness for anyone, and thus any conflict that arises from morality is a conflict within happiness. If one's full embrace of how one's life is going requires morality then any conflict due say to one's not being able to embrace morality is a conflict within what has to be embraced to be happy. It is not a conflict between embracing morality and being happy.

That happiness is the final good does not mean that it is a fixed un-revisable good. Flat out endorsing how one's life is going does not require one's endorsement to be irreversible and final. Even if I wouldn't flat out endorse my life to be going now the way I endorsed it to be going then, it doesn't follow that I wasn't then happy. Nor does its being the final good mean that it is temporally final (coming after other goods). One can be happy with how one's life is going in that one is pursuing things one values. The pursuit itself, that is, can have flat-out value, in which case achieving happiness does not require first that other values be achieved.

Finally, to say that happiness is the final good is not to say that my or your happiness in particular is the final good or that in relation to which anything can have flat out value. Possibly contributing to my happiness makes it a flat out good only for me. Something is flat out good if it can be a constituent component of happiness, or if it is a candidate for being such a component. This doesn't mean that if it cannot be a candidate for my happiness then it isn't flat out good. It only means it cannot be flat out good for me. It is only if something cannot be a constituent of anyone's happiness whatsoever that it cannot be flat out endorsed by anyone, and so cannot be flat out valued by anyone and so has no flat out value.

In sum, to say that happiness is the final good is to say that it is at the bottom of or at the end of the matter as far as goodness is concerned. To say that something is good in this or that respect, or to say it is good in so far as thought is concerned, or to say it is good so far as it goes, is not yet to get to the bottom of the matter or to the end of the matter regarding its goodness. The bottom of the matter is what is flat-out un-attenuated good—what is good absolutely, in all respects, and this in turn is what is good in respect of happiness.

The contention that happiness is the final good pertains specifically to happiness conceived as flat out stable endorsement and emotional embrace of how one's life is going. The contention lacks plausibility in regard to other familiar conceptions of happiness. Suppose, as Haybron holds, that happiness is being emotionally content. Such happiness may still be that in terms of which anything has flat out emotional value. But now something can contribute to and so have such emotional value and yet be thought to lack value. It can figure into one's contentment, that is, and yet not be part of what is endorsed for one's life, as when one's contentment is foreign to or un-owned by one's thoughts. I find myself being content in my life, where my life includes art, say, but I find no point in being an artist or in my art. It wouldn't then have value tout court, but at best value in respect of emotional contentment even though it is part of my happiness as Haybron understands it. For Haybron the endorsement of how one's life is going even by the subject's own lights is something apart from happiness. The only way to keep happiness as the final good when happiness is defined as emotional contentment would be to hold that all other things have flat out un-attenuated value in so far as they contribute to mere emotional contentment. One would have to hold this modified version of value hedonism, according to which pleasure contributing to deep emotional contentment is what makes anything flat out valuable, in order to preserve happiness as the final good. This isn't quite the view that contributing to any sum of pleasure is that by which anything has flat out value since one can have a preponderance of pleasures and yet not be emotionally content. It would be a modified version of value hedonism (according to which pleasure contributing to deep emotional contentment is the flat out value of anything) that one would have to hold to preserve happiness as the final good. One would have to hold that so long as something contributes to the production of this hedonic condition, it has flat out value. It needn't contribute by being thought worthwhile, since worthwhile contentment is no longer part of what it is to be happy. Even if no one could endorse it and so value it in thought as contributing to contentment that they can own, it would still have flat out value. Valuing it in thought, therefore would add nothing to its being valuable.

Another conception of happiness that would make it implausible as the final good is that happiness is constituted only by self-regarding values. I may value the survival of a forest but I do not or at least need not value it for myself. Kagan (2009) distinguishes interests from self-interests where the former encompass all the objects of my concern, whether the concern is for myself or not. Similarly we can distinguish what one values whether for oneself or not from what one values for oneself. Let us call the latter personal values. According to this second conception a person is happy with his life means he endorses and embraces how it is going so far as personal values are concerned. On this conception then clearly happiness is not at the bottom of all flat out value, unless one also holds that only personal values can be flat out good. The survival of a forest could only be flat out valuable if it produced something that was valuable to me personally. There is no denying that there is a notion of personal happiness that is often meant when we talk of happiness. We do sometimes talk of being happy ourselves or being personally happy even though much of what we value (not *for* ourselves) is unrealized. One can embrace how one's life is going personally even if one cannot embrace how things other than one's life are going (the destruction of the forest, etc.). However it seems also to be the case that this is not necessarily equivalent to happiness. One can fail to be happy with how one's life is going precisely because one can't endorse or embrace how things other than one's life are going. One's contemplation of the destruction of the forest is a dimension of one's life that can preclude being content in how one's life is going. It can matter to someone enough that it precludes his being content in how his life is going and matter not because of the malcontent but because of his valuing the forest. The malcontent is something he owns, and so something that precludes his being happy because of what he thinks of the forest. In such a case one's endorsement of one's life personally is not a flat out endorsement, but an endorsement only in respect of personal matters. Personal happiness is not equivalent to what it is to be happy per se, although it may be all there is to happiness for some self-centered people. What it is for such people to be happy is not the fact that they are personally happy, but that their personal happiness is enough for them to endorse and embrace how their lives are going. The "wider" conception of happiness as endorsed contentment allows that all value, including non-personal value, can be a flat out un-attenuated good as contributing to happiness.

Kagan (2009) holds there can be goods such as a redwood tree that come to be "possessed" in some manner and so contribute to well-being. He holds, that is, that well-being is wider than personal well-being. My contention, in addition is that for goods to be "possessed" is for them to be endorsed and emotionally embraced, and that being happy with how one's life is going is equivalent to well-being (at least by the subject's own lights). In particular one shouldn't hold that happiness is narrower than well-being so that it is well-being, and not happiness misconstrued as merely personal happiness that is the final good (the "home" of all flat out value). I am not at all claiming that this is what Kagan holds. Rather I am claiming that one shouldn't draw this conclusion from his discussion of non-self-regarding goods in terms of "well-being." Since we are allowing that a person's supposed happiness may be fully constituted by their personal interests, in order to show that morality, which involves other-regarding values, is necessary for all possible happiness, it will have to be shown that *non-defective* embracing of how one's life is going totally in terms of how it is going personally is not possible.

The plausibility of happiness as the final good seems to be undercut by the existence of what may be called inaccessibly transcendent values. The value of the awesomeness or simplicity of the universe for contemplation is not inaccessibly transcendent. It transcends only personal happiness as many other values do, but it is not inaccessible. It is there at least in part for the eye and the mind to behold. Spiritual values that go completely beyond what we can grasp in the way that some religious values are would be a paradigm of value that is inaccessibly transcendent. There are two ways of understanding the idea of an inaccessibly transcendent value. It may mean just that the content of the value (what about it makes for its value) is inaccessible, or it may mean further that valuing it (its force as a value) is inaccessible. The former holds that what its value is fails to be accessible while the latter holds the fact that it can be valued is inaccessible. The latter more extreme understanding takes it beyond having any human value at all in that it is absolutely inert in regard to any human valuing. For humans at least it is a value only in name – the bare idea that there may be a non-human kind of valuing and even some kind of non-human flat-out valuing. Such flat out values would indeed exist out of relation to all possible happiness, but this is not the kind of flat-out value involved in spirituality or religion. Consider the value of God's unfathomable will. The content may be inaccessible, but so long as it can be embraced and endorsed, it is not inert and so not outside the scope of contributing to happiness, This is perhaps the value expressed at the entrance to Dante's paradise "And His will is our peace" or the value expressed by St. Augustine when he says to God – Your will is more myself than I am. Taking this kind of value to be the limit of inaccessible transcendence of anything that can be a value in more than name, the issue is whether and how it can be incorporated into one's life so as to contribute to endorsing and embracing how one's life is going.

One way of incorporating God's unfathomable will is that contemplating it and doing one's work, loving others, etc., in terms of the contemplation of it is what can be embraced and endorsed. The contemplation that there is a God in whose will all value-content lies is then a predominant thematic value. It is not that work, loving others, knowledge, etc. have no value at all, but that they have value according to this theme. It seems that there are people for whom this indeed is happiness. They endorse and emotionally embrace how their lives are going for such contemplation being the background that accompanies all they do. Of course such people must hold that God's will is not totally unfathomable since working well, loving, etc. in their mind and heart fits into this theme. Such people hold that God's will includes elements of earthly human happiness.

Another way of incorporating God's unfathomable will is when contemplating it is the exclusive element of how one's life is going by which one flat out endorses one's life. It simply doesn't matter what else is going on. This was Augustine's happiness. Although profoundly close to his mother, when she dies he felt sad at the funeral and upbraided himself for feeling sadness at anything distinct from failing to contemplate God's will. Love, family, work, art, etc., are no part of Augustine's happiness. Two of Dostoyevsky's characters, Prince Myshkin and the Karamazov brother Alyosha are portrayed in this way. They each go through life and the world about them pretty much doing nothing, or at least not doing anything that they invest in or endorse. Other people are strangely drawn to them but they have no real human relation to others. Alyosha metaphorically goes through his life silent and with a smile. This kind of sheer embrace, serene, calm, and ecstatic at the same time is a variant of what Acquinas would have termed beatitude. Myshkin and Alyosha are "blissfully" happy. Such people hold that God's will, other than the fact that contemplating it is all that can be endorsed and embraced in one's life, is completely unfathomable. If they held it was unfathomable or inaccessible even as to whether contemplating it is to be encompassed in one's life or not, that would take it beyond or apart from all possible human happiness—but equally it would make it an unfathomable *value* only in name.

To Nietzsche characters such as Myshkin and Alyosha say "no" to life, fail to affirm life, etc. and so are nihilists. However these characters devalue not life, but anything in life other than contemplating what transcends life. Perhaps Nietzsche has good objections to that way of being happy, but it is not an objection to its being a way at all. The true nihilist is another of Dostoyevsky's characters, the underground man for whom there is no suitable, valuable vista of activity or caring to endorse and embrace.

Although transcendent value doesn't stand out of all relation to happiness since it is a way of embracing how our lives are going, if morality is to be necessary to all other flat out value by being necessary for happiness, it better be that at least "non-defective" beatitude involves morality. Rousseau says at the end of the *Social Contract* that the true Christian hardly cares about justice at all and so is "outside" the general will. This seems true, for example of Alyosha whose reply to Ivan's litany of earthly injustice in the Grand Inquisitor chapter of *The Brothers Karamazov* is that silent serene smile. If earthly morality is to be an overriding value, as I believe it is, then this kind of Christian beatitude had better be shown on some basis to be a defective endorsement.

Another set of values that seem to be flat out valuable apart from contributing to happiness are what can be called welfare values—absence of pain, health, protection from the elements, absence of hunger, etc. It seems that being pain free for example is flat out good or valuable independent of any contribution to how one's life is going. Anything as sophisticated as the flat out embrace of how one's life is going seems to have nothing to do with the value of being pain-free. Happiness, it seems is not the final good because welfare, whether contributing to happiness or not is flat out good. This objection confuses intrinsic value with flat out value. Being pain free is intrinsically good in respect of the way it feels-considering it just in its own feeling nature it is good or valuable. Suppose however that one does not endorse being pain free because one endorses running marathons as contributing to one's endorsing how one's life is going. The intrinsic value of being pain free is then not flat out valuable though it remains intrinsically valuable just in respect to its nature as a feeling. Even pain that is embraced within emotional contentment is intrinsically bad as it doesn't lose its character as pain. There is a certain level of being pain-free perhaps that cannot but be endorsed or embraced. Being free of chronic excruciating debilitating pain supposedly cannot but be endorsed. The intrinsic value of that sort of being pain free would also be flat out un-attenuated value, because it cannot but contribute to flat out endorsement of how one's life is going. Its contribution is to allow for any flat out embrace of how one's life is going. It needn't be explicitly intellectually endorsed in order to contribute to happiness. Nevertheless its flat out value is in this relation to being happy with how one's life is going. Its opposite has flat out negative value if it is supposed that this sort of pain cannot contribute to anyone's happiness. Welfare values, at least at some minimal level of welfare, may be intrinsically valuable in such a way that without them no happiness is possible. This doesn't make them flat out valuable apart from any connection to happiness, but rather flat out valuable in that by their intrinsic nature they allow for happiness.

Finally, what is valuable for animals or for the welfare of animals seems to have flat out value independent of any relation to human happiness, even if it can in addition have value for human happiness. The intrinsic value of being pain-free for the animal is just its emotional attractiveness as a feeling. The flat out value is that it contributes to the animal's being emotionally content in its life. The pain of a surgery that contributes to the health of an animal is not a pain that it is flat out valuable to be free of. The connection between happiness and flat out value holds for animals, only their happiness doesn't involve any endorsement on their part of their contentment. In Part Two it will be claimed that recognizing and valuing what has flat out value to animals is essential to anyone's non-defective endorsement of how their lives are going. For this reason animal welfare is an objective value.

In sum, something has flat out value, as opposed to value when considered in its own right out of relation to other things, or value only in certain respects or otherwise attenuated value, only if it can be flat out valued. It can be flat out valued only if it can be flat out embraced both emotionally and in thought. It can thus be flat out embraced only if it can contribute to endorsed contentment with how the life of a person is going, and so only if it can contribute to a person' being happy with their lives. This doesn't imply that it does contribute to any actual person's happiness or can contribute to every person's happiness— only that it is something that can contribute to human happiness. Something has flat out value to a particular person if it either does or, given what he also endorses, can contribute to his happiness, and something has objective value if it must be a component of anyone whatsoever being happy. It is this connection between happiness and value that makes happiness the final good – the final word on what is good.

(iv)

Besides being the final good happiness is also the final end or final aim that lies at the bottom of all we aim for or seek. Much of the discussion of happiness as the final good carries over to happiness being the final end.

For an aim to be endorsable in the sense of being something worth endorsing, its realization must be endorsable. If something aimed at is realized but that realization is not endorsed, then the aim was not something worth endorsing. The standard of success for endorsing an aim is not just that it be realized, but that its realization is thereupon endorsable. The standard of success for endorsing the proposition that my keys are on the table is that the proposition be endorsable in the face of the facts at the table. Similarly the standard of success for endorsing an aim is that it be endorsable when made a fact by being realized. The realization of the aim includes not only achieving it but also what goes into achieving it. The realization is the carrying out of the aim unto completion. Thus, issues of how costly it would be and how difficult it would be to carry out the aim are part of what goes into the endorsement of its realization. If the aim turns out to be too costly so that I no longer endorse it, then it fails in its realization being endorsable despite never being achieved. It is presumed in what follows that the aims are possible at least in the sense that it is possible to try to achieve them or do something that goes some of the way toward achieving them. This covers merely ideal aims such as world peace. In these cases the standard of success of the aim is again that it be endorsable when carried out—that one endorses one's having tried or having gotten somewhere.

The full standard of success of an aim includes not just the endorsability of its realization but its full embrace. If I cannot be emotionally content with regard to the realization, then the aim is a success only in regard to how I value its realization in thought. It is a complete success only if I completely value or embrace the realization emotionally as well as in thought. With this in mind we can say that an aim is endorsable (to be endorsed) exactly if its realization is embraceable. In this way the endorseability of aims is tied to the value of their being carried out. An aim is endorsable if its realization is valuable. It is this connection to value that allows much of what was set forth about happiness being the final good to carry over to happiness as the final end.

If the realization of an aim can be embraced intrinsically when considered just on its own, but cannot be flat out embraced then the aim itself is endorsable only intrinsically. For example the aim may preclude other aims or not fit in with other aims, so that its realization is not something I can flat out embrace (embrace when I think of what other aims I didn't get to realize by realizing the aim). It is a system of aims or ends whose realization can be flat out embraced in regard to how my life is going, and so a system of aims that is flat out endorsable. Any particular aim is flat out endorsable only as contributing to a system of aims that is flat out embraceable. But this is just to say that an aim is flat out endorsable only if its realization contributes to being happy with how one's life is going. Happiness therefore is the standard of success for flat out endorsability of any of our aims. It is that which finally lies at the basis and grounds any aims as flat out endorsable. It is in this sense that happiness is the final end or aim.

As with the case of happiness being the final good resistance to the claim that happiness is the final end comes from misunderstanding the relationship implied between happiness and all ends, or a faulty conception of the terms that enter into the relationship. Happiness is not the final end by being a specific end in addition to all other ends. I don't aim at happiness alongside my system of aims, and I don't have it as my specific overriding aim to which everything else aimed at is merely a means. To aim at happiness as a separate aim with its own separate successful realization would imply that its realization is embraceable separate from the realizations of all other aims. This would mean that I embrace how my life is going separate from embracing anything about it. To have happiness as a specific separate overriding aim would imply that any other aim is endorsable only as a means to, not as a constituent of, embracing how my life is going. But I can't embrace my life if I can't find anything in it (even if only thematic) that I can embrace in its own regard. I can hope just to be happy because to hope unlike to aim does not have any focus. I can remind myself that my aim is to be happy, that it is happiness that is important, but this is to remind myself that other aims of mine (approval, achievement) are only aimed at because of their contribution as constituents of happiness.

That happiness is the final end doesn't mean that it is what is aimed at finally in a temporal sense as something to be had after all other aims are realized. Happiness is not something I aim to realize at the temporal end of realizing my other aims. Since being in the process of carrying out aims can contribute to being happy with how one's life is going before these aims are completed, the flat out endorsability of an aim is not per se its being achieved so that happiness can come after. In a different vein, being the final end doesn't mean that future or later happiness trumps present happiness as an aim. I can flat out endorse aims for their realization contributing to shorter term present happiness. This doesn't mean that the continuation of that happiness is not a final end. Lasting happiness is always at the bottom of any aim that I can flat out endorse. I might hold that it is best however to work for it in a temporally piecemeal fashion, that it is best achieved perhaps by working for it short term and dealing with working for longer term continuing happiness later. Happiness being the final end does not mean that prudence, working only for the long term, is at the bottom of any aims that can be flat out endorsed.

That happiness is the final end doesn't imply that no aim is endorsable if it doesn't contribute to happiness. An aim may be endorsable because its realization, though not contributing to an unhappy person's happiness is a candidate for so contributing and is as close as they can get to happiness. Van Gogh flat out endorses the aim of painting in that its realization contributes to the only intermittent, unstable happiness in his life he can have. If the realization, however much he embraces it in its own right, was what precluded him from being happy with how his life is going, he could not flat out endorse it. Next, there can be conflicts between endorsements of aims within the compass of happiness. Oppenheimer may endorse scientific knowledge gained in building the bomb though he cannot flat out embrace its realization. This is not a flat-out endorsement, but an endorsement in regard to the aim of scientific knowledge just in its own right. There can be no conflict between flat out endorsement of an aim and contribution of its realization to happiness.

Finally, that happiness is the final end doesn't mean that before I flat-out endorse something as an aim I explicitly reflect on whether its realization will contribute to happiness. I have accumulated a system of un-discarded standing flat out endorsed aims in terms of which I endorse new ones or new ways of pursuing old ones. I have a relatively firm even if inexplicit grasp of what in regard to my life would make the new aim flat out endorsable; at least I do so if I have practical wisdom. I do not need to explicitly reflect on my life in order for what I now explicitly endorse as a new aim to be flat out endorsable.

If one thinks of happiness as sheer contentment, then happiness being the final end would imply that flat out endorsability of any specific aim would be that its realization contribute to overall contentment where that contentment itself is not necessary endorsed. But then the realization is attenuated in value—having only emotional value and emotional value that I cannot own in thought. The realization would be a success for my emotional state, but that state itself would not be a success for me if I cannot own it. It is the subsequent continued endorsement of the aim as it is being realized that makes the prospect of realizing it flat out endorsable; something fully attractive to me as a feeling and thinking being. A particular person's happiness may lie exactly in being content. Contentment that is as a thematic value is his only value. Such value hedonism would carry with it "psychological" hedonism, in that an aim is flat out endorsable for him exactly if its realization contributes to emotional contentment. This would be one case of happiness being the final end, but should not be confused with the general connection between happiness and ends. Similar remarks apply to a person whose happiness is fully constituted by self-focused value (personal happiness). Such a value egoism would carry with it "psychological" egoism. The person can only flat out aim for that whose realization contributes to self-centered satisfaction with how his life is going. Once again this is another case of happiness being the final end, but no part of what it means for happiness to be the final end.

The contention that there are no flat out endorsable aims outside the compass of happiness seems to call into question the possibility of transcendent aims. Since as we have seen, even unfathomably transcendent values, are within the compass of happiness as the final good, it is therefore possible for flat out endorsement of transcendent aims to be within the compass of happiness as the final end. Further, aims that risk great harm, even death, can be flat out endorsable by the realization of the aim which avoids the harm contributing to one's happiness. The more difficult case is aiming for the harm itself. There may be circumstances in which I come to flat out endorse dying in order to save a child, in order to promote a cause by being a martyr, and so on. These seem to be cases of flat-out endorsing an aim whose realization is opposed to all happiness. However, in such cases I value something more than my own life, which is a tragic conflict "within" happiness. I cannot be happy with my life going on and so my aim is not against happiness but against life in which happiness for me is no longer possible. I flat out endorse dying as the lesser of two ways of losing continuing happiness.

CHAPTER 3

Reason and True Happiness

(i)

So far it has been claimed that happiness is endorsed contentment with how one's life is going and that so understood it is the final good and the final end. The goal is to show that morality governs or "trumps" all other goods or ends by being absolutely essential to any happiness. If there is no happiness without morality, then something that goes against morality can have no flat out value and something that goes against morality cannot be flat out endorsed as an aim. In this way morality would be shown to be the condition of all flat out values and aims. So far, however, it hasn't been shown that the happiness of others is a condition of any happiness. From what we have claimed so far a person's happiness could for example be sheer contentment however gotten (hedonic) or it could be personal aggrandizement however gotten (egoistic). The happiness of others is not involved in any fundamental way adequate for morality in these cases. What we need to show is that such cases of endorsed contentment are defective – that they are not cases of real or true happiness. This requires showing that there is such a thing as true happiness and that it does involve the happiness of others in a fundamental way adequate for morality. If so then all flat out true values and flat out true aims (everything that can be non-defectively flat out valued or non-defectively flat out aimed for) would be subject to morality. In this chapter it is argued that there is such a thing as true happiness. Then in Chapter 4 it will be argued that true happiness, so understood, essentially involves the happiness of others in a certain way. In Part Two it is argued that the way it involves the happiness of others is adequate for morality.

The view of happiness that has so far been set out is basically Sumner's view (1996) of being satisfied with how one's life is going. Sumner goes on to demarcate what he calls authentic happiness. Authentic or true happiness according to Sumner involves both that one's satisfaction be based on a factual grasp of how one's life is going, and also that one's satisfaction be autonomous or subject to one's own reason. According to Sumner if one fails in important ways to grasp how one's life is really going, then one is only satisfied with how one thinks it is going, not with how it is going. Therefore according to Sumner one is not really happy with how one's life *is* going. Someone who is satisfied because he thinks he has dear friends and is admired for his accomplishments at work none of which is true according to Sumner is not happy with how his life is going at all. However, though perhaps true in a verbal sense this doesn't answer the question of whether or not being happy really requires a factual grasp. Why shouldn't being satisfied with how one *thinks* one's life is going be one way, so to speak, of being happy with how one's life *is* going, where the way it is going is that one fails to grasp the facts about it? Of course some people might fail to endorse false friendships and false admiration. These people will grant that illusions about their life mean they aren't really happy even if they think they are. For these people being "truly" happy requires a factual grasp of how their lives are going. But what of a person who specifically endorses even false friendships and even false admiration so long as they seem true? For such a person a factual grasp of how their lives are going is irrelevant to being happy with their lives. Contentment in accord with endorsement of things seeming a certain way is a dominating thematic value overriding any factual grasp of things. Why can't that be their satisfaction with how their lives are going? A mere terminological distinction between satisfaction with how one's life is going versus satisfaction with how one thinks one's life is going doesn't hold up if all that is significant to how a person's life is going as far as the person is concerned is how he thinks it is going.

One might say that the person who fails to factually grasp his life is liable to fail to have a stable, resilient happiness. His happiness is imperiled by finding out his dear friend isn't such a dear friend and that the admiration for his accomplishments was patronizing. That happiness is in peril in regard to change of circumstances, however, is not unique to this person's conception of happiness. In any case suppose that he avoids this peril as much as possible by insulating himself from the facts. This is the person who says "I don't want to know" and walks away when he suspects he might find out his best friend or spouse has betrayed him. The person in effect keeps himself inside a sort of Nozick (1974) machine, embracing emotionally and in thought the illusory life he makes for himself. It has to be admitted that so far as life satisfaction is concerned there is nothing obviously defective, unauthentic or unreal about the happiness of this person whose "real" happiness exactly lies in what may be unreal about his life.

Sumner's second component of authentic life satisfaction is that the satisfaction be autonomous in the sense of its being subject to the person's own reasonable consideration. Whereas the first component concerns a good grasp of the facts the second component concerns a good grasp of satisfaction; i.e., a good grasp of what to be satisfied with in one's life. Similarly Kekes (1982) identifies happiness as rationally evaluable satisfaction with one's life. Presumably he means positively evaluable satisfaction according to reason.

But now suppose reasonable consideration establishes that such-and-such is what to be satisfied with in life. Suppose further that a person is in fact satisfied with how his life is going in that such-and-such holds of it though this person hasn't himself reasonably considered things. Why isn't this person authentically happy? He is satisfied by what reasonable consideration would lead to. Such a person is like one of Plato's bronze or silver people who have true opinion about happiness but not knowledge. To Plato they are no less happy than the guardians who have knowledge though their happiness is not authentic in Sumner's sense. If reasonable consideration only subserves happiness by discerning what to be satisfied with then reasonable consideration is not a constituent of what it is to be happy and so true happiness does not require autonomy.

Both components of Sumner's conception of true happiness are correct I believe but we have yet to see why or how. The second component of autonomy or reasonable consideration by the subject has to be shown to be fundamental to what it is to be happy. It must be shown, that is, that well-considered satisfaction and not something such as true-opinion is part of what it is to be truly happy. To establish this we first turn back to what the relation is between contentment and endorsement that makes contentment belong to me as a thinking being. We shall then apply this to what makes endorsement in turn belong to me as a reasoning being.

What makes contentment, how I feel about things, belong to me as a thinking being is not just that it is endorsed as appealing to thought, but that the endorsement is from me as a thinking being. It is endorsed by how I think about the matter. This means that whether it is endorsed or not is determined by how my thinking goes. If endorsement is inevitably forced by the contentment itself then I, as a thinking being, don't own it—it owns me. If the contentment is actually produced by the endorsement then clearly the harmony between them is from me as a thinking being. If the contentment arises on its own, then it awaits what I can endorse before I own it. In either case the harmony is my own.

It is in owning it that the contentment fulfills me as a thinking being. The self as a thinker can only be fulfilled by something other than its thinking. It isn't fulfilled just in being itself. In that case failure to be fulfilled would be impossible. This something other (contentment) fills in the thinking self by being incorporated within that self, according to that self. Otherwise it is not fulfillment by the self, but the self being abandoned or lost to the something other. The contentment I feel is self-fulfilling contentment as far as the thinking self goes only if it is endorsed in terms of that self (what I think). The objection to Haybron's account of happiness in Chapter 1, that the contentment in my life can be foreign to me, not really mine, something that just happens in me, can be recast in present terms by saying that not all contentment is contentment that is fulfilling to me as a thinking being, and that what it is to be happy involves being self-fulfilled. I cannot both be happy with how my life is going and also not be self-fulfilled by its going that way. The alternatives to being self-fulfilled are being self-discordant or self-lost (other-owned), each of which seems inconsistent with *my* being happy. This doesn't mean that I cannot be engrossed when content, so long as being engrossed is not being lost to the contentment, but rather *my giving myself* over to it and so still finding myself in it.

Let us return now to the issue of authentic life satisfaction. What is missing from being satisfied with how one's life is going (what is missing from endorsed contentment) is whether the satisfaction is self-fulfilling or not. Only satisfaction with one's life that is self-fulfilling is true, authentic happiness. This requires not only that the contentment be self-fulfilling but that the endorsement is self-fulfilling as well. I am truly satisfied with how my life is going if my satisfaction is true to self-fulfillment. If there is going to be a place for reasonable consideration (autonomy in Sumner's sense) that is something more than subserving what is already happiness—something, rather, that is constitutive of what it is to be happy, it will be in reasonable consideration constituting self-fulfilled endorsement.

For me as a reasoning being, and not just as a being who has thoughts, to own what I endorse is for the endorsement to be in terms of how my reasoning about it goes. Whether what I endorse is caused by my reasoning or it just comes to me, it is encompassed by me as a reasoning being in so far as it arises or is retained according to what my reasoning about it is. The endorsement is the "something other" that is incorporated within the reasoning self, according to the reasoning self. The endorsement fulfills me as a reasoning being in that my reasoning encompasses the endorsement on its own reasoning terms. Likewise, for contentment to be self-fulfilling tout court, not merely self-fulfilling to me as a thinking being, the endorsement of it must be self-fulfilling to me as a reasoning being. It follows that to be self-fulfilling the satisfaction (endorsed contentment) with how my life is going must be in terms of my reasoning about the satisfaction; viz., that I find it reasonable upon due consideration. Reasoning about the satisfaction with how my life is going is reasoning about whether being thus satisfied with it is merited or not. The satisfaction will then fulfill me as a reasonable being to the extent that the reasoning does.

What it is for me to be a reasoning being is not simply that I reason by putting forth or entertaining reasons. If I do so without any standard according to which the reasons are accepted or rejected, then this putting forth and entertaining doesn't fulfill me as a reasoning being. Rather it just fills me up with reasoning or a sequence of reasons. Self-fulfillment requires a separation between what fulfills on the one hand and the self that it fulfills on the other. To be fulfilled as a reasoning being it must be in my terms that I give myself over to something other than my entertaining of reasons. But that in terms of which I own the reasons that come forth is simply the standard for good reasoning that I give myself over to. The conditions of self-fulfillment as a reasoning being are internal to my being a reasonable being because as a reasoning being I have standards that I hold myself to. In this way "regress" of self-fulfillment is ended. Contentment is owned or not in regard to me as a thinking being. Endorsements are owned in regard to me as a reasoning being. Reasoning and reasoning alone is owned by me, not in some further regard other than my being a reasoning being, but simply in me as a reasoning being having standards that I give myself over to. The realization of these standards is my self-fulfillment as a reasoning being.

In sum self-fulfilling satisfaction traces back to standards for that satisfaction to be reasonable. Let us say that considerations that conform to the standards I hold myself to make satisfaction in accord with those considerations "well-considered' satisfaction. Then the result is simply that self-fulfilling satisfaction, and so true happiness, is well-considered satisfaction with how one's life is going. So far the idea of a standard is purely formal. It doesn't say what, if any, standards there are. For all we have said so far the standard could be the perfection of our unique human capacities for work, play, etc. It could be God's will. It could be pleasure, contentment, or self-aggrandizement. The only point so far is that whatever the standard is, it can't be just in whatever reasons come forth. Following Wittgenstein something can be a standard or a rule (something normative) only if there is the possibility of failure to meet it. If the way we actually reason is per se what we hold to, then the reasoning has a grip on us. It is not something by which we can own the actual reasoning. This is true even if the actual reasoning includes criticism of some of our reasons. To think that self-critical actual reasoning is a standard is like thinking a second newspaper account of a robbery that corrects a first account is the standard of what took place (Wittgenstein). Since having a standard of reasonable satisfaction is at the core of self-fulfilling satisfaction, the normativity of reason that for Korsgaard (1996) is at the core of setting ends, is at the core, thereby of true happiness.

The idea that there is a descriptive notion of what it is to be happy on the one hand and a normative notion on the other is in one sense a false dichotomy. The "descriptive" notion of what it is to be happy is that it is self-fulfilling satisfaction, and normativity lies at the heart of any description of self-fulfillment. At most what it is to be defectively happy might be a purely descriptive notion.

An animal is truly happy in its life in so far as it is content in its life. For an animal being truly happy is no different than being happy because there is no normative "self" to be true to. Its happiness or contentment is true to the emotional creature the animal is, without the animal having to own that contentment or be self-fulfilled in having it. It is because we ultimately can own or fail to own satisfaction with how our lives are going that there is such a thing as defective satisfaction with how our lives are going. This doesn't make true happiness a non-descriptive notion. It is just that for humans being true to the reasoning, endorsing and emotional creatures we are devolves ultimately into the normativity of reason. The same holds for the notion of true contentment. For humans true contentment is contentment that is true to the more than just emotional creatures that we are. To be true to the creatures we are, however, involves normativity because (descriptively) we are normative creatures.

(ii)

In Chapter 2 the claim was that non-defective satisfaction with how one's life is going is at the bottom of all flat out value and all that is flat out to be aimed for. What value there meant was value in regard to us as emotional beings and as thinking beings. But we are also reasoning beings and so value has to also be in regard to us as reasoning beings. Tiberius (2008;138) puts this point as follows:

> To value something in the fullest sense is, in part, to have a positive affective response and in part to take our attitudes toward what we value to be justified.

Since to take attitudes to be justified is just to have reasons, the flat out value of anything (now for our reasoning nature as well) will involve taking those reasons to be flat out good reasons. The claim to be defended now is that something is a flat out good reason for valuing only in relation to well-considered satisfaction with how one's life is going. In this way by encompassing flat out good reasons within true happiness we will have encompassed not just value in relation to our emotion and thought but also in relation to our reason.

To begin with, something x is a good reason for something y to be an end or aim exactly if x is (also) a good reason for valuing or endorsing y's realization. It is not enough for x to be a good reason for y's realization that y's realization be valued or endorsed. Suppose I have a certain reason for aiming for wealth. Suppose that upon becoming wealthy I value my wealth but not for the reason I had in aiming for it, but for some other reason. The reason I had is now no part of the reason I value my wealth. Then the original reason never was a good reason for aiming for wealth; it only seemed so. Secondly, x is a flat out good reason for aiming at y if x is a flat out good reason for valuing or endorsing the realization of y. Suppose that being admired is my reason for aiming for wealth. Suppose upon becoming wealth I still value that wealth for the admiration that it brings, but I see that it has cost me too much in terms of my family life, etc. I see that I had better reason, that is, not to pursue wealth. Then my original reason is not and never was a flat out good reason for aiming for wealth – it only seemed so. Thirdly, x is a flat out good reason for valuing the realization of y only if x contributes to having an overall good reason for valuing how my life is going. The reason for valuing my wealth (admiration) is not a flat out good reason for valuing it because it doesn't contribute to having an overall good reason (which includes a rich family life, say) for valuing how my life is going. But now having an overall good reason for valuing how my life is going is what true happiness as well-considered self-fulfilling satisfaction is. Note that having an overall good reason is not having an overall reason *for* happiness—it is part of what it is to be happy. Hence for x to contribute to such an overall good reason is for it to contribute to happiness. We get the result then that a flat out good reason for valuing anything is that it is a reason that contributes to true happiness. Since a flat out good reason for having anything as an aim or end is that it is a flat out good reason for valuing its realization, it follows also that a flat out good reason for having something as an aim is that it (the reason) can contribute to happiness. In this manner true happiness is at the bottom of all flat out good practical reasons. Not only is happiness the final good and the final end, it is also the final reason.

We have already seen that having an overall good reason for satisfaction is having a standard for satisfaction that one, as a reasoning being, can give oneself over to, which standard when met constitutes one's being happy with how one's life is going. Thus a reason to value something is a flat out good reason for valuing it if the reason contributes to the standard for holding oneself to be satisfied with one's life, and a reason for aiming for something is a flat out good reason for aiming for it if it is a flat out good reason for the realization of that aim contributing to that standard. Thus what lies at the bottom of all practical reason is the standard which constitutes the conception that one can give oneself over to as a reasoning being, of what makes for one's being happy. Nothing regarding practical reason stands outside or beyond the issue, still to be resolved, of what standard one can give oneself over to as a reasoning being.

The claim that happiness is at the bottom of all flat out good reasons will not be plausible if the relation between happiness and good reasons is not interpreted in the right way, or if the terms of the relation (happiness, good reasons) are not properly understood. As to the relation itself, it is not being claimed that happiness determines all reasons as good or not. Happiness rather determines whether what are good reasons in their own right when considered by themselves are flat out good reasons. There may be good reasons to aim for an education that have to do with the worth of knowledge or with what an education can mean in its own right. These don't determine a flat out good reason for a person to aim for an education. The person may not have certain aptitudes, they may not be emotionally capable of achieving it without continued and extreme frustration, they may have to give up other aims which better contribute to their standard, etc. Raz (2004) says,

> an act could contribute to our well-being only when there are other *adequate* reasons [reasons other than contributing to our well-being] for taking it (italics mine).

If he means by adequate reasons flat out good reasons this seems to me a mistake. He must be saying that the reasons must be flat out good before they can contribute to happiness (well-being). But how can they be adequate while there is still an issue of whether they contribute to happiness? If he means by adequate that they are sufficiently good when considered in their own right (in regard to the particular matter at hand, in regard to a specific aim) then an adequate reason is something less than a flat out good reason. In a somewhat similar vein Raz says that people view their aims as sources of reason, not the contribution of them to their well-being. He is saying that a good reason to act has its source in what a person's aims are. This seems to me correct in that people act for or in accord with certain aims, and reasons for acting are in terms of what reasons there are for the aims or ends of acting. However I don't have flat out good reason to act unless I have flat out good reason for the aim. I may have plenty of good reasons for the aim, while yet these reasons don't fit together with other reasons I have for other aims into an overall good reason of what to aim for, and so how to act.

Happiness further is not at the bottom of all good reasons by itself being a good reason separate from all others and overriding all others. It isn't the fundamentally good reason. Rather it is fundamental to all other good reasons being flat out good. Just as truth is not a separate good reason for believing something, but rather that in terms of which what are already good reasons are at bottom adjudicated as flat out good (not just good given the position one is in, or good given what else what one knows, etc.) so too happiness is that in terms of which what are already good reasons are at bottom adjudicated as flat out good. If I ask someone what their reason is for acting so-and-so, for aiming at such-and-such and they say it is because it contributes to their happiness they haven't given me what good reasons they have. All they have done is to indicate that they have in fact flat out good reasons. Since happiness is not a separate reason at all it is not at the bottom of all reasons by being the one unrevisable final *reason* to which other reasons are responsible. What is "final" is that self-fulfilled satisfaction, which may come to different things at different times, is the standard for good reasons being flat out good. The contention that happiness is at the bottom of all flat out good reasons is not plausible in terms of other familiar conceptions of what it is to be happy. On a hedonistic view, for example, the claim becomes that pleasure or emotional contentment per se is at the bottom of all flat out good reasons. It is not however emotional contentment per se that can make good reasons flat out good, but rather such contentment being fulfilling to reason. What it is for a reason to be flat out good is that it contribute to what can be accepted by reason all things considered. If emotional contentment per se (just in itself, however gotten) is not one's standard of reasonableness, or is disavowed as such a standard, then contributing to sheer contentment cannot make any reasons flat out good reasons. It is because being fulfilling to reason has been built into what it is to be happy that happiness can be at the bottom of all flat out good reasons. This allows that for some people the standard of satisfaction they give themselves over to as reasoning beings might be contentment per se. Only so is contentment what it is according to a person to be happy. It doesn't imply that the only flat out good reasons there can be are those that contribute to contentment, unless contentment is the only standard possible for happiness. As far as we have gotten, contentment (just in itself) might be a candidate for being a standard, but it doesn't follow from our conception of true happiness that it is the only standard even though all true happiness involves contentment. I shall argue shortly that contentment however gotten cannot possibly be a standard reason gives itself over to. Similar remarks apply in relation to egoistic views of happiness. Only if egoism is avowed as a standard of satisfaction that one can give oneself over to does it follow that what is in my self-centered interest is at the bottom of all flat out good reason. Jay Wallace (2004) distinguishes what he terms "eudaimonistic" reasoning from prudential reasoning. The former pertains to all that we care about or all that is significant in our lives whether self-centered or other-directed, whereas the latter is egoistic. Someone's eudaimonistic reasoning might be fully prudential, but it needn't be. It is no part of what it is to be happy that one's reasoning be prudential. Thus to say that happiness is at the bottom of all flat out good reasons is not per se to say that only egoistic reasons can be flat out good reasons.

The contention that happiness is at the bottom of all flat out good reasons seems to be called into question, finally, by the apparent possibility of flat out good reasons that transcend any issues of happiness. For example one might hold that what makes something a flat out good reason is its harmonizing with the teleological unfolding of the universe or its harmonizing with God's will, etc. This can mean either one of two things. First it can mean that one's standard by which any reasons contribute to self-fulfillment is conformity to harmony of the universe, etc. This meaning doesn't take flat out good reasons outside the compass of happiness, but rather pertains to what (like hedonism and egoism) might very well be a standard of satisfaction one gives oneself over to, and so the happiness that flat out good reasons can contribute to. On a second reading it means that such conformity is a "metaphysically" objective standard for flat out good reasons even if such conformity is not what is or even can be anyone's standard of satisfaction. On this reading, roughly, there are flat out good reasons that no one can take as flat out good reasons for their aims and values. This would mean that as far as *practical* reason is concerned there are no flat out good reasons. This then would be tantamount to nihilism regarding practical reasons. Even if this is a possible position as held for example by Dostoyevsky's underground man it is consistent with our contention that happiness (which involves giving oneself over to a standard of being happy in how one's life is going) is at the bottom of all flat out good practical reasons.

We are working toward the idea that moral reasons are objective flat out good practical reasons by being essential to anyone's standard of satisfaction being something they can give themselves over to as reasoning beings. It would follow that any reasons for aims and values, no matter how good in their own right, cannot be flat-out good if they are not consistent with moral reasons. Any objectivity of moral reasons that goes beyond this would be irrelevant to *practical* reason. Whether moral reasons, that is, have a status in addition to their status as restricting what can be a standard of satisfaction self-fulfilling to persons as reasoning beings is irrelevant to the perfectly objective status that they have for our practical reasoning. Although there are differences between Kant's justification of morality and ours that I shall get to in Part Two both views hold that morality pertains to practical reason and requires a foundation only in practical reason. Kant further holds that the foundation of morality in practical reason is that consistency with moral reasons is required for any practical reasons to be flat out good reasons. He holds as well that this is so in turn because consistency with moral reasons is requisite for any self-fulfillment of our nature as reasoning beings. Despite these agreements we shall see in Chapter 6 that Kant's attempt at this defense of moral reasons does not succeed.

(iii)

The requirement for self-fulfilling satisfaction is that a person gives himself over to a standard in terms of which satisfaction with how his life is going can be owned by him as a reasoning being. So far this is a purely a formal requirement. We turn now to the issue of what substantively I can give myself over to as a reasoning being. One possibility is that there is some definitive, conclusive, un-revisable standard. For example, some hold that pleasure in itself is such a standard. Others hold that perfection of our unique human capacities is such a standard. Still others hold that satisfaction of egoistic desires is the absolute standard. Thus, reasons fulfill me if they accord with maximizing pleasure, perfection, or satisfaction of desires in my life. Note that these standards are not now being regarded as competitors to what our view of true happiness is, but rather as competing substantive completions of what it is formally to be happy. The claim is that pleasure is true happiness because and only because it is the definitive standard for a reasonable being to give himself over to in order to fulfill his reasoning nature and so in order thereby to own any satisfaction with how his life is going. The list of candidates for definitive standards goes on and on: conformity to God's will, Stoic acceptance of life's travails; health of mind and body; fitting in with the natural and social world, etc.

My contention is that only if a supposed definitive standard is provable by reason can it be a standard I give myself over to as a definitive standard. If a standard is not provable I can't as a reasonable being give myself over to its definitive status. Rather at best I would make it to be a definitive standard by sheer will of giving myself over to it definitively. Equivalently, without proof I don't make what is a definitive standard mine—I make it to be a definitively held standard, or make it up as a definitive standard. But then the definitive standard which lies at the basis of all self-fulfillment of reason is effectively whatever I decide to give myself over to or else whatever I find myself having as a definitive standard. The former would mean that all self-fulfillment is basically arbitrary, since the particular definitive standard is arbitrary. The latter would mean that I do not give myself over to the standard, but have been abandoned to it. In neither case are particular reasons ever flat out reasons I can own as a reasonable being. Suppose that I have certain reasons for a particular aim or certain reasons for valuing something. If the standard of reasoning is what I decide, then basically I own those reasons as flat out good or not depending on what I decide to hold to be flat out good reasons. If the standard is what I find myself having, then I own those reasons as flat out good reasons depending on whether I find myself holding them to be flat out good. The standard of reasoning drops out altogether other than as a general characterization

of what I decide to go along with or find myself going along with. My fulfillment as a reasoning being in either case would be whatever strikes me as reasonable. Rather than fulfilling me as a reasonable being, for reasons to be flat
out good depending exclusively on what I decide to approve or find myself
approving violates my nature as a reasoning being giving myself over to a standard other than simply what strikes me as reasonable.

It is sometimes held that un-revisable definitive standards for satisfaction
don't need proof. There are those who claim to feel God's will in their hearts
and those who claim to have direct experience of God's will. In each case they
claim to know what God wants for our lives and that constitutes a conclusive
standard. This standard which does not come from reason could fulfill us as
reasonable beings only if it were first provable by reason that reason can provide no standard for satisfaction. In that case we could fulfill our nature as
reasoning beings in preparing the way for giving ourselves over to standards
other than reason such as feeling or experience. This essentially is the way
Augustine proceeds in the *Confessions*. He claims to prove that reason shows
reason can provide no standard at all by which we could be satisfied with how
our lives are going, and then turns to contemplation of God (by feeling or experience) for a standard of satisfaction.

A second kind of supposedly definitive standard that doesn't need proof
replaces reason not with feeling or experience, but with sheer will or sheer
endorsement. I give myself over to what I once endorsed just in that it was
once endorsed. Originally it is a sheer act of will, choice, etc. to adopt a standard for satisfaction, but once adopted I give myself over to it definitively. That
I thus re-commit to an original endorsement can be regarded perhaps as being
self-fulfilled as a being with will. We can call this position "voluntarism" or
"volitionism" in that it is originally an absolutely voluntary adoption uncon-
strained by reason. Then to give that volition force, and so to fulfill me as a
volitional being, I am to continue to submit my will to it. At least approxima-
tions to such a view appear in Kierkegaard, Nietzsche, and Sartre. Once again
such a view fulfills us only when our reasoning nature has been given its due by
showing that reason can supply no standard.

I take now as a fundamental postulate that no definitive standard can be
proved by reason, and nor can one prove that any standard must go beyond
reason. This is equivalent to saying that neither definitive standards of reason
nor definitive standards based on feeling, experience or will can fulfill us as
reasoning beings. The very history of give and take over what the real standard
of happiness is (White 2006) is evidence for the first part of the postulate that
a standard cannot be proved. A provable standard would have no pros and
cons. Proof ends the matter. The perennial candidates for such a standard are

either subject to such give and take or else confuse formal components of what it is to be happy with substantive standards of what makes for happiness.

Perfectionism is the view that the development or enhancement of our capacities constitutes happiness. It is contentment with such enhancement that can be fully endorsed as self-fulfilling. To be happy we should be engaging in that which enables our powers to grow and flourish (Kraut 2007;169). The objection against this as a substantive standard is not that it is only the barest of sketches which Kraut (2007;140) admits when he says that the concrete realization "differs enormously from person to person." The objection rather is that perhaps simplicity in the exercise of our capacities is what should be endorsed. For example, contemplating "high" art may develop our powers of contemplation, but contemplating the simple things in nature and hence merely employing our powers rather than growing them doesn't seem to be provably misguided. Working at complex tasks has something to say for it but so does simple work. Kraut goes on to say (2007;202) that the powers of a human being are "a template on which whatever is good for us can be situated." This may be true but that the template is for developing, enhancing or perfecting doesn't follow from this. Perhaps what is to be endorsed is a simple life in which our capacities are not stretched. Instead of spinning one's wheels learning how the universe works, maybe realizing simple curiosities is the way to go. One version of this is that our happiness might consist in living the way animals or children live. Of course unlike animals and children we would have this way of living as a standard for endorsement so that it would still be a form of human happiness. If perfection of capacities means just an exercise of them that can be enjoyed and endorsed as being enjoyed, then we no longer have a substantive standard, but only the formal idea that to be happy involves engaging in life in such a way that allows for endorsed contentment. Kraut connects his developmental version of perfectionism to what it is to flourish. But then what is owed is a proof that happiness requires flourishing. One might say that failing to enhance one's powers limits one's possibilities. Someone who fails to develop powers for artistic appreciation doesn't know what they are missing. However the very enhancement might make the person unable to appreciate simple things any more. Everything we do in life precludes doing other things the true value of which requires doing them, so that not knowing what you are missing doesn't favor development of powers.

David Brink (2007;390–392) contends

> For a person with the normal range of…capacities, it is a very bad thing to lead a simple one-dimensional life…a person's good involves being engaged in activities which exercise…creative powers.

What he says seems to me perfectly reasonable, but how is it conclusive or definitive? A "one-dimensional" life dedicated to simple pleasures seems possible as a standard of satisfaction. Brink goes on to talk of the perfection of the exercise of our deliberative capacities and says,

> This kind of perfectionism, it seems, promises to explain the normativity of the good.

But if perfection of our deliberative capacities means perfection of our capacity to endorse aims in accord with their realization contributing to being satisfied with how our lives are going, this is simply the formal standard of being skillful in regard to the pusrsuit of happiness once one has a standard of satisfaction. It doesn't itself provide a substantive standard. This kind of perfectionism explains the normativity of the good only in the formal sense that one should do what is needed to attain the good. If perfection of our deliberative capacities means perfection of our capacity to discern the good, then again this is no substantive definitive standard. Mixing together formal standards which are definitive of what means to pursue happiness, with substantive standards of what happiness is does not make the latter definitive.

Another sort of supposedly definitive standard is that there is an objective list of what to go for that together even if only as a sketch constitute happiness. Rawls (1971;426), for example, lists

> personal affection and friendship, meaningful work and social cooperation, the pursuit of knowledge, and the fashioning and contemplation of beautiful objects.

Freeman (2006;68–69) says that there are a plurality of objective goods leaving open only the issue of which ones it is rational to pursue depending on a person's circumstances, capacities, etc. Unlike perfectionism this sort of standard doesn't unify or base the list on grounds of development and enhancement of capacities. Basically the list includes what is thought to have great intrinsic value. This is made clear by Freeman's separating the objective goods from issues of whether to incorporate them in one's life. The supposed substantive standard then is simply that one's life incorporates what has great intrinsic value. This is only a substantive standard, however, if it eliminates some things. For Rawls it eliminates counting blades of grass as contributing to happiness. Let us agree for the sake of argument, but only for that, that such an activity lacks intrinsic value. It may nevertheless contribute to a thematic value in one's life that one has reason to endorse as a standard. Such repetitive, pointless activity can be endorsed for keeping us out of the fray or out of the grind of having to deal with all the difficulties that arise with activities that in their own regard might have great intrinsic value. Counting blades of grass can function as a form of meditation, spirituality, etc. In one sense the lives of monks repetitive and basically divorced from any earthly point seems to be like a life of counting blades of grass, and there seems to be nothing provably inadequate about endorsing such a life. Any sort of thematic standard which is realizable independent of the intrinsic value of things would have to be proven defective for the objective list to provably be even a sketch of a standard. As another example, a Derrida-like "standard" of merely ironic playing at things undercuts intrinsic values, but seems possible as a substantive standard. How would one prove that this cannot be a reasonable standard for endorsed contentment? As an analogy, consider what happens in some twentieth century art. Rather than the Mona Lisa we have a red dot on a yellow background. Rather than the Pieta we have Duchamp's toilet. These latter have no intrinsic value as objects of art, but have artistic value perhaps in that they disabuse us of thinking the value of art lies exclusively in the object, or that art is a somber, serious thing rather than our own play, etc.

A third sort of supposedly definitive standard with affinities to both perfectionism and objective-list views is excellence in ways of being (Nussbaum 2011). There are dimensions of life such as work, play, social relations, etc. and excellence in these ways of being is the standard for being satisfied with how one's life is going. This is a purely formal standard if it simply comes down to saying that being happy with one's life is being happy with it in the dimensions of life. It comes down to this if excellence in a dimension of being means something like valuable or good in contributing to overall life satisfaction. It has more content if it means that there is intrinsic value to certain realizations of these modes of being-work of a certain kind being intrinsically valuable as work, friendship of a certain kind that is intrinsically valuable as friendship. It then becomes an objective list account with an explanation of the list as deriving from the natural dimensions of our being. Despite the explanation it, no more than objective list accounts, establishes that thematic values that are relatively independent of intrinsic value pertaining to specific dimensions, are not a cogent substantive standard. Nature gives us what the various dimensions of our lives are and so what living is, but not what it is to be happy with how we are living. Even if one defines flourishing in terms of the intrinsic value of the various dimensions, this does not establish that being happy requires flourishing, so understood. It seems that one can embrace certain endeavors that has one has no talent for being excellent in as contributing to one's being satisfied with one's life. Though this would not contribute to flourishing as excellence in various dimensions, it might well contribute to happiness. Flanagan (2007;11) says of art, science, technology, ethics, politics, and spirituality that these name

> familiar domains with which virtually every modern life intersects. They name places to go to make meaning and sense of things including ourselves.

Although he is surely right that these name places we can go, he gives no proof any of these are places we must go, except perhaps if "spirituality" signifies in part self-fulfilling satisfaction.

The Stoic standard for happiness is endorsing being content in the face of any circumstances. This doesn't mean that anything that happens is as good as anything else, but that nothing that happens should be bad enough to dislodge contentment. To a large extent what circumstances are bad is filtered through what we aim at and value. The Stoic claims that failure to realize our aims and values is not flat-out bad so long as we can nevertheless endorse being content with how our lives are going. Such endorsed contentment is the overriding thematic value that, running through our lives, constitutes happiness. But what is the proof that this value constitutes happiness? Can't a person endorse the realization of other values above this, so that without the realization of them they cannot endorse contentment? Of course this will mean that the person will be not be satisfied without the realization, but the issue is not whether we will be satisfied with our lives or not, but what the substantive standard is according to which we are satisfied or not. The Stoic might retort that on his standard you have stability to happiness that is missing on any other standard. You are insulated against the disappointments in life. But it is only endorsable stability that matters. This brings us back to needing a proof that contentment whatever else is the standard. What is the Stoic's proof against objective list accounts according to which any contentment is fulfilling, and so is owned by me as a being with standards, only in the realization of other intrinsic values? To those who adhere to such a standard the Stoic's contentment in the face of failure of realization is not endorsable. It won't do for the Stoic to say you might as well be content, since it is better to be content than not content. Even if this is so intrinsically in its own right as a sheer emotional condition, it doesn't follow that therefore contentment is always to be flat out endorsed. It is formally true that without contentment there is no happiness. What it is to be happy is defined in part by contentment. This doesn't imply that contentment itself is even a sketch of a substantive standard of satisfaction with how one's life is going.

Welfare conditions such as health, absence of pain, shelter and nourish-
ment are not even a sketch of a provable substantive standard for happiness
even if they are a provable substantive condition of the capability for happiness. To be a definitive substantive standard it would have to be proved that
welfare is sufficient for happiness. To some it might be enough for endorsing
how their lives are going that they have health, enough to eat, etc. To prove this
standard one would have to establish that it doesn't matter what one does with
one's being healthy and having enough to eat. One would have to prove that
the reasons in support of perfectionism, for example, are dis-provable. Egoistic
and hedonic standards which go beyond mere welfare nevertheless also fail to
prove that intrinsic values (excellence, perfection) don't matter for endorsement. They would have to prove that everything I want or everything that
pleases me is therefore worthy of endorsement.

The various considerations pro and con between competing substantive
standards don't seem to be due to ignorance, passion, or failure to understand.
They seem to be genuine considerations germane to whether they are standards I can give myself over to as a reasoning being. The existence of such give
and take between familiar standards makes it plausible to postulate that there
are no definitive, conclusive standards.

The second component of the postulate is that we cannot fulfill our reasoning nature by using it to prove there are no standards at all that reason can give
us. Such a proof would open the way for definitive standards in experience,
emotion or will to be sanctioned by our reasoning nature, and hence to fulfill
us as reasoning beings in the only way we can be fulfilled. Augustine in the
Confessions contends that we can so fulfill our reasoning nature. His proof is
based on the following considerations – we cannot know the purpose of the
universe and so our purpose, we are nothing but matter in motion, life is not in
our control, nothing we do makes any significant difference to the vast reaches
of the universe in space and especially in time. For Augustine this multi-
pronged proof paves the way for the emotional and experiential love of God to
be the definitive, un-revisable and conclusive standard of happiness. Much
of what Augustine says are genuine considerations that could temper any
supposedly definitive standard of reason – thus adding to evidence for the first
component of the postulate. Nothing he says, however, comes to anything near
a proof. That we don't know a purpose for us doesn't imply we can't give ourselves a purpose. After all I can give new purposes to artifacts that are distinct
and independent of whatever they might have originally been designed for.
Why can't I similarly give purpose to my life independent of knowing any
purpose I was originally designed for? Even if we are matter in motion, we are
the kind of matter in motion that has reason and feeling by which to value

things. Some matter in motion (us) can value other matter in motion going one way rather than another. It is true that much in our lives is out of our control, but it is an open question as to whether this should be troubling enough to preclude our embracing and valuing things. Why would the potential loss of things in our lives over which we may not have control even bother us unless those things were valuable to have in life? Nothing we do is significant on a grand scale. In time most, if not all of our projects will be swallowed up like the desert sands swallowed King Ozymandius' supposedly grand life. That our lives come to nothing in the long run doesn't mean that we can't be happy with how our lives are going. Our lives can come to nothing even in our own lifetime as when tragedy strikes our children after we have spent out lives in raising them. This doesn't mean that we were never happy with how our lives were going. It means only that this happiness didn't last. Tragedy befalling our children after we are dead similarly doesn't entail that we were not happy with our lives throughout.

Augustine asks us to contemplate an ideal story of life in the compass of the universe. This story, let us admit, has maximal intrinsic value in regard to contemplation. He presumes that fitting this story, or at least living completely in the hope of fitting this story, is the only true happiness. But an ideal can be what focuses our aspirations without its being something that, unachieved, destroys those aspirations. One could conclude from Augustine's story that in giving oneself over to a standard for being satisfied with how one's life is going, one must take into consideration the contemplation of what life is as a whole in the flow of the universe. This becomes part of what one may have reason to consider in establishing a standard, not a denial of any standard. One may find this contemplation inspiring, not as Augustine does as being something troubling enough to prevent any endorsed contentment.

(iv)

If the postulate is accepted then there is no standard provable by reason and no proof that we must go beyond reason to a standard based on feeling, experience or will. Actually for all our purposes the weaker postulate that no one has come up with either of these proofs is sufficient. It follows then that reason cannot be fulfilled either by giving itself over to a definitive standard, or by abandoning itself to other sources of a definitive standard. That there is no definitive standard in or out of reason implies that the only way for reason to be fulfilled is to be open-minded in whatever standard in or out of reason it gives itself over to. Reason, that is, can only be fulfilled by a standard that is other than its own ruminating by giving itself over to the considerations and information (though not the proof) regarding what to be satisfied with in life that others, as well as oneself, can provide. Any of the standards we have looked at—perfectionism, objective-list etc.; standards based in feeling, will, etc.—can fulfill reason so long as they are held in an open-minded way. As I look for reasons to contribute to standards for how my life is going, even reasons for going to feeling or will for a standard, since I have no definitive reasons the considerations that others present and how things go in other people's lives according to their considered standards are pertinent to my considering as a reasoning being. They are pertinent either as calling my considerations into question, or as deepening and reinforcing my considerations, or as being thought to be irrelevant and so not having to be taken into further account. The substantive standard then is any open-minded standard. Such open-mindedness satisfies Wittgenstein's requirement that a norm must allow for conditions of failure in order to be a genuine norm. If I give myself over to such a norm of open-mindedness then my own personally developed actual reasoning including my own personal correcting fails to conform to it if I neglect or ignore others' reasoning. If reasoning could prove a standard then open-mindedness would not be something to give oneself over to as a reasoning being. When a mathematician definitively proves a proposition, it seems a perversion of reason to be open minded about the proposition. Once we accept the postulate of no-proof, however, being open minded seems a norm that reason must give itself over to and so a norm that fulfills our nature as reasoning beings. If the postulate is accepted, that is, then the only satisfaction with how our lives are going that can be fulfilling (including fulfilling to our nature as reasoning beings) is one that is answerable to an open minded revisable standard. Note that this doesn't imply that one can never be happy with how his life is going because the standard is open to revision. The satisfaction with how my life is going can be well considered and so belong to me as a reasoning being during one period, even if new considerations and information make a different standard well considered at a later period. The fact that I now understand that my standard may have to be later revised does not mean that as a reasoning being I can't be committed to it now. It is possible for a person to revise their standards through their lives while yet being happy throughout their lives.

We said that true (non-defective) happiness is well considered satisfaction with how one's life is going. We can now say that well considered does not mean definitively established. Rather it means open minded or adjudicated in terms of considerations and information available from others. From now on when I talk of well-considered satisfaction it is to be taken in just this sense. Here is what Kraut (2007;203) says,

> Every account of what is good for a human being must be a sketch...further elaboration and further inquiry is always possible...the story we tell about our powers is always subject to revision and expansion...we can always find new insights about what is good for us.

All that I would add is that the sketch itself may have to be abandoned for a different sketch and that what has to be included in what makes the story subject to revision and expansion are others' considerations for their story and others' information gotten by carrying out their story. Kekes (1982) similarly holds that happiness is rationally evaluable satisfaction with one's life and that there are no standards outside of inter-subjective rational evaluation. He doesn't quite go far enough however since for him what evaluation pertains to is only feasibility and consistency, whereas I claim it pertains as well to the elements of value.

According to Rousseau and Kant our autonomy consists in being bound by a law of reason that we ourselves give to ourselves. I have now claimed that self-fulfilling life satisfaction is satisfaction according to a norm of reason (being open-minded about one's standards) that we as reasoning beings give ourselves over to. Explicating Sumner's idea of authentic life satisfaction as self-fulfilling satisfaction, we get that authentic non-defective happiness must be autonomous as Sumner holds. The supposed objection to Sumner's requirement of autonomy, recall, was that Plato's citizens have true happiness by having true opinion from the guardians, and so have true happiness without autonomy. The objection fails since there are no guardians who have proof or conclusive grasp of what happiness is and so there is no way of being happy by having true opinion. For better or worse we are "saddled" with having to author our standard of satisfaction based upon our open minded reasoning.

Sumner's other component of authentic happiness was that we have a good factual grasp of how our lives are actually going in support of our satisfaction. The objection, recall, was that if one's reasonable standard for how it is going is exactly that one merely thinks it is going according to one's standard then a good grasp of how it is actually going seems irrelevant and even deleterious to authentic happiness. Let S encapsulate any particular standard. Then the standard we are to consider is not S but S': thinking-my-life-is-going-S-based-on-my-experiences, where the veridicality of the experiences is beside the point. Suppose that finding love is a component of S and I have experiences such that I think I have found love with Mary and that these experiences are not veridical since unbeknownst to me Mary cheats, lies, etc. I experience only her fake "loving" self. Now for me to be open minded in my standard S' I must be open to considerations that others offer me regarding the standard S that is part of my standard. The following would be such considerations: Someone says to me that Mary is cheating and lying, that it is hard to find true love, that one must aim for a person of character and not be swept away, that love requires mutual respect. But if S' is my standard I will just brush off these considerations or pretend verbally to take them into account. In either case I continue on without any pause in my love for Mary since all I care about are experiences and I am getting them. This response is quite different than if I say that I don't care I love her anyway, which is a response that takes the considerations into account and rejects them. In brief I will insulate myself against genuinely taking others' considerations into account. But now the other is put at a loss as to how to communicate with me. What they say is just brushed off or responded to verbally without any modification of my behavior that shows the verbal response to be anything more than a pretense, or perhaps an inability to genuinely respond. The point is that others communicate considerations from the vantage point of how my life *is* going, whereas my response is not from that vantage point-making genuine communication impossible. But now a standard S' that puts others at a loss as to how to genuinely communicate considerations regarding the key S component of the standard implies that the standard S' cannot be held in an open minded way. Hence it cannot be a standard that is self-fulfilling to me as a reasoning being. Thus S' is defective as a standard by being inconsistent with what it is to be truly happy. The basic defense of Sumner's requirement is that a standard S' cannot forgo having a good grasp of how one's life is going and yet be open minded because having such a grasp is necessary in being the only vantage point from which others are able to communicate their considerations.

People are not usually willingly self-deceptive in regard to all aspects of how their lives are going. Usually they make communication impossible only in regard to one facet or another of their standard (S) for being satisfied. Someone who holds to the fully deceptive standard S' would have their standard satisfied by being in a Nozick machine that filters out all their experiences in life that go against S. In a sense such a person tries to put himself into a Nozick machine of his own making. The reason against entering a Nozick machine is not per se that we want our experiences to be real, because the question the machine example raises is exactly why we want that. My suggestion is that it is because being in such a machine puts others at a loss as to how to communicate with us over what our standard *within* the machine is. This cuts a person off from his existence as a reasoning being and hence precludes authentic life-satisfaction.

Returning now to the idea of well-considered but never definitive standards, it may seem that for reason to operate there has to be a final, definitive standard, even if it can't be reached, for otherwise reason is getting nowhere.

An analogy to aesthetic appreciation should help to see that this isn't so. Simply liking a piece of music by finding it emotionally satisfying is not yet to appreciate it. That requires that the liking be sensitive to considerations about the piece by which the liking is aesthetically endorsable. There seem to be no definitive, un-revisable standards which determine for me finally what the overall value of the piece is. Being open to the considerations of others as the basis of endorsability whether these considerations are duly rejected or duly incorporated enriches one's grasp of the basis of endorsability. This enrichment is internal to aesthetic reasoning without requiring that there be some final definitive appreciation. There is no such thing as finally being done with appreciating a Brahms symphony.

The analogy between the aesthetic appreciation of a work and well considered satisfaction with one's life goes beyond sheer lack of conclusiveness. Considerations leading to endorsement are not enough for aesthetic appreciation if they don't bring forth or at least allow us to own an emotional response in, say, hearing a symphony's performance. Similarly considerations favoring endorsement are not enough for life satisfaction if they don't bring forth or at least allow us to own an emotional response of contentment. The analogy is strong enough to say that being truly happy is a matter of appreciating, as opposed to merely liking, how our lives are going. For Kant aesthetic judgment is objective without being responsible to any object other than considered judgment itself. Its objectivity is the determination of its richness by the mutual interchange between subjects. This likewise is what judgments of happiness are responsible to.

That a standard for self-fulfilling satisfaction is never definitive does not mean that it can't ground strong commitment. It is just that no well-considered satisfaction is perfect. If the postulate is correct then there is no such thing as perfect happiness. This doesn't imply that one can only be tentatively happy. It is just that one's whole hearted reasonable satisfaction is subject to revision. Nor is open mindedness the same as vagueness or incompleteness. The content of one's present standard of endorsement and its reasons if too vague or incomplete means that one is short of true happiness. That it is revisable means it is short of chimerical perfect happiness, not true happiness. Finally it may be that the subject's reasons for his standard of satisfaction are not explicit all at once to the subject. It is often the pressure of reasons and endorsements of others which force explicitness. For the most part I have only a tutored sense of how my standard is justifiable to me. A comparison of each of these points with the case of aesthetic appreciation should make them clear.

As mentioned, the description of what it is to be happy includes normative elements. The real distinction between a supposedly descriptive versus a normative conception of what happiness is concerns how far the normative conception is actually instantiated in people's lives. Especially in regard to true happiness as involving a non-definitive standard and so a norm of open mindedness, there is a great deal to doubt about its being widely instantiated. At least a large portion of many people's standards are held definitively. This is true not only of many religious people, but of people religious or not who are bound to cultural standards and of scientific people who claim knowledge of what constitutes happiness. These people are not truly happy – their supposed happiness is defective. This discrepancy between what it is to be happy and how people live is no different than the discrepancy between what it is to be moral and how people behave. If one defines happiness as what people take to be the final good and the ground of all flat out good reasons in their lives, then of course people with closed minds can be happy. It seems better to say that such people are falsely happy.

(v)

In sum to be happy with how one's life is going is to be satisfied in a self-fulfilling way with how one's life is going. Any contentment or endorsement that fulfills me as a reasoning being must conform to a standard that I as a reasoning being give myself over to. Further there is no definitive or conclusive standard that I can give myself over to other than one that accords with the (second-order) norm of being open-minded toward considerations for or against any standard of satisfaction. This is what constitutes well considered satisfaction with how my life is going which is the only kind of satisfaction that is self-fulfilling. In Chapter 4 the claim will be that respect and care for others' pursuit of happiness is a necessary component of anyone's happiness. No one, that is, can be happy who fails to respect and care for the pursuit of happiness of all others. Before turning to this key claim it is well to review how the notion of happiness that has been set out relates to notions such as eudaimonia, flourishing, well-being, and welfare.

It has been argued that happiness is the final good, the final end and what is at the bottom of all flat out good practical reasons. In these respects it agrees with Aristotle's conception of eudaimonia. For Aristotle eudaimonia is excellence of activity in accord with practical wisdom. This includes an emotional component that is at least akin to contentment in that such activity for Aristotle will be pleasant (un-impeded, non-troubling). Since practical wisdom endorses a standard for what is to be aimed for, being content in activities that conform to this standard constitutes eudaimonia as emotional fulfillment that is also fulfilling to our nature as reasoning beings. In this regard our understanding of happiness agrees with Aristotle's eudaimonia. As to the substantive standard Aristotle seems to accept some sort of perfectionist view according to which our activities must have excellence in their own right in order to accord with practical wisdom. Roughly I must be engaging in activities that I am good at or can become good at in a way that only human beings can so engage— a good friend, a good craftsman, a good citizen. The activities, that is, must develop unique human capacities of intelligence, ingenuity, etc. If this is Aristotle's view then there is disagreement with our view over the substantive standard. For Aristotle practical wisdom consists in being responsive to objective standards while on our view it consists in being responsible for standards that it can be responsive to as a reasoning being. In sum at the formal level eudaimonia agrees with our view of happiness, whereas substantively there is a great divide. It turns out to be a deep and significant divide in relation to morality.

Eudaimonia is often equated to flourishing. Flourishing I believe has a connotation of doing well or excellently in worthwhile activities in a way that embodies our happiness, or our final good or final end. If so, then flourishing is equivalent to Aristotle's full formal plus substantive understanding of eudaimonia. But other ancient philosophers had a different substantive standard for eudaimonia (for happiness as the final good or the final end). For this reason it seems to me best to use the term flourishing not for eudaimonia per se but rather for a substantive way that eudaimonia can be realized. On our view flourishing is not definitive of happiness. A person could be happy without flourishing. For some of us playing the piano badly, getting only passing grades at school, etc. may contribute to happiness, though we would hardly be said to be flourishing in our activities. Chekhov describes one of his characters as having no talent other than a talent for living, which is just to say that being excellent in particular activities is not essential for happiness.

Aristotle in his discussion of the life of contemplation has a notion that goes beyond flourishing – namely leading an *exceptionally* happy life. This doesn't signify an exceptional degree or kind of emotional feeling, but rather engaging in an activity that has or produces great intrinsic value and which is difficult and so not an activity people commonly have talent for. It seems possible for people to lead exceptional lives without being happy at all. Van Gogh would seem to be an example. A student at the top of all his classes, the captain of the football team, and so on is leading an exceptional life even if he is troubled and morose. Although they are exceptional in their artistic and student activities and so exceptional in their lives neither are happy. The inversion of Chekhov's character would have an exceptional talent for everything except for living.

Despite the even exceptional excellences it does not seem to me that either Van Gogh or the student is flourishing *in their lives.*

As far as what pertains to the characterization of our lives, these considerations suggest that eudaimonia be equated with happiness as the final good or the final end, that flourishing be equated with a way of being happy that involves excellence in particular dimensions of life which leaves it open that one can flourish in his art without flourishing in life. This leaves the case of lives that, though excellent or exceptional in activities, yet aren't happy. If all activities were productive we could use the terms productive and exceptionally productive lives to cover this case. Since not all activities are productive the best I can think of is living an accomplished life or a life that is exceptionally accomplished. Flourishing then would be living an accomplished life that one is happy with.

The term well-being is sometimes used in contrast to being happy. For example Sizer (2010) says that happiness can fail to track well-being. For Sizer a person is happy if he takes himself to be living well. Happiness, that is, is well-being as reckoned by the subject. This is only well-being tout court if the subject's reckoning is axiologically and factually justified. Her distinction is basically Sumner's contrast between happiness and authentic happiness. I prefer to mark the distinction as one between a person's thinking that they are happy versus his being happy. A person's life is going well if the person is satisfied in a self-fulfilling way with how it is going, whereas a person merely thinks his life is going well if he is satisfied with how it is going, but this satisfaction is not self-fulfilling (is defective). On this terminology happiness is equivalent to well-being. Annas (1995) equates happiness with living well and contrasts both to pleasure, desire-satisfaction and life-satisfaction. This seems to me correct for life satisfaction that isn't authentic.

The term welfare is sometimes used as a synonym for happiness. Thus Sumner (1996;172) says,

> Welfare consists in authentic happiness, the happiness of an informed and autonomous subject.

I believe that this is an inflated use of the term. If someone is faring well in their lives they are not necessarily happy. Rather things are good enough for them to be capable of pursuing and being happy. If I ask someone how they are doing (faring) they may say they are all right or doing well, meaning not that they are happy, but that things are going good enough. Faring well includes such things as health, absence of debilitating physical or emotional pain, absence of debilitating poverty, etc., as well as absence of debilitating circumstances such as tragedies too great to let them get on with their lives. There is a minimal level of how our lives are going below which happiness and its pursuit is not possible. There are misfortunes of hunger, sickness, tragic loss that debilitate us emotionally or otherwise preclude any pursuit of happiness unless and until they are overcome. This level of misfortune may be different for different people. Above this level a person's life may or may not be happy. It is important to keep some such notion of welfare distinct from notions of happiness and well-being, since our relationship to those who lack welfare is significantly different than to those who lack happiness.

To summarize, I suggest that happiness, living well and eudaimonia signify that which is at the bottom of all ends, values and reasons, which in turn I have claimed is self-fulfilling satisfaction with how one's life is going. Flourishing is happiness that also realizes intrinsic value in the dimensions of life. Living an accomplished life is realizing intrinsic value whether happy with how one's life is going or not. Welfare or good fortune is one's life going well enough to be capable of being happy.

CHAPTER 4

The Happiness of Others

(i)

Nothing so far has been said about how, if at all, the happiness of others is relevant to what it is for a person to be happy. The claim in this chapter is that others' pursuit of happiness is constitutive of what it is for any person to be happy. It is the task of this chapter first to defend this claim and then to clarify what it comes to.

Recall that for a person to be happy is for his satisfaction with his life to be something he owns. It must be something that fulfills him as a reasoning being. Hence the satisfaction must conform to a standard he can give himself over to as a reasoning being. Since by our postulate there is no definitive or conclusive standard he can give himself over to, it follows that for a person to be happy he must give himself over to being open-minded about standards for satisfaction he comes to or has. Only in this way does his reasoning conform to the non-conclusive nature of what he is reasoning about. Now to be open-minded is not just a condition of being tentative versus being dogmatically fixed. It is a condition of being tentative "for" further considerations. Any standard, that is, is subject to further considerations which either re-enforce it, modify it, or lead to its abandonment. Further being open-minded is an active condition not a passive one. I as a reasoning being do not give myself over to the non-definitive nature of the standard by avoiding pertinent considerations and information and thus continuing on with the standard. That would be to treat it as a definitive standard or at least to fail to treat it as the non-definitive standard that it is. The issue then becomes what is the pertinent information and the pertinent considerations that I must give myself over to in order to give myself over to open-mindedness? Note that if open-mindedness is to be something that I give myself over to then, again following Wittgenstein and Korsgaard, the pertinent considerations can't be just how I actually consider and re-consider things on my own. This would not allow for failure and would be a matter of self-congratulation not self-fulfillment. It must be then that the pertinent information and pertinent considerations that I give myself over to are other than my own. The issue more exactly is what is the pertinent information and considerations beyond my own that I must be open to in order to give myself over to open-mindedness regarding standards of satisfaction?

© KONINKLIJKE BRILL NV, LEIDEN, 2014 | DOI 10.1163/9789004283213_005

Since I have no definitive knowledge of any specific standards of satisfaction, the considerations that others have for or against standards of satisfaction are pertinent. These considerations of others include not just their reasoning about what might be a standard to adopt, but how standards they adopt pan out in practice – whether realizing the standard reveals it to be one that brings satisfaction or not, what new considerations its being realized bring forth, etc. But now the pursuit of happiness at its core is just coming to reasoned standards, seeing how they pan out, revising or modifying them according to further considerations, etc. Thus since I have no definitive knowledge, what is pertinent is exactly others' pursuit of happiness. If I am to give myself over to the open nature of standards of satisfaction in order to own any satisfaction with how my life is going then I must give myself over to being open to what comes from others' pursuit of happiness.

To give myself over to what comes from others' pursuit is to give myself over to regard for others' pursuit. An analogy should make this clear. Suppose that I give myself over to voting by the club members as the standard for how I as treasurer shall spend the club's money. Suppose however that I have no regard for their actually voting. I attempt to block voting, to get the members not to hold a vote, etc. Then I really do not give myself over to the standard of being open to voting. The disregard makes it a charade. Similarly suppose that I give myself over to being open to the considerations of others in their pursuit— being open to taking such considerations into account and holding or modifying my own standard of satisfaction accordingly. But suppose I have no regard for their pursuit. I keep myself open-minded, but block or sabotage the pursuit of others. I sabotage what there is to keep myself open to. This is to sabotage or defeat the norm of open-mindedness one is supposedly giving oneself over to, and so again is a mere charade. It follows then that if I am to give myself over to the norm of open-mindedness and so own any satisfaction with how my life is going then I must give myself over to regard for the pursuit of happiness of others.

Note the claim is not that since I don't know what will make me satisfied with how my life is going I should be open to and so have regard for the information about satisfaction that others can provide. This is true but the claim goes deeper than that, for it says that whatever satisfaction with my life I may have it is not truly owned and so is not happiness unless I own it in accord with being open to and having regard for the pursuit of others. The claim is not that regard for the pursuit of others is a means to my finding happiness, but that it is constitutive of what it is for me to be happy—to own satisfaction I might realize.

According to Chapter 2 something is flat-out valuable to the extent that it can contribute to happiness. Since now regard for others' pursuit contributes to happiness it is flat-out valuable. Since it is necessary for happiness and so necessary for anything else to be able to contribute to happiness, regard for others' pursuit is a value that other values cannot contradict if they are to contribute to happiness and so be flat-out valuable. Thus regard for others' pursuit is not only valuable, but a condition of anything else being flat-out valuable. In this sense it dominates or takes precedence over all other values. For example, however great the intrinsic value of knowledge or art may be if it is achieved by violating regard for others' pursuit then it has no flat-out value. Regard for others' pursuit is also objectively valuable in that it is not just a component of happiness, but an essential component of the happiness of anyone whatsoever.

The result then is that regard for others' pursuit of happiness is a necessary constituent of anyone's happiness. No one no matter what they achieve in life, no matter how satisfied they are with how their lives are going can be happy if they don't incorporate as a predominant value regard for the pursuit of happiness of others. Again according to Chapter 2, something is a flat out aim or end if its realization is flat-out valuable. Suppose that one of my ends or aims violates regard for another's pursuit of happiness; it blocks their coming to their own standards or realizing standards they come to in order to see how they pan out, etc. Then the realization of my end or aim cannot be flat-out valuable since whatever satisfaction with my life the realization contributes to will not be satisfaction according to a standard that is well considered. Since the realization cannot be flat-out valuable neither can the end or aim. Hence nothing is to be flat-out aimed for that contradicts regard for others' pursuit. Regard for others' pursuit takes precedence over all aims and ends and does so for anyone whatsoever. It is an objective constraint on anyone's aims or ends.

Finally from Chapter 3 there is no flat-out good reason for doing an action if its being done is inconsistent with the overall good reason it takes to endorse how my life is going. But any action that violates regard for others' pursuit of happiness by blocking it, sabotaging it, etc., is an action that being done is inconsistent with the overall good reason it takes to endorse satisfaction since that overall good reason involves conforming to open-mindedness. Thus there can be no flat-out good reason for doing anything that violates others' pursuit of happiness. Considered on its own I may have good reason to steal from you which we may suppose interferes with your plans for your life. It will get me the money I need to buy a car or take a trip. However I am not thinking things through. Buying a car or taking a trip matters only if it contributes to self-fulfilling satisfaction with how my life is going. By thwarting your pursuit however I close off your considerations involving the use of the money for what is perhaps a standard of satisfaction you have that I could learn from and so I am being closed minded. I may be satisfied with having the car, but I can't claim that satisfaction as well considered. Thus regard for others' pursuit takes precedence over all other reasons for acting in the sense that there can be no flat-out good reasons for acting that contradict that regard.

In sum since being happy with how one's life is going is at the bottom of all flat-out values, flat-out aims and flat-out good reasons for actions and regard for others' pursuit of happiness is an essential constituent of anyone's being happy with how their lives are going, it follows that regard for the pursuit of happiness of others is at the bottom of all values, all aims and all reasons for acting. This is the fundamental result of our entire discussion of happiness. Before turning to the clarification of what regard for others' pursuit comes to, I review step by step the argument for the fundamental result.

1. To be happy with how one's life is going is to be satisfied in a way one can own (in a self-fulfilling way) with how it is going.
2. One can own satisfaction with how one's life is going only if one owns the reasons for being satisfied.
3. One can own reasons for it (and so be self-fulfilled) only by giving oneself over to a norm of what is reasonable in regard to being satisfied.
4. There is no proof of any specific standard for being satisfied and so no definitive standard that one can give oneself over to as fulfilling one's reasoning being.
5. So one can own reasons for satisfaction only by giving oneself over to a norm of open-mindedness regarding reasons for satisfaction.
6. From 1, 2, and 5 to be happy with how one's life is going one must give oneself over to a norm of open-mindedness.
7. To give oneself over to a norm of open-mindedness is to be open to and to have regard for (as worthy of consideration) pertinent reasons (considerations, information) beyond one's own reasons for satisfaction (Wittgenstein).
8. What other people take to be reasons for being satisfied and whether these reasons pan out or have to be modified as they live their lives accordingly are the only reasons there are beyond my own reasoning.
9. From 7 and 8 to give oneself over to a norm of open-mindedness is to be open to and to have regard for other people developing reasons for what would satisfy them and modifying them or not according to how things pan out.
10. Other people developing reasons and holding or modifying them according to how things pan out just is their pursuit of happiness.
11. From 9 and 10 to give oneself over to a norm of open-mindedness is to be open to and have regard for others' pursuit of happiness.
12. From 6 and 11 to be happy with how one's life is going one must be open to and have regard for others' pursuit of happiness.

Since regard for others' pursuit is an essential component of what it is for me to be happy it is also an essential component of my pursuit of happiness. No pursuit of happiness that violates regard for others' pursuit can possibly lead to happiness. To violate regard for another's pursuit is to block, distort or otherwise preclude their consideration of standards of satisfaction. But this means that any satisfaction I get from the violation closes off pertinent reasons for being satisfied despite the fact that I have no proof of my reasons. I cannot as a reasoning being own such satisfaction and so be happy. Whatever my reasoned conception of what might be satisfying and whether or not it pans out in the realization of the conception (viz., whatever my pursuit is) it cannot ensue in a conception I can be satisfied with except by also having regard for others' pursuit. Since a pursuit that is flat-out inconsistent with achieving or maintaining happiness is not a pursuit of happiness at all but only a defective semblance of such a pursuit it follows that I cannot pursue happiness without regard for others' pursuit.

This result that I cannot pursue happiness without regard for others' pursuit makes the pursuit of happiness inevitably an inter-subjective enterprise. There is no such thing as my pursuit separable or isolable from others' pursuit. A separable pursuit would leave me with nothing but my own reasoning without any norm for my reasoning. It would leave me "open-minded" without there being anything in regard to which I was open minded. Much of the account of morality in Part Two and of freedom in Part Three depends on this idea that no one's pursuit of happiness is divorced from anyone else's, so that the pursuit of happiness is not an individual enterprise but an inter-subjective one. It will be helpful to have a similar example of such an enterprise to refer to as a model.

Consider the enterprise of becoming a good chess player. The goal of this enterprise is not just to win games, but to win games well—to become an excellent chess player. Being satisfied with winning, even consistently winning, will not be enough. One wants to win in challenging, intelligent, and innovative ways. We postulate that there is no definitive or conclusive standard for how to play which guarantees winning no matter how intelligent and challenging one's opponents are. We postulate, that is, that there is no decision procedure for winning at chess. Because there is no definitive or conclusive standard developing one's chess play involves regard for the play of others. I could sit alone and run through pretend games where I take the part of both opponents. This could go some of the way toward becoming someone who wins well at chess. Taking the part of an opponent may help me to see certain weaknesses in my strategies but it won't help me see my weakness as an opponent of my strategies. Individualistic self-correcting will go only so far. To become one who wins well at chess one wants challenging opponents with their own strategies who are clever and innovative in their play. During games each party may even clarify what his strategy is and point out to the other what better moves the other might have made, so that each comes to a better understanding of what was involved in winning that interesting game. Each party, that is, has regard for the well playing of the other in that game and so for the others' pursuit of winning well in chess. It is within this mutual regard that each pursues winning well at chess. Although chess is a competitive game whose point is to win, the enterprise of being excellent at chess has a higher level cooperative aspect in which each has regard for the well playing of others. Each walks away from the competition as a winner in the respect of chess excellence. If I win without regard for your well playing, say I try to psych you out, divert your attention, etc. then I may be satisfied with my win, but I cannot be satisfied in a well-considered way – in a way that I can own, and that can fulfill me as chess-playing being. It may be that in real life what matters most is simply winning any which way so that if I become expert at unnerving my opponents that is a way to chess supremacy. It is not however a way to chess intelligence innovation and winning in well considered ways according to the nature of the game itself. Henceforth when I talk of the enterprise of chess I mean the enterprise of pursuing well considered satisfaction with one's play in winning—viz., chess-happiness.

(ii)

The question now is what does regard for others' pursuit of happiness come to? In what follows the pursuit of happiness includes those who are happy as well as those who are not. The person already happy with how his life is going still pursues the continuance of happiness. In pursuing happiness a person seeks or has his own reasoned conception of what would constitute well-considered satisfaction with how his life is going. Equivalently a person seeks or has a standard of satisfaction he can claim as a reasoning being. Even if the person is already happy with how his life is going this standard is subject to revision in accord with further consideration. This revision may come either prior to any realizing of the original standard or it may come during or after the realization of it. In the former case the person is prospectively reconsidering what he aims to realize, while in the latter case he is retrospectively reconsidering based on how the attempt has been going so far or how it seems to him after achieving the realization. In either case being subject to revision does not mean actually revising. Further considering may lead to a modification or rejection of his standard, but it may also lead to a more well-considered holding to the standard. The question is what regard must I who thus pursue happiness have for another who likewise pursues happiness?

Both the others' prospective and retrospective considering are pertinent for me to take into account in my ongoing seeking or having a standard for satisfaction. Others' considerations in both regards are exactly what I give myself over to in being open-minded. This doesn't imply that I accept or agree with those considerations. Rather I take them into account or incorporate them as leading either to a more well-considered holding to my standard or to a modification or a rejection. For example if their standard and their considerations (reasons) for it oppose mine in certain ways I will take this as an opportunity to perhaps come up with counter-considerations which thus enrich the standard that I hold to. It is by incorporating others' prospective and retrospective reasoning rather than disregarding it that I give myself over to a standard of open-mindedness and so make any standard for satisfaction that I have or can get self-fulfilling to me as a reasoning being.

What is outside or beyond my own actual considerations is the arising or existence of prospective and retrospective considerations of others. It is others coming up with their reasons (reasons I myself might not ever come up with) that give me something to be open to beyond my own reasoning. Their prospective "imagination" of ways of living and what would or would not be appealing about such ways is different than mine. Their retrospective reasoning especially provides considerations that I would not come up with. Retrospectively they see how the standard for satisfaction they have pans out in practice (in being attempted or realized). Not everything about the cogency of a purported conception of happiness can be prospectively worked out. The proof as they say is in the pudding. One's prospective ideas of what makes certain personal relations attractive as part of fitting into a satisfaction with one's life may be modified strengthened or weakened upon the realization of these relations. Tiberius (2008;76) puts this point succinctly:

> it is (at least in part) by being a friend, daughter, sibling, parent that we discover what is valuable in these relationships.

Now I cannot possibly come up with what retrospective considering can provide in relation to all potential candidates for standards of satisfaction. I can only live one life. Others however can provide test cases for how standards different than mine pan out. Equivalently others provide me with experiments in living that I can't carry out, and so with retrospective considerations I cannot come to on my own.

In order to be open-minded I must let the prospective and retrospective considerations arise from others themselves – I cannot be the one directing or producing them. As an analogy consider a particular researcher running experiments to get considerations about a cure for cancer where such a cure is not yet known. They prospectively have ideas about what might work, and run that kind of experiment that would lead to retrospective considerations about how they may need to modify their ideas. Since the cure is not yet known they have no proof of what experiments should be run and so should be open to other researchers running their own experiments according to their own prospective ideas. Not only is it closed minded to refuse to consider information gotten from other experiments, but equally it is closed minded to direct which other experiments should be run. As regards the pursuit of happiness the standard of open mindedness for me requires that prospective and retrospective considerations of others arise from them. I must have regard for their being the authors or the sources of their pursuit of happiness within which prospective and retrospective considerations are generated or arise. This regard does not extend to those who are not open minded in being the source of their considerations. If they hold to a specific standard as definitive or conclusive any considerations that arise that are skewed by their holding to this standard are not considerations I must be open to in order to be open-minded. Being open-minded doesn't require being open to closed-mindedness. That element of their authorship of their lives does not demand regard. We have then the result that being open-minded requires full regard for the being of others as the open-minded source of the arising of prospective and retrospective considerations.

Further this regard is for others *exactly* as such open-minded sources. The regard is not mitigated by other factors such as the other not being intelligent, talented, creative, gregarious, etc. Recall that in our defense of the postulate that there is no proof of a standard of satisfaction we claimed that there seem to be pros and cons to all standards. Being talented in various ways is not necessarily having more "talent for living" as Chekhov puts it. Simpler lives have something to say for themselves and so are to be duly regarded as sources of considerations arising as much as the lives of geniuses. Nor is regard to be mitigated by another's life not seeming to be particularly unique or novel. It is not the case that one butcher, baker or candlestick maker more or less makes no difference to my open-minded consideration. Each may have distinct considerations and each may constitute significantly different "experiments in living" despite surface similarities. The resources of each individual for reasoning and for emotional possibilities, let alone the variation in circumstances, make each life something I, as open minded, must have regard for. One should no more hold that one more butcher-life is not going to make a significant difference than one who is trying to come to a rich aesthetic sensibility should hold that one more impressionist garden is not going to make a difference.

My regard for another's pursuit is a generic regard for his very being as someone authorizing his own pursuit of self-fulfilling satisfaction. It seems fair to say that this is a regard for the other as a person, a regard for the other's human dignity as the author of their lives in accord with their emotional, thinking, and reasoning nature. In Korsgaard's terms (1996) it is a regard for the practical identity of the other just as it pertains to being human. The proof that such regard for the other is integral to one's own open-minded pursuit of how to live, is a proof then that the personhood or dignity of the other is integral to one's own personhood or dignity, that one's own personhood or dignity is inseparable from regard for the personhood of others.

(iii)

Regard for others' pursuit comes in two broad categories one of which is respect for their pursuit and the other of which is care for it. Respect pertains to how one is to refrain in acting toward others while care pertains to what one is to do. Respect pertains to how one is not to intervene while care pertains to how one is to intervene. Roughly the distinction is between not doing harm versus helping or aiding. Suppose that there is a valuable ancient vase on a pedestal. Respecting it includes not playing racket ball in the room not picking it up and juggling with it, etc. Caring for it includes placing it more securely on the pedestal if it is partly over the edge, encasing it in glass, etc. Respecting it so to speak is hands-off whereas caring for it is hands-on. Although it is not a hard and fast distinction and not an easy one to make out precisely it is nevertheless a significant one as we shall see.

A person's pursuit of happiness exists in his considering values in an open-minded way and his acting to realize values. If the consideration of values includes not just what is intrinsically valuable but also what is flat out valuable (Chapter 2) then considering values is tantamount to forming a standard for satisfaction, holding to a standard revising a standard, etc. The considering as we have seen can be prospective or retrospective. To fail to respect another's pursuit then is to fail to respect either their open-minded consideration of values or their acting to realize their values or both. One sort of failure to respect is by interfering, blocking, or getting in the way. For example if I manipulate another's considerations for my own purposes or if I deceive them about pertinent facts then I am interfering with their open-minded considering of values. If I injure their leg I interfere with their realizing their value of being a champion ice skater. In the first case I fail to have regard for the arising of their prospective considerations and in the second I fail to have regard for the arising of retrospective considerations. In either case I thereby fail to give myself over to a norm of open-mindedness. However I "benefit" from the interference I cannot claim that benefit as contributing to a self-fulfilling satisfaction with how my life is going. Thus, in demoting their pursuit of happiness I demote mine as well.

People can have competing values so that one person's realizing his value of working as a lumberjack precludes another from realizing his value of saving the forest. People can also have the same value, say to advance in the company they work in, but in such a way that one person's realizing his value is inconsistent with the other's realization. Let us suppose the competitive situation cannot be resolved by either giving reasons to the other that convince them to abandon their value. What I claim is that although one person's realizing their value interferes with the other's realization, it need not interfere with the other's pursuit of happiness. It is just a fact about life and about anyone's pursuit of happiness that we find ourselves in competitive situations. The question is how this can be made consistent with the regard of each for the other's pursuit of happiness. The mutual regard implies that for each the goal is not to realize their value (to win) but to realize it in a way that respects the other's pursuit of happiness (to win well).

Let us consider the case of competition between two people for a higher position in an organization. What is required is that after the competition is over both parties "walk away" with their pursuit of happiness intact. If I manipulate you or sabotage you to achieve the goal, you walk away with diminished trust in regard to how others behave which will skew your considerations as to whether to compete in the future at all. Given that competition is a fact of life this greatly diminishes what standards of satisfaction you will consider and so closes off your considerations in regard to your standard for satisfaction. That is a loss for me in that I achieve the goal at the cost of cutting off your considerations and so the achievement cannot be for me part of an *open-minded* standard of satisfaction (a standard for satisfaction I can own as a reasoning being). Thus I have interfered with your pursuit of happiness and have not contributed to my own happiness. If the manipulation or sabotage is surreptitious then I will not have reduced your trust. However I have skewed your considerations as to whether you are competent to pursue such a job in the future making you falsely think you must lack some merit, and even skewed your confidence in discerning your own merit about anything. Once again this diminishes your considerations in regard to your forming a standard of satisfaction.

This implies that I have achieved a goal that cannot contribute to my happiness (my *open-minded* standard of satisfaction).

On the other hand if the competition proceeds so that each of us goes for the job according to what is involved in our meriting it (no manipulation or sabotage) and in a way that is above-board (no deception of the other) then I claim we can each walk away with our pursuit of happiness intact. If you don't get the job you come to better understand what your competency is, what merit you lack, and so perhaps improve your skills or go for something else you are more suited for. In this way your revised standard is more likely to be realized and so lead to retrospective considerations regarding the worth of the realization. Hence I get the job without demoting your pursuit of happiness. If your pursuit of happiness is skewed or demoted, it will be because you haven't made the best of it upon losing the competition. It won't be because I have demoted your pursuit. In this case my getting the job (winning the competition) interferes with your getting the job, but not with your pursuit of happiness. Thus not all cases of interference with another's achieving a goal or realizing a value are cases of interfering with their pursuit of happiness. Being good at prospectively and retrospectively considering standards of satisfaction takes precedence for each of us over achieving a specific goal or not, just as in the chess analogy coming away from the competition being better at pursuing chess excellence takes precedence for each of us over winning or losing a specific game.

Another sort of failure to respect another's pursuit that is distinct from flat out interference is to tamper with the other's pursuit. Whereas interfering is a matter of harming, tampering is a matter of putting in harm's way. Breaking a vase is one thing, throwing it up in the air and its perchance landing unbroken on a pillow is another. To tamper with another's pursuit is to play reckless with it. A basic way of playing reckless with another's pursuit is to induce less than optimal circumstances or conditions that don't, or at least might not, on its own interfere with another's considering and acting to realize values, but nevertheless put it at risk. For example suppose that for my own purposes I discourage someone from continuing to advance their career in the job they have. I tell them I don't think they have what it takes, that such a career isn't what I would go for etc. I am not interfering with their pursuit if they continue on with it, but I am still tampering with their pursuit in the sense of putting it at risk by producing a less than optimal circumstance of their having to deal with my discouragement. As another example suppose I belittle another person. I am tampering with his pursuit by producing the less than optimal condition in him of wavering confidence in his continuing on with his pursuit. Similarly if I inflict emotional distress on another I am tampering with his capacity for emotional contentment making his pursuit of happiness more difficult in multiple ways. Note I am not saying that what is harmful or bad about wavering confidence or emotional distress is just that it can be debilitating to the pursuit of happiness. They are each intrinsically bad apart from this. It is bad on its own as an emotional condition to lack confidence or be in distress. What makes it not just intrinsically bad, but flat-out bad or harmful is how it tends to degrade the pursuit of happiness by being a condition that makes the pursuit more difficult than it otherwise need be.

Instead of emotional pain consider the case of inflicting physical pain. This too is intrinsically bad and can make a person's pursuit of happiness more difficult. Nevertheless if I inflict great pain on you in re-setting your broken leg when no anesthesia is available I am not producing a decrease in optimal conditions for you to pursue happiness. In this case a less than optimal condition already exists. The choice is great pain now or perhaps chronic pain later on. The pain I inflict on you is intrinsically bad (horrible, terrible) and the memory of it may make your continuing pursuit of happiness more fragile. Although I am inducing a less than ideally optimal condition I am not inducing a less than optimal condition given the circumstances.

To induce less optimal circumstances or conditions in another's pursuit is to play reckless with his prospective and retrospective considerations even if it doesn't go so far as to interfere with them. But then I am playing reckless with my own open-mindedness which is directed toward such considerations. I am failing therefore to fully give myself over to open-mindedness regarding my standard of satisfaction, and so precluding my self-fulfillment as a reasoning being. Again that doesn't mean that the whole badness of inflicting emotional or physical pain on another is that it separates me from self-fulfillment as a reasoning being (Cohen 1993). It is because such pain is already intrinsically bad that its infliction can upset or unsettle the other making his pursuit more difficult.

It is certainly true that not every case of discouraging another, belittling another, inflicting emotional or physical pain on another makes their pursuit more difficult or, by itself, puts their pursuit at risk. There are small day to day slights of these kinds that seem to leave the other's pursuit intact. However by such slights I am still playing fast and loose with their pursuit in that they can add up over time to weaken and even devastate a person's pursuit of happiness. I don't know how many of these small slights a person has suffered and how many more they may continue to suffer at the hands of others. As an analogy consider again respect for a valuable vase. Suppose conditions of temperature, humidity and amount of light are factors that individually might not erode or crack the vase but together can be quite damaging. If I vary the thermostat away from optimal temperature I am being reckless with the vase. I am failing to respect it because I am upping the risk of its being damaged if the humidifier breaks down or if the window blinds fall off, etc. To thus play fast and loose with another's pursuit by these small slights even when individually they don't tamper with it, is to play fast and loose with my own commitment to open-mindedness. But that commitment, in being my self-fulfillment, is not something to be bargained with on the chance that my small slights turn out to be harmless. Such bargaining is failing to fully commit myself to open-mindedness.

Respect for others' pursuit of happiness, properly understood, is not the same as respect in general for others' pursuits in life. Consider a person whose pursuit of certain goals involves killing others or stealing from others or manipulating others. This person may be satisfied with how his life is going partly because of the realization of such goals. What he cannot be however is satisfied in a self-fulfilling way. He is interfering with others' pursuit of happiness by killing them, etc. Hence he is not giving himself over to open-mindedness which requires respect for others, not interfering with them. In our terms his pursuits in life aren't a pursuit of happiness (a pursuit of self-fulfilling satisfaction). If I interfere with him therefore I am not interfering with or failing to respect his pursuit of happiness. Bok (2010;176) says,

> There is no one view of happiness that should exclude all others...[but] pursuits of happiness that abide by fundamental moral values differ crucially from those that call for deceit, violence, betrayal.

On our conception of happiness there is no pursuit of happiness when one's pursuits in life call for deceit, violence or betrayal. We can rephrase Bok's point as saying that pursuits of happiness that abide by respect for others' pursuit of happiness differ crucially from those that do not so abide. The crucial difference is that I can interfere with another's killing, stealing, etc. while yet keeping to the standard of open-mindedness. Although there are many considerations regarding happiness that I must be open to, I know conclusively that some considerations of what to pursue in life are positively, flat-out inconsistent with pursuing happiness. Therefore keeping an open mind doesn't involve being open to such considerations. I need to be open-minded about what to value as a contribution to a standard of satisfaction because there is no definitive standard. This doesn't mean I need to be open-minded to what I know contradicts open-mindedness. There is nothing to be open-minded about in regard to whether to involve killing and stealing in my standard of satisfaction. Thus if I interfere with a person who kills or steals I am in no way abandoning the standard of open-mindedness. In sum, the crucial difference is that disrespect for others' pursuit of happiness is integral to or internal to my own pursuit, while disrespect for those whose pursuits already disrespect others is in no way integral to my own pursuit of happiness.

(iv)

The second broad form of regard for others' pursuit is to care for it. Caring is to be understood not in the sense in which I can care about something while doing nothing about it, but in a sense that involves acting (Noddings 1984). To care for others' pursuit is to tend to it, to come to its aid, to protect it from being harmed and so on. This involves caring for their consideration of values as well as their realizing their values. I do not give myself over to open-mindedness if I sit and watch others' prospective and retrospective considerations being destroyed or damaged and I do nothing about it when I can easily help. To do so fails to tend to and so have regard for potential considerations that open-mindedness is supposed to be open to. As an analogy consider two teams of researchers each pursuing in their own way a cure for cancer. If the one team fails to respect the other team's pursuit by sabotaging their experiments then they are not pursuing a cure in an open-minded way since they are blocking considerations which, for all they know so far, may have to be taken into account in making progress (either by being rejected and so keeping them from going down a wrong path, by modifying their own research, or by setting their research off in a completely different direction). The same is true if they fail to care for the other team's research by not sharing information with them, not recommending them for grants when asked, etc. In failing to promote the other team's research they close themselves off from pertinent considerations that might be provided by it. This analogy is by no means perfect since in this case each is working toward a definitive answer which will settle which, if either, of the two teams was on the right path. It is the answer's not yet being known that demands open-mindedness. In the case of open-mindedness about a standard for being satisfied with how one's life is going there is no definitive answer that each is working toward. What each is working toward rather is a shared well-considered character of each of our standards. This dis-analogy aside the point remains that failing to care for another's working toward such a standard diminishes our working toward it.

Although respecting others' pursuits may interfere with our pursuits or goals, it does not take us away from pursuing happiness. If I continually refrain from breaking other ice skaters' legs, such respect may interfere with my goal of an Olympic medal, but it doesn't interfere with pursuing a medal whose realization can contribute to a self-fulfilling satisfaction. Unlike respect, caring for others' pursuits is open-ended and can take us way from pursuing happiness. If I continually go around tending to other skaters, making sure they get to practice, sharpening their skates, getting their lunch, I have no time or resources left to pursue an Olympic medal as part of my happiness. For the most part it is the case that one can be *fully* respecting of others while yet fully pursuing happiness, but not fully caring for or tending to others while yet pursuing happiness. But it is open-mindedness to considerations *in the pursuit of happiness* that matters, not sheer abstract piling on of considerations. The caring for others that this entails cannot be such as to preclude the very pursuit I give myself over to being open-minded about. The pursuit of happiness for the most part involves fully respecting others but only caring for others to some extent depending on how much it takes away from my pursuit. Despite the vagueness of what caring to some extent comes to there are clear cases where caring is demanded of me in pursuing my happiness. If I am an excellent swimmer and see someone drowning in a pool, I must surely rescue them and save their pursuit of happiness. Small kindnesses such as giving encouragement to others in their pursuit, offering advice, being pleasant to others, and otherwise contributing to their positive emotional state surely are called for as part of the extent of caring that doesn't cost our own pursuit of happiness.

That my care for others doesn't extend to what costs too much for my own pursuit is not an issue of self-centeredness versus compassion. My pursuit of happiness is valuable to others. Recall that something is flat-out valuable if its realization contributes to happiness or to self-fulfilling satisfaction. My pursuit which provides others my prospective and retrospective considerations contributes to their *well-considered* standard for satisfaction the realization of which is constitutive of their happiness. For people who do not require costly care in order to pursue happiness, my caring only to some extent while yet pursuing my happiness is best for them. Among this group of people it is best for each if the care for each other is limited in extent. Equivalently it is best for the enterprise of pursuing happiness that each only care for the pursuit of others to an extent that is not too costly for their own pursuit. If one calls this self-centeredness it is a self-centeredness that has flat-out value for others, not a self-centeredness opposed to what is good for others.

There are large groups of people who do require enormous care in order to pursue happiness. The sick, the weak and the destitute need help, and the oppressed need protection from their oppressors. Let us say that such people who lack the conditions and circumstances for pursuing happiness at all lack welfare. There is no question that their situation is dire; i.e. the lack of welfare in these regards is intrinsically awful. Considered in its own right it is terribly bad to be very sick, infirm, wracked with hunger or oppressed. For me to not actively care to alleviate or improve the situation of such people, even at the cost of abandoning my own pursuit of happiness seems to be an awful lack of compassion. Tending to their intrinsically horrible suffering it seems should take precedence over my pursuit of happiness.

Certain considerations mitigate this supposed lack of compassion. Although suffering is intrinsically terrible it is not flat-out terrible. Consider a group of terrorists who are starving or who have serious injuries. To fail to leave food or medical supplies for them so that they can continue on in their terrorist ways is no lack of compassion. What makes suffering flat out terrible is that it keeps the person from pursuing happiness or equivalently it keeps the person from partaking in the enterprise of the pursuit of happiness. Now for all those who already partake it is indeed valuable for others to enter into the enterprise. Additional prospective and retrospective considerations become available which promotes everyone's well-considered standard of satisfaction. However if in order for others to enter into the enterprise those who already partake would have to give up their pursuit of happiness there would be no enterprise for the others to enter into. As soon as someone entered the enterprise they too would have to give it up in order to help others enter. It would be as self-defeating as everyone on a sinking ship helping others to life boats where, as soon as they get in, they go back and help others into the life-boats. We would have continuing rotation of people into and out of life boats without their ever moving away from the dangerous ship. Since for those who do partake the pursuit of all others who partake is valuable, there is universal value in nobody who partakes abandoning their pursuit of happiness. This together with the value of others entering into the pursuit calls for a common division of the caring needed for others to enter the enterprise which leaves each still to pursue happiness. What we have then is a socio-political issue of how to organize care for those who lack welfare in such a way that each who don't lack welfare can substantially get on with their lives.

The simple analogy of the enterprise of chess mastery or winning well at chess is instructive. For those already partaking in the enterprise it is valuable both that other partakers sharpen their game and that novices be helped to enter the enterprise. Suppose that the latter requires playing many games with novices to the point at which they become good enough to partake in the enterprise. For each partaker to spend all their time instructing novices would remove the supposed fruits of the instruction (an enterprise for the novices to enter into). This is a problem of organization among those who already are in the co-operative enterprise where each values the continued participation of all those who partake. A fair distribution of the "burden" of caring for others balances "compassion" for the less chess-fortunate with the pursuit of mastery by those who already partake.

In sum the full value of compassion is realized in the organizational distribution of caring among those for whom each other's pursuit of happiness is valuable, so that each individually may continue with their pursuit by caring to some extent for others. Organized charities, governmental agencies for promoting welfare, etc. allow each to contribute care to an extent that doesn't undermine their pursuit of happiness by contributing to and promoting organized efforts. This by no means solves the problem if the work of those charities and agencies is corrupted by those who carry out the work or by oppressive or uncaring political institutions which prevent such work. This presents a further problem for those already within the enterprise of how to promote an end to oppression and corruption – which makes contributing to still further organized efforts (political movements) a mode of caring. However intractable all this seems to be in practice the point remains that welfare (food, shelter, health) however intrinsically valuable doesn't take precedence over pursuing happiness but has its full value in regard to pursuing happiness (Sen 1993).

(v)

The picture we have drawn of being open-minded about one's standard of happiness makes the idea of having formulable general standards for one's life and considering them for potential revision central to happiness and its pursuit. The picture involves a person considering others' prospective and retrospective considerations and adjusting his own formulated general standard accordingly. Apart from issues of whether people's formulable general standards and considerations are fully determinate there is the more basic issue of whether formulated general standards and considerations play a significant role at all.

For Aristotle wisdom and living well so as to attain eudaimonia is modeled on being skillful, say as a carpenter or a soldier. The pursuit of happiness on this model does not proceed by formulating standards and the give and take of considerations about standards between persons. Rather it proceeds by observing others who live well in particular circumstances and developing thereby the skill to likewise live well in particular circumstances. There may be occasions where things are not going well or circumstances are novel where even the most expert carpenter may have to explicitly consider how to modify his practical wisdom about carpentry. Even in such cases however the consideration is not so much formulating modifications of formulated general standards. Rather it is something like imaginatively rehearsing various ways he may have to employ in order to carve pieces so as to fit a certain shape and discerning in his imagination which of the ways appears to work. It is by training, experience, and imagination not by formulated general rules or standards that he proceeds and develops his carpentry. Further the skillful carpenter may look to the work of other skillful carpenters to see how they solved similar problems, or he may ask another carpenter to show him by doing it or by going through the motions in outline of how to do it (=imagining in public). This inter-subjective aspect of the enterprise of carpentry is not one of reasons for or against formulated general norms or standards. What I wish to claim is that there is no fundamental opposition between this picture of skills and the picture of formulating considerations in regard to formulated general standards. The latter I claim completes or adds to the former in a crucial way. Before proceeding to this claim note that even if we abandon general norms or standards, the enterprise of carpentry as characterized above involves being open to the input of others in pursuing one's own craft as a carpenter. Therefore it involves respecting and caring for others pursuing this craft. In this regard our fundamental result that pursuing happiness involves respecting and caring for the pursuit of others holds up even if the pursuit were not to involve formulated general standards for living as a whole and formulated modifications of such standards.

To get at the importance of complementing skills with general standards consider again the pursuit of chess mastery. The player in a game may consider his next move by imaginatively rehearsing or picturing how the game may proceed from each of various moves he can now make. This rehearsal of possibilities holds with it pros and cons of making any of the moves without any formulable general rules or norms of good play. We can say that each such rehearsal of possibilities is an individualized considered norm for making a move *in a particular situation*. But now a chess player may have stored within him a whole host of templates for such rehearsals, so that in games where the configuration easily fits a stored rehearsal the move can be made directly without the rehearsal coming to the fore. The rehearsals may get modified by an unexpected or ingenious move or sequence of moves by the opponent that take the game beyond fitting any of the player's system of stored rehearsals. His system of stored rehearsals, that is, can get modified by failures or successes of moves made in accord with it without the system having to come to the fore. When a modified rehearsal does come to the fore for the first time in an imaginative episode it supplies the player with pros and cons (reasons, considerations) he never came to by explicitly considering general standards for good play. The modifications further can "reverberate" across other stored templates which thereby get adjusted, giving a more holistic character to the development of the player's skill. The player then has a fund of stored templates many of which come to the fore for the first time and so provide him with new reasons for moves that he never before explicitly considered. In this way the mutual modification by each player of the others' system of stored templates by moves each makes is an "exchange of reasons" that doesn't invoke general norms or standards of good play. As noted, even if this is the entire model of the chess mastery enterprise, it still calls for each to respect and care for the play of the other.

The system of templates is surely too complex to come to the fore in the form of all the multifarious individual imaginative episodes of rehearsing possibilities. What this implies is that when the opponents move made with a particular public rehearsal influences the player's system the influence is only from that fragment of the opponent's skill. The rest of the opponent's skill or competency in chess is "wasted" as far as influencing the player is concerned. Similarly even if I watch the carpenter rehearse the possibilities for dealing with the particular problem of how such pieces can be fit securely into a certain shape all I pick up from him is that portion of his skill. The only way to pick up his skill as a whole (the system of stored templates) would be to interact with him over long periods of time in all sorts of circumstances the way a novice might pick up on his skill. But now there are general features or patterns of inter-relations within a chess player's system which together characterize his system and tie it together as an overall strategy of play (e.g., an aggressive queen-centered strategy). Since this generality is about a system of individualized *norms* for dealing with particular circumstances the generality itself is a general norm or standard. Further since it is a generality about a system of individualized considered norms (each rehearsal of possibilities being a consideration in regard to which possibility is best) general *patterns* of such considerations come with the overall norm or strategy. Suppose that the opponent could formulate such a generality. Then he could on the occasion communicate his overall skill, not just his skill as it deals with a particular move. This allows the player to modify and enrich his skill (his system of templates) according to the general overall pattern of his opponent's system rather than just to piecemeal particular elements of it, without having to engage his opponent in numerous (hundreds of?, thousands of?) chess matches. This is an exponential increase in the scope of open-mindedness in regard to the cooperative enterprise of chess-mastery.

Generalities about inter-relations between individual norms and inter-relations between individual considerations are bound to lose details of the system of stored templates. Hence the generality, the overall strategy with its general sort of considerations, does not fully formulate the chess opponent's or the carpenter's skill—their ability to produce imaginative rehearsals for what would work best in particular circumstances. The modifications the formulated generality induces in the player or a second carpenter are modifications in the details (the individual components) of the player's system. The communication is of patterns from the opponent's detailed system to modifications of the player's system including modifications in the details of individual stored templates. This is just to say that I "understand" the significance of his generalities in my own terms. This explains why the unskilled who don't have a stored system of templates fail to understand the general strategy that is formulated. Since the exchange of considerations regarding a general norm is from one skill-constituting system to another, formulating general types of reasons or considerations for a general norm is not opposed to a skill-constituting system of what-will-or-will-not-work-in particular-circumstances. Nor however are skill-constituting systems an alternative to the exchange by general formulations, since the full fruit of mutual skill modification lies in this type of general exchange.

The picture we have developed with respect to skills such as carpentry or chess applies as well to the skill of pursuing happiness. An individual in deciding what to do or aim for envisages alternative possibilities of doing or aiming-for, the comparison of which gives pros and cons for what the best move is. This rehearsal of possibilities is an imaginative deliberation. As with the case of chess it is an individualized considered norm for a particular move in life. The system of stored templates constitutes the individual's skill in pursuing things. An overall system-wide pattern of inter-relations then is a generality about particular considered norms for doing and aiming, and so is itself a general norm with general inter-relations of considerations constituting the individual's overall strategy for doing and aiming well. It constitutes that is his considered standard of satisfaction. For example, his deliberation about whether to go to work has inter-relations with the rest of his stored templates for deliberating. The general pattern of these inter-relations is how going to work measures up in regard to his other individualized norms for doing other things in life, etc. giving thereby the place of this deliberation in his overall considerations of a strategy for dealing with life. The influence now of a second person's particularized considered norm on a person's skill-constituting system corresponds to how the second person's deliberation, restricted to a particular action or aim, modifies the first person's system of individualized templates for deliberating. Once again much of the second person's skill is "wasted" in that it exerts no influence on the first person. The influence of the second person's general considered norm corresponds to the other's general standard of deliberation in regard to actions and aims which in full generality is just his considered standard for satisfaction with how his life is going (whether that standard is already met or yet to be met). This standard can come to the fore by the first person probing further and further for the second person to formulate the basis of deliberating that particular way, thus revealing the large-scale system-wide pattern of his skill set and thus revealing his standard of satisfaction and his considerations for it. In this sort of exchange the enterprise of pursuing happiness reaches its full fruit of mutual development of each party's fund of templates (skill for pursuing happiness). Perhaps with lovers or friends over long periods of interaction we can pick up on the holistic patterns of their fund of templates without much explicit general formulation. Other than that, however, there seems to be no substitute to such formulation for discerning another's skill-set holistically. Since there are varying degrees of generality of inter-relations some of which are patterns only of subsets of our skill-constituting system of templates for imaginative deliberations, the general standards we express or formulate need not be fully general. Thus I may express reasons for the standard of overall satisfaction only in respect of certain aspects of my life. The standard does not have to come to the fore in its full generality and perhaps does so only when the system as a whole seems to be in question (think of a person in crisis in an extended discussion of the meaning of life with another person). The picture we have drawn explains why a fully general standard of satisfaction is bound to lose some of the specific details of a person's pursuits. It also explains what a "standing" (implicit, unformulated) standard of satisfaction is, since the pattern of inter-relations is ongoing whether formulated or not. In other words having a considered standard of satisfaction is an ongoing condition and doesn't just exist in judgments. Likewise then this ongoing standard being satisfied is an ongoing condition in line with the claim in Chapter 1 that life satisfaction and so happiness exists as an ongoing condition – not as a formulated reflective judgment.

Unlike the enterprise of chess mastery the enterprise of pursuing happiness includes an emotional component of contentment as part of the "skill" itself. My standard of satisfaction can come to naught as far as happiness is concerned if its realization doesn't bring with it emotional contentment. The picture of a system of rehearsal templates underlying general principles is particularly apt in this regard. In an imaginative rehearsal of possibilities (imaginative deliberation) I get a sense of what might or might not please me or be emotionally appealing—somewhat as an imaginative rehearsal of being face-to-face with a bear can give me a sense of how fearful or not I might be. In line with Chang (2004) such prospective emotional appeal is internal to reasoned normativity for actions and aims. Thus patterns of emotional appeal as part of the general pattern of templates are internal to the general types of overall reasons. If the templates are in part ones selected for emotional appeal then the overall strategy will have a built in bias toward emotional content-ment. Finally, the skill of pursuing happiness like most skills involves action-control components. The chess player doesn't need a steady hand to make his move like the carpenter does, but he does need perhaps the courage of his convictions, perseverance and concentration. On a much grander scale some-one could have a well-considered standard of satisfaction and fail miserably in his pursuit of happiness for lack of those action control qualities involved in realizing those standards (Tiberius 2008).

Although the development of the account of happiness has been carried out basically at the level of fomulable generality of reasons for a general stan-dard, nothing in that account is inconsistent with the picture of this level hav-ing an underlying foundation in a skill-constituting system of particularized templates. This picture perhaps softens the apparent intellectualist exaggera-tion of the account. Embedding the account in such a picture leaves intact the main result of Part One that integral to anyone's happiness is respect and care for others' pursuit of happiness.

PART 2

Morality

∵

CHAPTER 5

The Fundamental Principle of Morality

(i)

Suppose we define an action to be wrong just in case it fails to respect or care enough for the pursuit of happiness of others. According to this definition it is sometimes wrong to act to achieve one's aims or goals, as when such acting fails to respect or care enough for others' pursuit of happiness. This I take to be the minimum requirement of a definition of an action being morally wrong. Presuming that the fundamental principle of morality is to avoid doing wrong then according to the definition the fundamental principle of morality is to do what respects and cares enough for others' pursuit of happiness. By the results of Part One it follows from the definition that for a person to do what is wrong goes against their own happiness. In the face of doing what fails to respect or care enough for others' pursuit a person cannot be satisfied in a self-fulfilling way with how their lives are going. The definition then is a characterization of what it is to do wrong that is at the same time a defense or justification for not doing wrong. Equally the fundamental principle of morality according to this definition to do what respects and cares enough for others' pursuit of happiness is a principle whose violation goes against a person's happiness. Hence the definition results in a fundamental principle of morality that is justifiable. The defense or justification is not that morality has some important place in our lives, but that it has the supremely important place of not being contestable by anything else that may have a place in our lives such as our values, our aims, what we have reason to do.

The definition of an *action* being wrong in terms of its failing to respect or care enough for others' pursuit seems to imply that actions themselves can respect or fail to care for others' pursuit. Although actions can harm or contribute to harming others how can they themselves fail to respect others? One could equally question how an action itself can be wrong. It can harm or contribute to harming others, but how can it itself be thereby wrong? It seems rather that it is persons that can fail to respect others by the harm they do or who are wrong for doing the harm and so it seems that the attempt to define actions as wrong is misguided from the start.

Let us grant that what makes an act wrong is that it is an act people can be held or charged to not do. This doesn't mean that anyone who does the act can be so held or charged. Someone who is tricked or manipulated into doing harm to another does what is wrong even though they can't be held to not doing it, because it is the kind of act that those who can be held responsible can be charged to avoid. If so then the definition of a wrong act becomes in fact *what* those who can be held responsible are always charged with avoiding in being charged with avoiding an act. With this in mind the definition can be recast as follows: An act is wrong just in case what those who can be held responsible are charged to avoid by not doing the act is a failure to respect or care enough for the pursuit of happiness of others. It is not a mistake then to define actions as right or wrong so long as the definition is understood in this way as defining actions we can be held to avoid doing in terms of what we are being held to avoid.

The reason I believe that what makes an act wrong is that people can be charged or held to avoid it is that morality concerns avoidable misfortune. There are all sorts of natural misfortunes or naturally produced harms in our lives. This much is a fact of life. The point of morality is to not add misfortunes that are avoidable. A misfortune originating from a person that is unavoidable is a natural misfortune of our nature. It is too bad perhaps that people cannot foresee all the harm originating from their acting, but such unforeseeable harm counts only as a natural misfortune. Rocks after all can foresee none of the harm their falling can originate when they are falling toward a person's head, and so rocks fail in a necessary condition of being charged with the harm. In relation to what people cannot foresee the harm they produce is a natural misfortune like a rock falling. A person with a true compulsion to rape if there is such a thing is a natural misfortune in the lives of others, but the rapes he commits are misfortunes avoidable by people. Thus though the compulsive rapist cannot be charged with avoiding rape but can only be prevented from doing it, it is nevertheless a wrong act. If this is correct then there is no morality without avoid-ability. Supposing that avoid-ability is tantamount to responsibility and freedom then there is no right or wrong without responsibility and freedom; there is only fortune and misfortune. Freedom and responsibility are considered in Part Three.

According to the definition an act is wrong if it fails to care enough for *anyone else's* pursuit of happiness. But consider people whose prospective and retrospective considerations will never become available to me. It seems that I cannot be open to considerations that are not available to me. The open-mindedness essential to my happiness seems limited to others whose considerations I come across. If so then failing to respect or care enough for people whose considerations I don't come across doesn't go against my happiness. To preserve the connection between doing wrong and going against happiness it seems that the definition has to be restricted in scope to anyone else whose pursuit of happiness I happen to come across. If I am sitting in a café in Paris and by snapping my fingers can cause the death of a person in rural China what is that to my well-considered satisfaction with how my life is going? What considerations do I close myself off to that aren't already closed off by circumstances of distance and lack of even indirect communication?

My happiness requires that I as a reasoning being give myself over to the open-ness that belongs to any standard of satisfaction for how my life is going. If I don't give myself over to the open character *that belongs to the standard* then giving myself over to being open-minded would not be something I do in that open-mindedness is called for by reason. Hence it would not be something that I submit myself to as a reasoning being. But for me to give myself over to the open-ness that belongs to my standard itself is for me to have regard for any considerations pertinent to that standard *whether I come across them or not,* since the open-ness of the standard is not that I may come across further considerations but that there are further considerations. Hence to be self-fulfilled as a reasoning being in relation to my standard of satisfaction and so to claim that satisfaction as belonging to me requires having regard for *there being* further considerations. As in Chapter 4 to have regard is to respect and to care enough, and so it is essential to my happiness to respect and care enough for all considerations whether they are available to me or not.

Considerations exist in other people's having them. There isn't a fund of considerations in Plato's ideal reality. To have regard for any considerations there are is to have regard for any prospective and retrospective considerations that anyone comes up with in their pursuit of happiness. Their pursuit of happiness, recall, just is their coming up with considerations. Hence the scope of the definition is unrestricted. It pertains to the pursuit of all others and only as so pertaining does it keep the equation between doing wrong and going against my happiness. It is both wrong and against my happiness to snap my fingers in that Paris café even if by doing so I can in some manner profit by promoting my goals; even if, that is, someone offers me some means to achieving my goals if I do it. The person in rural China is the source or repository of pertinent considerations that I must respect and care for to be happy.

Not only does the scope of the definition extend to all others' pursuit of happiness, it extends as well to the pursuit of as yet unborn future generations. To have regard for what belongs to the open-ness of my standard of satisfaction in its own right is to have regard for pertinent considerations that belong to it simply in that it is open, This extends beyond the totality of actual prospective and retrospective considerations of all people now alive and all who have ever been alive. Unless I can prove that there are no considerations beyond all these actual ones, the standard remains open for further considerations beyond these actual ones. Again these considerations don't exist in a Platonic ideal reality but in the potential pursuit of future generations. This doesn't mean of course that I can't be happy until considerations of future generations arise, but rather that I cannot be happy if I don't respect and care enough for their arising. For one example to destroy without a trace a painting by Leonardo or a novel by Tolstoy is to block pertinent considerations from arising in future generations. On this account such destruction is morally wrong and goes against our happiness. As another example to fail to care for the environment is to make circumstances under which future generations pursue happiness less optimal than they would otherwise be which is to fail to care enough for that pursuit. Again on this account it is both morally wrong and against our happiness to fail to protect the environment. This doesn't mean that the intrinsic value of a painting or a novel or the environment is that they foster the pursuit of happiness. It simply means that the flat-out, all things considered value is in the fostering.

To a large extent the relation of morality to future generations on the present account parallels the relation of truth to future generations on Peirce's account of truth. Truth for Peirce is what is "destined" to be agreed to by inquiry. Inquiry is an enterprise that goes beyond how inquiry has proceeded so far and hopefully beyond how it will proceed after all who are now living are dead. Nor is inquiry for Pierce something existing ideally in Plato's ideal realm. It is people who determine what inquiry is and how it is to proceed. For Peirce this implies that there is no such thing as giving oneself over to truth as the standard of theoretical reasoning, and thus no such thing as being fulfilled in one's nature as a being with theoretical reason, without valuing continuing inquiry by future generations. Whatever the virtues of Peirce's account the parallels should be clear. The pursuit of happiness as involving regard for the open nature of any standard of satisfaction is an enterprise not restricted to how it has proceeded so far, but goes beyond it not to Plato's realm but to people who determine what considerations there are for standards. There is no such thing as giving oneself over to the enterprise without valuing, respecting and caring enough for future generations. Hence there is no such thing as being fulfilled in one's nature as a being with practical reason without valuing continuing pursuit of future generations.

Justifications of regard for others such as Brinks' altruistic egoism (2007) which make others' deliberations about how to live pertinent to my own deliberations fall short in the scope of which others we are to have regard for. Even if my own deliberating is improved by exchanging considerations with others why should I have regard for those who are not available to me for such exchange? They can't improve my deliberating. That they would or might improve my deliberating if they were available only implies that I should have regard for them *if* they were to cross my path. On our account my living well involves giving myself over to the open-ness of my standard for how to live. This is a regard for reasons or considerations there may be whether or not they are available to me and only so is a regard for my nature as a reasoning being. The issue is not just "improving" my deliberating by making it more well-considered, but claiming my deliberating as belonging to me as a reasoning being. This claim, involving as it does regard for considerations whether available or not, is part of what it is to live well or to be happy. It doesn't improve my chances for living well – it is a constituent or a necessary condition of anything that comes to living well.

(ii)

It is not clear that one can separate the question of what something has to be in order to serves as a fundamental principle of morality from the question of how it can be justified as having value in our lives. Take the question of whether a fundamental principle of morality has to extend in scope to all people or just to persons within a community, culture, or tradition. Should it extend to all people equally so that each person counts for as much as any other? Should it allow friends and loved ones to take complete precedence over others? Should it put respect for each individual above the greatest good for the greatest number? Should it require that it is always wrong to put one's goals above other people? I am not sure how to answer these questions as to what should or shouldn't go into a fundamental principle of morality apart from the question of what makes morality valuable. I am not sure, that is, that the question over the content of a fundamental principle can be separated from the question of what value in our lives justifies the principle. If so then a fundamental principle of morality has to be based on an account of value that justifies the principle. In any case in this chapter I will not try to separate these questions. Instead I will try to develop that the fundamental principle should be to respect and care enough for the pursuit of all others in tandem with the view that happiness in our sense is the value to be realized by it and so what justifies it.

For Plato a definition of morality is responsible to a proper account of value. Thrasymachus' definition is that what is right or just for the weak is to act in accord with the rules the strong set up, while what is right or just for the strong is to act so as to appear to be in accord with those rules. Plato's criticism of this supposed fundamental principle of morality is that it is based on a flawed understanding of the good or of what is valuable. Thrasymachus is presuming that achieving one's goals or getting what one wants is what is supremely valuable. For the strong person this means keeping the weak in line so as to keep them from getting in the way of achieving his goals, while also harming the weak by breaking the rules so long as his doing so is consistent with keeping them in line. For the weak the supreme value of achieving one's goals means achieving them as much as possible in the face of the sanctions set up by the stronger. Given that some are by nature weak that is as much happiness as the weak are capable of. Socrates in Book I of the *Republic* doesn't provide counter-examples to Thrasymachus' definition as he did to previous definitions. He doesn't object to Thraymachus' view that is by showing it is not in reflective equilibrium with what most or many people believe are cases of right versus wrong actions. Rather Socrates resets the issue as one of whether Thrasymachus' view is based on a true account of what is valuable. To respond to Thrasymachus one must show that what he supremely values is not supremely valuable, that even if one had the ring of Gyges making one invisible so that one could perfectly act the way Thrasymachus endorses, one would still not want to act that way. There is another way of understanding the issue Thrasymachus raises for Plato. Rather than giving a definition of right or just action Thrasymachus is simply denying that morality which requires refraining from doing harm to others and benefiting others exists. It is a sham or a lie— a system set up to deceive and induce fear in others. On this understanding some sort of grasp of morality apart from issues of value is presupposed, and so the question of what morality is becomes isolated from what is valuable about it. What is isolated however is what most people call 'moral'—what they call 'right' or 'wrong'. However as Glaucon and Adeimantus make clear in Book II people themselves are suspicious that what passes for right or wrong may be nothing but seeking to avoid harm, all the while finding it valuable to harm others if they could. Reflective equilibrium as a criterion of a supreme principle has to include the value of conforming to cases of that principle because people take what they think are cases of doing wrong to mark out what is valuable to avoid; otherwise they take them as mere labels for something else.

I won't go into Plato's account of the good by which he thinks he can respond to Thrasymachus. Instead let us consider the response that is based on the account of value and happiness in Part One. Thrasymachus is presuming that getting what you want is valuable; i.e. will lead you to be satisfied with how your life is going. It may very well fail however when you find that you can't endorse having all that you want when you have it. Further, even endorsing it may seem empty and estranged in relation to one's reasoning nature; one's reflective considering of what the basis of the endorsement is. If happiness then is not getting what you want but rather being satisfied in a self-fulfilled way with your life and if the value of getting what you want is that it will make you happy, and if being thus satisfied requires respecting and caring enough for the pursuit of others even if it goes against your aims or goals to do so, then Thrasymachus' definition and the supreme principle for how to live one's life that derives from it is all based on a bogus account of value. In response to Thrasymachus then even if one could appear to respect another's pursuit while not really doing so by surreptitiously embezzling their money it would have no value since by detracting from their pursuit of happiness it abandons one's own commitment to open-mindedness by which alone one can be happy in the sense of owning satisfaction with how life is going. Even if I had the ring of Gyges I wouldn't want to abandon my commitment by disrespecting the other, since the ring of Gyges doesn't give one a proof of what the standard of satisfaction is which alone would enable me to abandon this commitment to open-mindedness and yet be satisfied in a self-fulfilling way. Even with the ring then it is supremely valuable to respect and care enough for the pursuit of others. Against Thrasymachus respecting others isn't a means to the value of achieving one's goals since the achievement has no value without respect for others. Further there is no division between the strong versus the weak when it comes to being open-minded to others' considerations as to how their lives are going. Finally in regard to Glaucon and Adeimantus respecting others is no burden that we put up with for the sake of avoiding harm from others. It is no burden to restrict one's achieving one's goals by respecting others if that gives that achievement any value as contributing to self-fulfilling satisfaction.

The lesson to be drawn from the response to Thrasymachus is that a proper account of value in terms of self-fulfilling satisfaction leads to a supreme principle of morality according to which if an act is wrong it is so whether or not one can do it without being found out. If it is wrong it is so even if it goes against achieving one's goals. If it is wrong then even if one is weak and so particularly vulnerable to sanctions from others one needn't be motivated by fear to avoid doing it; that it is wrong is sufficient motivation.

(iii)

Consider next the utilitarian account of a supreme principle of morality. A utilitarian account is any account which defines what is good or valuable independently of how we are supposed to relate to one another and then holds the supreme principle to be to act in such a way as to promote the greatest good for the greatest number of people. The principle can come in various modified versions—to promote as much good as is foreseeable, to promote greater good than other options available for acting, to act in line with rules that being in force promote the greatest good, etc. These modifications are not important for the point I want to make that a utilitarian supreme principle is based on a faulty theory of value.

What is good for a certain person let us presume is that they obtain pleasure. This doesn't mean that their attaining it is what makes it good. Pleasure we can presume is of such a nature that it is good or valuable for the person to attain it. Suppose now that this is what is also good for a second person. It doesn't follow that both people attaining pleasure is better or more valuable than one person only attaining it. Who after all is it better or more valuable for? Unless one begins by presuming that what is good for the one person or for each person is that both attain pleasure it does not follow from its being good for each that he attains pleasure that it is good for anyone that both attain pleasure. The utilitarian will argue that what sums up values or goods is objectively more valuable than the individual values or goods that enter into the summation. As was claimed in Chapter 2 however objectively valuable means must be valued by everyone. If a person needn't value another's pleasure then he needn't sum it into what has greater value than his own pleasure alone, and so he does not violate the principle that what sums up values or goods must be more valuable than what enters into the summation. One cannot argue *by this principle alone* that more people having pleasure is more valuable for anyone than his own having pleasure. The utilitarian needs some sort of argument that everyone must value the overall attaining of pleasure. What goes for pleasure goes for any other supposed value. Though it may be a truism that each person should act in a way that is most valuable, or at least more valuable than other ways of acting, it doesn't follow that each person should act in a way that promotes the greatest value for the greatest number unless it is already established that for each person the realization of value in others goes into what is most valuable for him. The utilitarian's supreme principle of morality then depends on a bogus account of value for its justification. In effect it closes off the very issue of a justification of morality in terms of what, if anything, I should value in others by a bogus claim that greater good has meaning apart from its being greater good for anyone.

The account of value in Chapter 2 is an "agent-relative" account; value exists in being valued by agents. Once we accept this account it is no longer the case that when it is settled what the good of each is it is thereby settled that each should promote the good of all. That may be so because of the specific nature of the good for each, but it is not so generally no matter what the good of each is. For example the egoist (Thrasymachus) contends that the good of each is getting what he wants and so only if others getting what they want serves or is consistent with his getting what he wants is another's good to be promoted. Bernard Williams (1995) holds that some of a person's goals are so important or valuable to him that only if what others value is consistent with his reaching these goals must the person value what others value, or at least value it enough to act accordingly. Each of these positions contrasts with the utilitarian who holds that one must value all values of others equally with one's own values enough to act accordingly. Some account is needed of value or of the good that decides between these variants, and so decides between potentially great differences in the fundamental principle of morality regarding how much to value others that each would support. Since what is of value to a person is what contributes to his happiness the issue basically is what happiness is.

In Part One it was claimed that happiness is self-fulfilling satisfaction with how one's life is going and that as such everyone must value as part of their happiness respecting and caring enough for the pursuit of happiness of others, since without this a person cannot claim any satisfaction as belonging to him as a reasoning being. Since a person's goals are only valuable or important to the extent that they can contribute to his happiness, valuing the pursuit of others takes precedence over achieving one's goals no matter how important those goals are to the person. This doesn't imply however that a person is wrong to pursue goals as opposed to doing all he can to help others or to promote the general welfare since only caring *enough* is built into the definition of what is wrong in accord with the rationale of why helping others has value to others and why we have value to others. Thus Williams seems right after all that it is not incumbent upon us to abandon our central goals to care for others. The point against Williams is not that by our definition and its accompanying fundamental principle of morality we have an algorithm for determining what caring enough means. Rather the point is that without our conception of what it is to be happy we can get a quite different general understanding of what caring enough means. Suppose we take achieving one's most central goals or projects to be what happiness is. Then the egoist about happiness (Thrasymachus) can accept Williams' point that it is not incumbent upon us to abandon our central projects. If a competitor for a job is in the street bleeding to death then the egoist can say it is not incumbent upon him to come to the competitor's aid. One might respond that the egoist is not being asked to abandon his career goals – only to abandon achieving them in certain ways. But what if his central project is to achieve career advancement easily and without hard work? What if this is more important to him than the advancement he would be capable of achieving against the competitor? On our account it is his supposition that such a goal contributes to happiness that is his mistake. Suppose that in order to circumvent the egoist's co-option of Williams we accept some sort of perfectionist or objective-list account of happiness. Then those who do not or cannot measure up to what is thus required for happiness can have no goals or projects important enough to hold onto versus ceaselessly caring for others. This would lead to a two-tiered system where the "excellent" people pursue their projects while the non-excellent care for and serve the excellent in their pursuit. To avoid this it seems that one would have to define happiness as satisfying one's central goals whatever they are so long as satisfying them values others' pursuit of their central goals enough. This would avoid egoism and elitism, but only by smuggling in care for others in one's definition. What does tempering achieving one's goals by caring enough for others have any more to do with happiness than the utilitarian idea of tempering one's goals by complete caring for others? If partial tempering adds to happiness, why doesn't full tempering add to it more? It is hard to understand why my happiness involves tempering my goals without first understanding why the goals of others have any value to me. Without this happiness would no longer be a fully agent-centered notion, leaving the door open to the utilitarian. There is no *principled* connection between pursuing my goals and caring for others that by-passes issues of how and to what extent happiness (the agent-centered notion) requires valuing others' pursuit.

(iv)

There are aspects of morality that have seemed to some to be fundamental that seem to require a separation from any issue of happiness. It has seemed to some for example that the worth of all persons whatsoever simply in that they are persons. The worth of persons as ends not merely as means, the intrinsic worth or dignity of persons beyond all price are all notions fundamental to morality hardly to be validated in terms of happiness. This nexus of notions is clearly emphasized by Kant and just as clearly fails to be emphasized by Aristotle. I wish to claim that an account of the fundamental principle of morality incorporating this Kantian nexus cannot be validated without set-tling issues of happiness.

Bloomfield (2008) contends that the immoral person cannot respect or value himself as a human being in terms of what is common to the human condition since he doesn't respect others. Joyce (2008) responds that even if self-respect which is not also respect for others is irrational that doesn't show that such irrationality harms me. Suppose however that someone lies to me or steals from me. It seems that the harm in that is that they interfere or thwart my goals. But that harms me only if I can be satisfied with those goals according to how I think and reason about them. It is this last, let us say, that constitutes self-respect or a respect for myself as rational author of my life and so contra Joyce all real harm is in relation to self-respect as a rational being, the rationality of which is contradicted by failure to respect others. In defending Bloomfield we have had to elaborate his notion of being oneself as a human being specifically in terms of an account of happiness as realizing goals I can be satisfied with as a rational reasoning being. What I respect or value in myself is the human *capacity* to pursue such happiness; to author my life in accord with achieving what I can claim as reasonably satisfying. However, suppose that as a rational being I can establish definitively that certain specific goals are the only ones that can be reasonably claimed as satisfying upon being achieved. Then the only rational *exercise* of the capacity is to aim for those goals. I cannot as a rational being respect others who do not aim for these goals. It is true that they have the capacity to pursue happiness, but they fail to exercise it in the only way that gives it value. Thus Bloomfield's claim would be consistent with a perfectionist or elitist fundamental principle of morality—the exact sort of principle his contention is meant to avoid.

In general any consideration of parity between valuing others as persons and valuing myself as a person needs to explain what valuing-as-a-person means. If it doesn't mean valuing the capacity to pursue happiness then why should I value myself as a person over valuing the capacity to pursue happiness? In the spirit of Joyce's response what would be the harm of not respecting or valuing myself as a person? If it does mean the capacity to pursue happiness then the capacity is valuable only if the exercise of it is valuable. But if there is one true happiness, either getting what you want as per Thrasymachus or accomplishing excellent things as per the perfectionist, then the capacity in others as well as in myself is to be valued or respected only if exercised this way. Thus Bloomfield's contention as it stands is compatible with Thrasymachus' fundamental principle of morality—for each of the strong to do whatever they can to achieve their goals. A fundamental principle of morality then as respect for others as persons cannot be justified by Bloomfield's contention until one settles what it is to pursue happiness as a person.

The classical locus of justifying a fundamental principle of morality in terms of self-respect or self-valuing requiring respect for or valuing others is Kant himself. I shall criticize Kant's justification in Chapter 7. The contemporary locus is Korsgaard and in Chapter 7 I shall argue that with certain shifts of emphasis and terminology her view is equivalent to the justification in terms of the conception of happiness set out in Part One. For now I wish to claim that the fundamental principle we have justified by settling the issue of what it is to be happy does indeed incorporate the Kantian nexus of notions; respect for

the dignity and worth of all others-treating others never only as means but also
as ends, etc.

The definition is that it is wrong to fail to respect or care enough for others
simply in that they pursue happiness. It doesn't matter to the pursuit of happiness as set out in Part One what race or gender they are. It doesn't matter what
their talents are or what their intelligence is. It doesn't matter whether or not
they share my goals or beliefs. So long as they pursue happiness it is wrong to
fail to respect or care enough for them. Their pursuit of happiness is a matter
of all that they aim at, value, and are satisfied with being subject to their standard of what to aim at, value, and be satisfied with. Their pursuit of happiness
thus is a matter of their being the author of their lives in what they do, aim for,
and value. But to pursue happiness involves as well that their standard be
something they can give themselves over to, can claim as belonging to them,
etc.—not something they abandon themselves or lose themselves in pursuing. Only so is any satisfaction with how their lives are going self-fulfilling.
Others then pursue happiness just in case they are authors of all they aim at,
value, and are satisfied with in accord with a standard that they themselves
authorize. In short to pursue happiness is to be the author of one's life. The
definition in terms of the conception of happiness in Part One then holds that
it is wrong to fail to respect or care enough for others being the author of their
lives. Further, to so fail precludes my being the author of my life. The only standard I can give myself over to as a reasoning being is one generated and held in
an open-minded way which requires respect and care for others being the
authors of their lives. In one good sense the worth or dignity of a person is
exactly his being the author of his life. Hence to fail to respect or care for others
being authors of their lives is to fail to respect or care enough for their dignity
or worth as persons. Further this is a dignity or worth beyond all price. Nothing
is to be flat-out aimed for at all or flat-out valued at all if it goes against being
able to claim these aims or values via authorizing one's standard. Hence dignity of authorship is beyond all price in the sense that it is at the bottom of
anything else having a price (having flat-out value). Since the dignity of authorship of anyone is essential to the dignity (open-minded authorship) of anyone
else, it follows that the dignity of each person has worth beyond all price for
themselves and all others; viz., the dignity of every other person is at the bottom of anything that has value or a price for me. Hence the fundamental principle is that it is wrong to fail to respect or care enough for the dignity of others
precisely because that dignity is beyond all price.

Suppose someone is not pursuing self-fulfilling satisfaction because they
dogmatically hold as a standard of satisfaction say God's will according to a
certain religion. Because they dogmatically hold what has no proof they don't

give themselves over to their standard as reasoning beings but rather abandon themselves to it. They then do not have full ownership or authorship over their lives. They lack dignity to the extent that their dogmatism governs their lives even if they may be open-minded in certain other regards. I cannot respect dignity that isn't there and our fundamental principle doesn't imply their dogmatic pursuit is to be respected. I can however care for a dignity that doesn't exist by one way or another attempting to remove their dogmatism. In a way this is like caring for someone whose welfare status is so low, they are so sick, hungry, etc., that they are unable to author their lives. Whereas such people lack bodily health in a wide sense of health the dogmatist lacks mental health in a wide sense of health. In these cases although I don't respect the dignity they have as persons, by caring enough to restore them to a condition in which they can assume full authorship over their lives I care for the dignity they are capable of as persons. To fail to care enough to restore goes against the pursuit of happiness of others who need no restoring because it fails to bring into existence prospective and retrospective considerations that could arise from the restoration. Hence the fundamental principle entails that it is wrong to fail to care enough to restore persons who need it. Further in doing so I fail to give myself over to reasons that are pertinent to the open nature of my standards of satisfaction which goes against my own happiness. What it is to care *enough* in these cases and how exactly one is to care are issues of "detail." The principle however is clear on this matter—one is to have regard for the dignity of others as persons both in the sense of the dignity they in fact have and in the sense of the dignity they can become capable of having.

The definition and the fundamental principle it leads to implies that it is wrong to treat others merely as means to attaining one's goals. What treating them merely as means comes to is having regard for them only in so far as it helps one to attain one's goals without at the same time treating them as ends, where to treat them as ends means to respect and care for their authorship of their lives, for their being a locus of authorizing ends, values, and aims for themselves. Often this will be a matter of informed consent on their part as to how they are being treated, whether this consent comes immediately or through an exchange of considerations.

The fundamental principle incorporates these various Kantian elements because, as with Kant, it is a categorical imperative to act in accord with a law that one, as a being with reason, prescribes to oneself. On our account however the law is not fundamentally the universalizability of one's maxims, but rather regard for the open-ness of the standard for the ends, aims, values embedded in one's maxims. For Kant one's autonomy, dignity beyond price, being an end and never just a means all derive from one's being subject to a law that one as a being with reason subjects himself to. To the extent that subjecting oneself to such a law involves respect for others who subject themselves to it, one's own dignity is tied to the dignity of others, and one's own being an end is tied to others being an end. For all this to be so it is not essential that the law is fundamentally one of universalizability rather than a law of open-mindedness. This is not to say that the law of open-mindedness is not universalizable. Since it is a law I give myself over to in order to be fulfilled as a reasoning being, it pertains to all reasoning beings. That lacking any definitive proof requires one to give oneself over to open-mindedness is a law for any reasoning being. The difference we shall see in Chapter 7 is that ours is a law for reasonable beings internal to first enabling their happiness whereas for Kant it is a law for reasonable beings which puts limits on their happiness.

(v)

So far the contention has been that what a fundamental principle of morality is and should be is not separable from issues of the nature of value which in turn are not separable from the issue of what happiness as being at the bottom of all value is. The utilitarian who accepts this connection I argued has a mistaken "agent-neutral" conception of value; overall happiness having value only in a bogus agent-neutral free-floating sense. I then argued that once we switch to a proper sense of value, the issue of whether a fundamental principle should be one of regard for all others, only for others who have certain perfectionist values, or only for others who serve my values needs to be settled. I then argued that the connection of a fundamental principle to what happiness is as the bottom of all values is consistent with Kantian elements of a fundamental principle because, Kant aside, elements such as autonomy and dignity are anchored in what it is to be happy. What now of what we may call the extreme de-ontologist who finds moral prohibitions such as don't kill, don't steal absolute no matter what, and so apparently prohibitions apart from any connection to happiness?

The kind of view I have in mind is one according to which the fundamental principle of morality is a body of absolute constraints no matter what the consequences for others or for oneself. One is never to kill, to lie, etc. It is wrong to kill someone in self-defense or to stop them from killing others. It is wrong to lie to the police at my door coming after an innocent person as to his being in my home. Thus any value pertaining to persons is secondary to the value of conforming to these constraints. It might or might not be a secondary principle to come to the aid of others when doing so doesn't violate these constraints, but as far as the fundamental principle goes what matters is conforming to these constraints. On this view it seems that my happiness or the happiness of others is one thing whereas moral duty and moral value is something totally different. As I understand it something close to this view is held by Quakers and elements of this view at least inform many religions (Judaism's commandments, Christ's admonition not to resist evil). Philosophically it is the extreme de-ontological view of morality according to which the value of doing right or wrong is independent of all consequences. Note that this is a view about the value of doing wrong or not—not a view about the moral worth of persons. One could hold that the moral worth of a person is in his avoiding what is wrong to do simply because it is wrong (duty for duty's sake) while yet holding that what is wrong or not is tied to consequences. Further it is not the view that moral prohibitions have precedence in most cases over coming to the aid of others to the extent that such precedence in general has good consequences. My claim now is the de-ontological view does make sense on certain conceptions of value and happiness and so its supreme principle like the others we have considered is subject to defense or not according to what is or isn't defensible as an account of value.

Suppose one holds that our lives unfold according to and within the provenance of God's plan and that our happiness or felicity and so the value of anything in our lives is in our lives unfolding this way. To come to each other's aid seems a secondary value if a value at all since God doesn't need our mutual aid for each of our lives to unfold according to His plan. Since we don't grasp what the plan is it is not clear what coming to another's aid would even mean. It is each person's relation to God that matters as far as happiness is concerned. A person's relation to other people only matters in our not interfering with others' lives unfolding under God's provenance. For me to kill, torture or lie to another is to disrupt the course of their lives, but more importantly it is to disrupt God's provenance over their lives, and this is a violation of my relation to and respect for God. It is not that God won't take care of victims of wrongdoing, but that his doing so requires a change of course or an adjustment in his provenance. He has to step in to repair damage. If only we don't kill, lie, etc. then everything about each of our lives is ultimately our happiness according to God's original provenance. Our compact with God concerns justice, not goodness. Goodness is completely within God's provenance; justice is in part within our provenance.

Consider a custodial parent's relation to his several small children. The children don't know how to care for each other. They don't know what each other's good or happiness is. This is the parent's provenance. While in this condition each child knows enough by the "law" given by the parent to not stomp on the others to, to not take toys from the others etc. These operate as absolute constraints. A particular child's toy might be dangerous but the others do not understand well enough to be charged with coming to his aid by taking the toy away and disposing of it. The prohibition against taking toys away is not tempered by a requirement of care. The basic relation of each child is to the parent and only secondarily to the other children. In this manner perhaps we are children of a custodial God.

A different sort of underpinning for an extreme de-ontological fundamental principle of morality is in the idea that self-sufficiency or self-reliance is the definitive standard for being satisfied with how one's life is going. Self-reliance as a "thematic" value (Chapter 2) makes which goals one has inessential so long as going for these goals and getting them fits the overall theme of living self-reliantly. This is somewhat akin to Nietzsche's will to power. What it is for a person or at least a super-person to be happy is to be a locus of exerting power. On this view no one is to take care of anyone else for to do so diminishes the other's self-reliance. But nor is anyone to kill, steal or lie to another for the sake of achieving goals since having to employ others as means to achieving one's goals is a lack of self-reliance (will to power) not an expression of it. This latter distinguishes the view from Thrasymachus' account. Whereas in the previous religious account we are each too feeble and unknowing to care for each other so that all care is in God's hands, on the present account we are each in a sense to be gods; self-sufficient caretakers of the course of our lives.

The religious account depends on our not being able to discern by our own considering what the standard is (viz. God's plan) for being satisfied with how our lives are going. The second account depends on self-sufficiency or self-reliance being the definitive standard for being satisfied. The claim in Part One was that each account over-reaches. Even if the standard is God's plan there is no proof, Augustine's arguments notwithstanding, that part of his plan isn't *for us* to come to well-considered standards. There is no proof that God the parent doesn't want his children to grow up. Because there is no proof one can only hold to a modified version of the religious account. On this version one's happiness does involve caring enough for others' pursuit although tempered by the Augustinian contemplation that perhaps all this comes to naught in the scheme of things; such contemplation being a thematic component of one's standard of satisfaction. As such there is something, perhaps even a lot, to be said for such a modified view, but it no longer under-pins an extreme de-ontological alternative to our fundamental principle of morality. The second account depends on self-reliance being the definitive standard which would require proof. Nietzsche for example holds the proof to be in the nature of things, wherein everything, including us, is will to power. Even if this were so however something's being in the nature of things doesn't make it satisfying in a self-fulfilling way. As Scheler (1962) emphasizes we by our unique person-hood can say no to nature as far as value is concerned. Since there is no proof of self-reliance one can only hold a modified version of the account. On this version one's happiness involves holding one's standard of self-reliance in an open-minded way and so requires caring enough for the considerations that constitute others' pursuit of happiness. As such there is something and per-haps a great deal to be said for such a modified view, but it no longer underpins an extreme de-ontological principle of morality.

(vi)

Several alternatives to our fundamental principle have been considered. Thrasymachus would have us respect and care for others too little, only when it suits our goals. Extreme agent-neutral consequentialism would have us care for others too much. Perfectionism would have us respect and care for others selectively depending on the other's pursuit being worthy enough. Finally the extreme de-ontological account would have us respect too much (in not resist-ing evil) and care too little. All these alternatives in one way or another contra-dict the account of happiness and the concomitant account of value set out in Part One. Without settling what happiness is and what value is there is no set-tling on a fundamental principle of morality. Such settling takes precedence over any issue of reflective equilibrium with cases of "ordinary" thinking of what is or isn't wrong to do. Firstly there is important disagreement among us as to cases—even as to what some consider core cases. For some it is perfectly okay to interfere with others who have opposing religious values. For some only those of one's tribe or community are to be cared for. For some great art-ists or scientists are to be cut slack so that what is wrong for others is not wrong for them. It is perhaps true that something so core as the prohibition against killing, inflicting pain, and so on appears in anything that can be called a moral view for the reason, we can suppose, that it is universally recognized that killing, inflicting pain and so on are cases of harming. However harming is one thing and doing wrong is another, and there are central differences over which cases of inflicting such harms are wrong or not. Secondly, ordinary moral thinking itself is laden with ideas of what the value of morality is in relation to our happiness. For some moral value opposes happiness but nevertheless takes precedence. For others being moral is important for happiness but so are other things that may oppose it. For still others being moral is at the core of what it is to be happy. One can limit one's settling on a fundamental principle by retreating to equilibrium with one sub-class of moral thinking about moral value. For example a liberal fundamental principle of morality has to preclude elitism, treat all persons equally as persons in certain regards, etc. This seems to be Rawls' (1971) understanding of what reflective equilibrium is. This is a significant undertaking for those whose thinking is within this sub-class, giving them an understanding of how their thinking about cases and their thinking about moral value all hangs together. This may very well make their commitment to their way of thinking more attractive to them and may even convert others to this way of thinking. If one wants more in order to settle on a liberal fundamental principle as Kant and Rousseau do it is best I suspect not to go to a listing of cases that ordinary liberal thinking endorses as wrong or not, but to go to how these cases connect to ordinary liberal thinking about moral value, and then unify the latter into a conception of human existence as to living well or being truly happy, which conception based on universal facts about who and what we are undercuts alternatives to the liberal principle. Such facts would include our being reasoning, valuing and emotional beings seeking self-fulfillment in which case abandoning reasoning as the locus of such self-fulfillment would fail to accord with living well. Such a basis not only integrates and re-affirms the attractiveness of liberal thinking, it defends or justifies it. The liberal should dialogue with the illiberal over what makes for living well or happiness. His liberal view in a sense wins if there is genuine dialogue, since his moral view is validated just by there being genuine dialogue, by its being an open question of what it is to live well. The liberal view is the only view such that if the opponent accedes that it might possibly be true they thereby accede that it is true.

Wallace (2004;406) says that the "ambitious" version of showing the eudaimonistic value of morality would be to establish that moral life

> is a universally necessary condition for a meaningful human life such that no life can be counted worthwhile which lacks a commitment to moral ends.

It is telling from our point of view that Wallace holds the ambitious justification of morality to reside in its absolute eudaimonistic value. The conception of happiness set out in Part One coheres, I believe, with Wallace's understanding of eudaimonistic value in terms of a meaningful and worthwhile life, for according to that conception to be happy with how one's life is going is to be satisfied in a way that one can claim as one's own with how it is going, and hence to find meaning and worth with how it is going according to one's emotional, evaluative, and reasoning nature as a human being. The ambitious version then is to show that morality is a universally necessary condition of happiness. Not everyone agrees that such an ambitious version of justifying morality is possible or even desirable. One might hold that there is no such complete and final end as happiness and that even if there is any justification of morality in terms of it will have to smuggle in morality as part of one's conception of happiness. More seriously, even if circularity can be avoided the very nature of morality as sufficiently overriding all other considerations seems to preclude justifying it in terms of considerations beyond it which latter considerations would then be the overriding ones. Finally a justification in terms of anything else would apparently be inconsistent with a commitment to morality for its own sake (Brock 1977).

It has already been argued in Chapters 2 and 3 that being satisfied in a self-fulfilling way is a complete and final end in the sense that it is that in terms of which all other values or aims are flat-out valuable or flat-out to be aimed for, and that resistance to this idea of a final and complete end is due to misunderstandings of what it means. Of course the view of happiness set out in Part One was designed or tailored to be such that it could serve to defend morality. This by itself doesn't make the justification of morality circular since that view didn't incorporate specifically moral notions. However the question arises (Brock 1977) as to how that conception of what it is to be happy is to be justified. If its justification is that it implies and so justifies morality then we would be going in a circle. The question therefore is why the complete and final end is to be identified with the view of happiness set out in Part One? The answer is that the conception of happiness in Part One incorporates fulfilling us in regard to everything about us – so that it leaves nothing unfulfilled (it is complete) nor anything by which it is open to further issues (it is final). What fulfills us as emotional beings, and further as valuing beings who decisively endorse things, and further still as reasoning beings who give themselves over to the norms of reason is that which ends all issues. The conception of what it is to be happy is justified by its being that conception alone that *is* eudaimonia, the complete and final end. This is also the sense in which the conception was tailored to be that conception that can serve as a justification of morality. Since morality overrides all other values it can only be justified in terms of that which itself overrides all other values; viz. the complete and final end in terms of which anything else has flat-out value. Just as Plato held that justice could be established or defended only in terms of the well-functioning of all elements of the soul: desire, commitment, and reason we are holding that morality can be established or defended only in terms of fulfillment of all the elements of the soul: emotion, decisive endorsement, and reason.

As Brock (1977) points out since what is to be justified is the overriding nature of morality, it can be justified by something else that is also overriding only by showing that morality is necessarily and not just contingently in line with that something else. For example, if morality were only contingently related as being conducive to happiness then morality would lose any overriding nature that supposedly belongs to it itself as morality. It would no longer be overriding in its own right, but overriding to the extent that it connects to happiness. In Part One we attempted to show not only that happiness is overriding by being at the absolute bottom of things, but that respect and care for others is necessarily part of what it is to be thus happy, not something merely in fact conducive to it. In this way the overriding nature of respect and care also is shown to be unquestionable in that it essentially connects to what is more obviously, though not more stringently, overriding.

The questioning of the overriding nature of morality comes from its demand that one go against one's other goals no matter how cherished; i.e. that one goes against other components of one's happiness which as such are themselves overriding. Since these are apparently left aside by moral value it is not clear morality can be overriding completely and finally without incorporating them. But then as incorporating them it is no longer morality in the sense of being that which demands that we go against other goals. This dialectic between morality and happiness is resolved by the conception of what it is to be happy which likewise demands that we sometimes go against our own cherished goals for the obvious and easily recognized sequence of reasons that achieving self-fulfilling goals overrides even one's most cherished goals, that such self-fulfillment entails having well-considered goals and that having well-considered goals entails open-mindedness about them which entails respect and care for others. In sum the existence of other considerations regarding happiness in terms of which morality is justified doesn't imply that morality is not overriding since those other considerations don't obtain independent of morality to temper or condition its overriding nature.

If the justification of morality is that it is absolutely necessary for me to be happy then isn't the real motive for avoiding wrong by respecting and caring enough for others the selfish or self-serving one of caring for my own happiness? Even if a particular person doesn't think about their being happy when they avoid doing wrong so that *their* motive for avoiding it perhaps is just that it is wrong – still this wouldn't be the true motive. By the true motive I mean that which would be the motive of a reflective person who understood that avoiding wrong is unquestionably necessary just in its being necessary for him to be happy. Annas for one denies that the further understanding of morality as part of my final good makes the true motive for being moral a selfish one. She says (1995;127–128),

> ...the good of others matters to me *because it is the good of others*, and it is part of my own final good. It is quite unwarranted to think that the second thought must undermine the first. (italics mine)

But if the good of others matters to me also because it is part of my own final good that seems to undermine the purity of my motive for promoting the good of others. The pure motive, that is, would be to promote their good *just* for their sake apart from its being part of my good. This would make the good of others something I value intrinsically considered just in its own right. As an analogy consider protecting a painting. If my motive is to protect it for the sake of what it is then my motive is pure, whereas if it is also my motive in that it is part of my good to protect it for the sake of what it is then part of my motive is extrinsic to what its worth is. We need to backtrack and ask what it means to say that it is also my motive in that it is part of my final good. My motive for protecting the painting is also my motive in that it is part of my final good means that my motive is part of a system of motives the realization of which constitutes what I require to be satisfied with how my life is going. This doesn't undermine the purity of my motive in protecting the painting. Rather it establishes that motive as important enough to have a central place in my life. Equivalently it establishes my motivation to protect the painting when considered in its own right as important enough to be my motive all things considered. This doesn't mean my motive to protect is no longer pure: it means that my motive to protect the painting for its nature holds up when all things are considered. If my motive is pure to begin with (to protect it for what it is not for the prestige it brings me to own it) then it remains pure when it is also my motive in that it is part of my final good.

Suppose now that I am motivated to tell the truth because it is right to do so and suppose this means that I do it because it conforms to a rule of respect and care for others that I authorize as a standard for conducting my life. Analogous to the intrinsic value of a painting the intrinsic values that motivate me to "protect" telling the truth might be that it is fair, just, gives others their due, etc. That telling the truth is also my motive in that it promotes my final good adds no impure content to my motive—it simply incorporates my motive into a system of motives I require in order to be satisfied with my life. It establishes my motivation to tell the truth just for its intrinsic value as being the right thing to do just for its own sake because it is right as important enough to hold up as my motive all things considered. Rather than adding content it elevates the motive to a central place in my life. That telling the truth is also my motive in that it is part of my final good doesn't mean that my motive is or becomes selfish. It means that my final good is unselfish. Understood in this way Annas is right that if the good of others matters to me for their own sake (considered just in terms of its being good for them) then the thought of its being part of my own final good is just that it continues to matter when all things are considered. It doesn't add any impure consideration to its mattering. It sustains its mattering all things considered.

The justification of morality as *essential* to my final good doesn't contradict being motivated to do what is right for its own sake. What it does is justify my motive for doing what is right for its own sake also being my motive in that it is and has to be part of my final good. It justifies, that is, my motive for doing what is right for its own sake as being irrevocably central in my life. To think that morality on its own according to its own intrinsic nature of being a fair, just unselfish standard of conduct should be my motive but not at all in that it is part of my final good is to think it has in itself an intuitively apprehended flat-out value apart from being valued as contributing to my final good. It would make flat-out value something that first pertains to morality as some property of it and only thereby to be valued for our lives. This I argued in Chapter 2 is a mistaken account of what value, including moral value, is. By itself, of course, a justification of morality will not ensure that I will be motivated to do what is right, let alone do what is right for its own sake, but nor does it undermine doing what is right for its own sake.

In sum then a justification of morality in terms of happiness is consistent with the overriding nature of morality and with a commitment to it for its own sake. This leaves the question of how the account of the justification of our specific fundamental principle of morality relates to how people might ordinarily account for its justification. A person might say when pressed to account for why we should respect and care enough for others' pursuit of happiness that others matter as much as he does, that others have the same right to pursue happiness, that he is just one person among others; all of which is to say that he should allow for or respect others' pursuit. A person might say that he cannot be happy while others are suffering, that the happiness or not of others matters to his happiness, etc.; which is to say he must embrace and care for others' pursuit. All such ordinary accounts of justifying the principle certainly follow from our justification. No one would ordinarily say however that it is because such respect and care is part of giving oneself over to the open-ness of standards of satisfaction by which one fulfills oneself as a reasoning being and so can claim any satisfaction with how one's life is going as their own. However it is not a constraint on a justification of a principle of morality that it be exactly how people would ordinarily justify it. The whole point is that the ordinary justifications don't seem fully adequate. They seem to be in need of a further accounting or elucidation to be complete and to close the matter. If they did seem fully adequate then Glaucon and Adeimantus and the rest of us who do care for this moral principle would not be asking Socrates and all the philosophers following for an accounting.

There is far more to the phenomenology of morality, to how avoiding doing what is wrong seems to be to the truly moral person, than being motivated toward it simply in its own right. Following Kant, for example, the truly moral person is humbled in the face of the moral law. On our account I give myself over to the moral law as part of giving myself over to the open-ness of standards of satisfaction by which I claim anything as being self-fulfilling. I am humbled in the face of the moral law then in that I give myself over to it. A truly moral person will be or feel unable to live with himself if he does wrong. On our account if I do wrong I am divorced or estranged from how my life is going no matter how otherwise satisfied I may be with it because I fail to commit to that by which I can claim any such satisfaction as my own. A truly moral person is diminished in his own eyes by doing wrong. On our account I am diminished to being a valuing and emotional being as I have abandoned what belongs to me as a reasoning being. I leave it to others to fill out the phenomenology of being a truly moral person. Since that phenomenology however should track the true worth or status of morality if it is to be the phenomenology of the *truly* moral person it is something to be derived from an account of what that true worth is, what the justification of morality is, not a test for it.

To sum up, in this chapter a definition of doing what is wrong was given that according to the account set out in Part One makes doing wrong something that goes against our own happiness. The fundamental principle of morality to respect and care enough for the pursuit of happiness of others that follows from this account is thereby justified or defended. It was claimed that it is only by settling the issue of justification that one can settle the issue of what, if anything, the fundamental principle of morality is, and that only an account of value and what is at the bottom of all value (only an account of happiness) can settle the issue of justification. Fundamental principles of morality opposed to ours it was claimed fail to give a proper account of value or of happiness. Finally, justifying morality in terms of happiness need not be circular and need not conflict with morality being an overriding consideration or with it being something to be committed to for its own sake. I turn now to what the content is of this fundamental principle of respect and care for others' pursuit of happiness.

CHAPTER 6

The Content of the Fundamental Principle

(i)

Any fundamental principle of morality is responsive to what in general is harmful to people and what in general are the needs of people. Fundamental principles will differ as to which inflictions of harm and which failures to meet needs are wrong. Any fundamental principle establishes some "reflective equilibrium" with the mutually understood field of harms and needs. What underlies moral principles is not a field of universally agreed to intuitions about what is wrong to do, but a field of universally understood ideas of what are harms and needs—the field that constitutes the topic of morality. For example, Thrasymachus will agree that killing another person is to harm him, only by his fundamental principle if it is advantageous to one's goals it isn't wrong. Someone who does not hold an extreme act-utilitarian principle will agree that failing to aid as many people as possible fails to meet what are genuine needs but that such failure isn't wrong. To understand the content of a moral principle is to understand how it categorizes various kinds of infliction of harm and failure to meet needs into those that are wrong and those that aren't.

We begin with cases of killing others and failing to save others' lives. For one to kill another for the sake of achieving personal goals clearly fails to respect their pursuit of happiness; indeed it destroys it. It has this consequence whether or not I am found out and so violates the fundamental principle whether I am found out or not. The point in regard to the justification of the principle is that any of my personal goals can contribute to my happiness only if achieving them is part of a standard of satisfaction I can give myself over to as a reasoning being. As far as happiness goes my standard being held in an open-minded way is lexically prior to any achievement of specific goals. In destroying another's further prospective and retrospective considerations any standard I hold is closed-minded and hence any goals I achieve are no part of what it is for me to be happy. I may "get away with" killing the other in the sense of achieving goals I wouldn't otherwise have achieved without any sanctions from others, but I cannot escape the sanction of what I do going against my own happiness. This is true whether my goal is the selfish one of getting a competitor out of the way to get a job or the lofty one of promoting art or scientific research. The same applies to killing another for the sake of my friend's goals. It violates not only my own open-mindedness but the open-mindedness of my

© KONINKLIJKE BRILL NV, LEIDEN, 2014 | DOI 10.1163/9789004283213_007

friend who loses the same prospective and retrospective considerations as I do. His standard is less well-considered by my act.

One might think that the sanction of going against my own happiness is not so great. After the wrong is done I can always re-commit myself to being open-minded and so continue on to pursue happiness. This kind of cynicism lets Thrasymachus in through the back door. To thus re-commit oneself so long as it no longer conflicts with my achieving goals is not to commit myself at all. It cannot fulfill me as a reasoning being to commit myself to a standard of reason when it is convenient. There are people however who after killing someone do genuinely and categorically commit themselves to not doing wrong; people who are born again or born for the first time morally. They still have lingering that they have closed off considerations. They may genuinely want to commit themselves to open-mindedness, but how can they if any other goals from now on are tarnished by those considerations not being able to be taken into account? Those destroyed considerations have to somehow be compensated for or resuscitated before there can be commitment to the openness of standards of satisfaction. Of course if I kill someone there is no complete resuscitation of the destroyed considerations. It won't do for me to re-create in my own mind what the considerations might have been. This would be to substitute my own considerations as to what they might have been which, for Wittgenstein-like reasons, is not committing to a *standard* of reasonableness that my reasoning, including my reasoning about how others might have reasoned, conforms to. The killer who truly wants to categorically commit can do no better than (and must do no less than) carry on in some way the projects of his victim. That is as close to resuscitating the victim's considerations as he can come, or as close to "paying back" the common enterprise of pursuing happiness for what he has cost it and cost himself, and thus as close to committing to open-mindedness as he can come. The "sanction" then is that his life is no longer his own. It is no longer to pursue happiness according to his considerations of a standard that would be satisfying. This is not a sanction that has to be imposed by anyone to be real. It is the unavoidable consequence of his killing. It is in this sense that he must pay with *his* life for killing another. Prisoners who go before the parole board and claim that they are genuinely repentant and so should be left free to now pursue their happiness contradict themselves. Genuine repentance for killing requires rather a life-long pursuit of compensation. It is not so much that once one kills he is no longer worthy to be happy. Rather once one kills one has in fact abandoned the worth (the dignity beyond any price) of giving themselves over to a standard of reason that is essential to *being* happy (not to deserving to be happy). At least metaphorically the biblical injunction of an eye for an eye and a tooth for a tooth, a life for a life is the truth. In the case of killing doing wrong is its own life-long punishment.

On the other hand if I could not have foreseen how my action of using my remote to unlock my car would set off a planted bomb killing an innocent bystander there is no failure of mine or of what I do to respect the life and the pursuit of happiness of the bystander. I may feel terrible, but I can feel terrible when a lightning bolt hits my neighbor's house killing him while I get to walk away unharmed. I do not have to compensate for unforeseeable wrongs or for natural harms in order to be fully committed to open-mindedness.

Attempted killing of another that doesn't succeed still fails to respect the other's pursuit of happiness. Even if it doesn't close off the other's considerations it tampers with them. It may not do any harm to the other, but the idea of avoiding doing wrong is not just to avoid harm that we can be charged with avoiding, but to avoid initiating foreseeable harm, which is covered by our principle of respect. Again, I fail to respect the value of a vase in attempting to push it off the pedestal even if it doesn't fall. In relation to the justification of the fundamental principle, to attempt what might close off pertinent prospective and retrospective considerations is to fail to give myself over to open-mindedness. The analogy from Chapter 4 to giving myself over to the voting by club members in regard to how to spend the club's money makes this clear. To try to block voting, even if it fails to stop it, is inconsistent with giving myself over to voting as the standard for spending money.

Suppose that another person is trying to kill me and I can only prevent this by killing him. If I do so I do not fail to respect his pursuit of happiness since he is not pursuing happiness. Anyone who kills as a means to their goals or as itself their goal is not giving himself over to the open character of standards of satisfaction and so is acting in a way inconsistent with being happy upon achieving the goal since they cannot claim any satisfaction with achieving the goal as belonging to them or being self-fulfilling as a reasoning being. But now to act in a way absolutely inconsistent with any chance of happiness is not to be pursuing happiness. Similar remarks apply to killing someone who is trying to kill others. One might contend that in killing the about to be killer one is closing off his prospective and retrospective considerations. However those "considerations" are made irrelevant by including killing. Since I already know outright that considerations including killing cannot be part of a well-considered standard I am not being closed-minded in closing off those considerations. For me to be open-minded does not require that I be open to closed-minded considering.

In a lifeboat scenario I am on a boat with B and C and if we all remain on the boat it will sink and we will all drown. B and C together by remaining on the boat are threatening my life. They can be charged with avoiding it even if they are not to blame for failing to avoid it. As such by their remaining they are failing to respect my pursuit of happiness which is wrong even if they are not to blame for it. Because of this in remaining they are not pursuing happiness since their pursuit involves failing to respect mine. Hence saving my life by throwing either one off is not interfering with his pursuit of happiness and so according to our fundamental principle is not wrong. Since the same analysis applies to each of B and C it isn't wrong for any of us to throw one of the others off the boat.

The cases so far exhibit certain principles or laws about wrong doing that derive from the fundamental principle. First if an act is wrong it is so whether one is found out or not. Second if an act is wrong so is attempting the act. Third whether an act is wrong may depend on whether it prevents other wrongdoing. Fourth doing wrong is its own punishment requiring not just repentance but atonement that, as far as possible, compensates for the wrong. These are not intuitively demonstrable principles governing right and wrong that any fundamental principle of morality must be responsible to or must be in reflective equilibrium with. Any intuition of the truth of those laws or principles must derive from an underlying fundamental principle. If a person has these intuitions the question is what unifies these intuitions and then what justifies them. What is intuitively clear prior to any fundamental principle is that killing is a harm and so morality must deal with it one way or another. How it deals with it when there are apparent gains to be gotten from the harm, when the harm isn't actually inflicted, and when the harm prevents that very harm are not "intuitively" clear. There is always Thrasymachus, extreme act utilitarianism, elitism and the extreme de-ontologist whose intuitions need to be deconstructed.

A more interesting, though no less core case of doing wrong is killing someone who is not attempting to harm anyone in order to save my life or the life of several others – such as, for example, taking both of a person A's kidneys to implant in two other people B and C thus saving their lives. This case merits protracted discussion since, as we shall see, it brings out a crucial anticonsequentialist result regarding the relative worth of persons. Supposedly if I take A's kidneys I disrespect his pursuit of happiness and so do wrong according to the fundamental principle. However if I don't take them then it seems that I don't care enough for the pursuit of B and C supposing it is "easy" enough to get A's kidneys. The fundamental principle which says to both respect and care enough seems to be violated either way. Thus, apparently it is both wrong to take A's kidneys and wrong not to. This is not an impossible result per se, but it is not I claim the result that actually follows from the fundamental principle, which is rather that it is wrong to take A's kidneys and not wrong to fail to take them. The issue that this case presents is whether and on what grounds respecting takes precedence over caring enough when there is a conflict. Although the fundamental principle is seemingly silent on this matter it may be that there is still an asymmetry between respecting and caring enough as regards the pursuit of happiness that settles the matter in favor of respecting A.

To have regard for others' prospective and retrospective considerations is to have regard for conditions being favorable for such considerations. This includes being able to rely on and trust others to behave in certain ways. If we cannot trust each other to keep hands off each other's kidneys then the pursuit of happiness is greatly damaged by having to constantly take care not to lose our kidneys, which gets in the way of considering how to live according to considering the value of projects and goals. For roughly Hobbes-like reasons it is essential to our pursuit of happiness that there is agreement to keep hands off kidneys. Even B and C who need kidneys have to agree to a universal principle against kidney-napping as part of a regard for conditions being favorable to prospective and retrospective considering. Note that the principle includes the case where taking kidneys saves others' lives. If we cannot trust each other to keep hands off each other's kidneys even when taking them saves lives then we never know when our kidneys might be in danger and so all our goals and plans have to be tempered or skewed by the threat rather than considered in terms of value. On the other hand it is not essential to the pursuit of happiness to be able to rely on others to provide kidneys when one's life is at stake, The pursuit of happiness can proceed quite well under social conditions which do not include any such principle of kidney-supplying. One would not have to walk around worrying about not getting kidneys any more than one might walk around worrying about kidney failure. One's setting and considering of goals wouldn't be tempered by a constantly present threat. Kidney failure happens; it is a part of life. Any over-worrying about it is an issue of how much one values health, etc. Regard for the social conditions for pursuing happiness favors a principle against taking kidneys even to save lives over an incompatible principle of providing kidneys to save lives. It also favors this principle against not having either of the two principles. In this case at least a principle of trust as to respecting each other's pursuit of happiness takes precedence over a principle of trust as to caring enough for each other's pursuit of happiness.

It follows that if a person is to give himself over to the norm of reason in regard to considerations of a standard of satisfaction he must give himself over to the principle against taking kidneys since this latter principle protects each of our prospective and retrospective considerations. As usual this implies that adherence to the principle is essential to being happy because only by such adherence can a person be satisfied in a self-fulfilling way with how his life is going. Anyone who pursues his life in violation of this principle then is not pursuing happiness, since he is pursuing his life in a way that is inconsistent with what it is to be happy.

Suppose now that I take A's kidneys to save B and C and suppose first that B and C agree to it either before or after the fact. Then B and C fail to give themselves over to the norm of reason and so fail thereby, as they continue to pursue their lives, to be pursuing happiness. Although then B and C's lives are saved, their pursuit of happiness is not. Hence I don't fail to care enough for their pursuit of happiness by not providing them with A's kidneys, though I do still fail to respect A's pursuit by taking his kidneys. Hence I do wrong according to the fundamental principle of morality only if I take A's kidneys. Not only is it wrong to take A's kidneys but it goes against my own pursuit of happiness to do so. I as well fail to give myself over to the norm of reason. Suppose next that B and C are kept in the dark. They get kidneys but don't know how they were obtained and are kept from finding out. Even so, B and C only at best *seem to themselves* to give themselves over to the norm of reason because of their ignorance. They are not perhaps to be blamed for this ignorance if they make serious efforts to find out but it remains the case that *in fact* they don't give themselves over to the norm. Whether a person gives himself over to the norm of reason in his life cannot depend on his ignorance of the fact that the norm is not really governing his life. B and C have been placed in a variant of a Nozick machine (Chapter 4). If so then B and C still fail as they continue their lives to be pursuing happiness – it only seems to them that they are. But the fundamental principle of morality doesn't require caring enough for others' seeming pursuit of happiness. Hence again I do not violate the caring component of that principle in failing to save B and C's lives by failing to take A's kidneys.

According to the above analysis a principle of not taking kidneys is essential to the norm of reason that derives from the open nature of standards of satisfaction. Crucial to that analysis is that once a principle is essential to the norm one must give oneself over to it in order to give oneself over to the norm and so pursue happiness. One cannot make exceptions to the principle, such as whether one will be found out or not, without violating the norm of reason. But now note that the entire defense of the principle being part of the norm is that it protects and secures people's considerations. It is the fostering of conditions for considering standards and so the fostering of prospective and retrospective considerations that is the rationale of its incorporation into the norm of reason. However, there seems to be a problem with this rationale; namely, in failing to take A's kidneys two entire sets of considerations (B's and C's) are lost, whereas in taking A's kidneys only one entire set of considerations is lost. This it seems undercuts the rationale of adding the principle in the first place. It would seem rather that one should add the principle of preserving more sets over less sets; a principle incompatible with the principle against kidney-napping. It seems, that is, that at least there is no rationale for adding one principle over the other, and if one adds the principle of preserving sets of considerations then it is failing to take A's kidneys which would turn out to be wrong.

This line of thinking holds that full sets of considerations are comparable as to the worth they hold for me in being open-minded. In particular it holds that two sets of considerations have greater worth in regard to my standard of satisfaction being well-considered than a third single set. But there is no basis whatsoever for this comparison. What is it about the considerations of B and C together that make my incorporating them a *better* considering of what is satisfying than incorporating A's considerations instead? Is there any conception of grades of worthwhile considerations? If there were such a thing as a true standard of satisfaction to be approached then at least the idea of greater or lesser worth to certain considerations as opposed to others would make sense in terms of which considerations get me closer to the truth. But according to our postulate in Chapter 4 there is no such approach. The baker's set of considerations is no more or less to be considered than the scientist's unless there is some idea that some considerations take precedence over others. If there is no "true" satisfaction there is no dimension of approaching the truth by which to order or compare considerations. Because of this incomparability there is no sense to the idea that A's considerations are less worthwhile than B's and C's together. But this is just to say that each person's pursuit of happiness is beyond any price by which it can be bargained, even against the pursuit of several others. Previously it was claimed that each person's dignity as pursuing happiness has a worth that cannot be outstripped by any of my goals or aims. Now I am claiming that each person's dignity has a worth that cannot be outstripped by the dignity of others.

An analogy with the aesthetic appreciation of painting should clarify this point. There is no such thing as the definitive truth in regard to appreciating painting. All there is are considerations which enrich appreciation. I may compare a painting by Botticelli with one of Picasso's paintings in order to enrich appreciation, but there is no such thing as coming to the resolution that Botticelli's painting is better or more worthy of respecting and caring for since there is no dimension or scale of an approach to a finally true appreciation. Each painting has worth to be considered that is not outstripped by the other. Nor if we add a painting by Rembrandt can we say that it together with the Botticelli has more worth to be considered than the Picasso. In relation to the enterprise of aesthetic appreciation the status of each painting as something to be considered is completely separate and insulated from this status of other paintings. Similarly the status of a person's pursuit as something to be considered is completely separate and insulated from this same status of other people. The very nature of the pursuit of happiness, that since there is no approach to a final truth there is no scale according to which different sets of considerations can be compared or graded, implies this absolute separateness of each individual's pursuit.

Once the principle of preserving two sets of considerations over one set is seen not to be a part of the norm of open-mindedness the rationale for incorporating a principle against taking kidneys holds up and so finally we can say that at least in this case respect for A's pursuit takes precedence over saving B and C's lives because to save their lives in this manner by taking A's kidneys is *not* to fail to care enough for B and C's pursuit of happiness.

Suppose that person B is highly inventive about proposing various satisfying ways of living and ingenious at coming up with prospective supporting reasons whereas person A is much less so. Again the fact that there is no "true" satisfaction implies that there is no sense to the idea that A's more limited prospective and retrospective considerations are less worthwhile or further from the truth than several sets of considerations, this time all in one person B. Hence A's pursuit of happiness is no less worthwhile than B's and thus it goes against reason to respect and care for A's pursuit less than B's simply because B is more imaginative, inventive, clever, and so on. In particular it goes against reason to take A's kidneys to save B and C no matter how imaginative and inventive B and C are.

Consider next the trolley case. Similar to the case of taking A's kidneys to save the lives of B and C this is the case of diverting a runaway trolley to a second track which kills A in order to save the lives of B and C who are otherwise in its path. The only difference so far as I can tell is that this case is extremely rare. Such circumstances hardly ever arise. What this means is that a general principle of trust that we don't kill each other in these circumstances is not an essential social condition of pursuing happiness. Because the situation is so rare I don't have to constantly take care not to get myself into such a situation and so skew my considerations away from what is valuable to pursue in life. The circumstance is like other potential natural disasters in this regard. I could just as well be hit by lightning. It is just a fact of life that once in a while such things may happen. Because no such principle is part of a norm of regard for others' pursuit of happiness, if I fail to kill A then I indeed fail to care enough for the pursuit of B and C, while if I kill A I fail to respect his pursuit. Furthermore the inestimable and incomparable worth of a person even in relation to several others precludes calling in a principle of maximizing sets of considerations to avoid disrespecting A by killing him. Hence it is wrong to kill A and wrong to fail to kill A. This result holds as well if the case is varied so that I have to throw A on a single track to stop the trolley from crashing into and killing B and C. If this latter situation were somehow a more ever-present or common kind of situation it would be different as then it would revert to the kidney case. So long as it is rare however the conclusion follows that both options are wrong. What we have is a moral tragedy that cannot be avoided by any sort of (even unanimously agreed to) "fair" procedure for determining what to do, such as drawing straws which favors B and C two-to-one. Such a procedure is not essential as a social condition in the pursuit of happiness and has no rationale other than to mask the fact that whatever is done goes against the pursuit of happiness.

Euthanasia encompasses a family of different kinds of cases. I consider only those where the person is now incapable of consent or not as to being killed but has previously expressed wishes. If the person's previous wishes were to have his life ended, then to fail to end it disrespects the pursuit *of others* who have a standard of satisfaction that includes such an ending. These others' considerations for such a standard would be skewed, even perhaps destroyed, if they had no trust that their wishes would be carried out. My failing to end or to help end a comatose person's life breaks the trust by which others may have and consider such a standard for their own end of life. Since I have no proof that a standard of satisfaction shouldn't include this end of life I am failing to respect others who are living. If the person's previously expressed wishes were to continue to live on then killing him similarly breaks the trust and so fails to respect the pursuit of happiness of others. This same analysis applies to honoring the wishes of a dead person. I have no proof that a standard for being satisfied with how one's life is going should not include working toward what involves expectations for how things go after one is dead. Note that this standard is not the absurd one of realizing goals after one is dead – which couldn't possibly be a standard for being satisfied with how one's life *is* going. If I don't honor a person's wish that his cat be provided for by his estate then I fail to respect those others living whose standard of satisfaction includes making or having achieved enough money to provide for their cats after their death by undermining the trust that having such a standard requires.

To sum up our discussion of killing, the principle that it is wrong to respect or care enough for the pursuit of others implies that killing another for personal goals is always wrong, that it is not wrong to kill another to keep him from killing, that it is wrong to kill another without his consent even if it saves several other lives, and that killing another in accord with their previous consent is at least in some cases not wrong. The point of the discussion was not to match even core intuitions that people have about killing. The core intuition of some people is that killing is always wrong no matter what. For others a core intuition is that it is always wrong to kill an innocent person no matter what. Each of these intuitions conflicts with our fundamental principle. As in Chapter 4 it is possible to give accounts of the nature of human existence, value and happiness according to which such intuitions are principled ones. The point of our discussion was simply to establish that our fundamental principle is not intolerably amorphous, vague or indeterminate as regards when the harm of killing another is or isn't wrong.

(ii)

We turn now to cases of saving others' lives. If someone is choking in a restaurant and I know the Heimlich maneuver I fail to care enough for their pursuit of happiness if I fail to at least try to save their life. If someone is drowning in rough seas and I am not a strong swimmer and have no other way of helping them than to swim to them then I do not fail to care enough for their pursuit when I don't even try to swim to them. The cost to my pursuit of happiness in this case is too great or at least great enough for it not to be wrong to fail to save them. Suppose there are two people B and C each choking in a restaurant and there is time only to save one by applying the Heimlich maneuver. In going to B and applying the maneuver I do not fail to care enough for C by not saving him since it is not possible to. If I sit there and save neither then I fail to care enough for B and for C. As to the choice of who to save, neither choice, and so neither act, is a failure to care enough for the other's pursuit. Suppose now that B is my wife. If I save C I not only fail to save B but I also fail to care enough for the special bond of trust and care I have with B. Unlike the previous case where saving C makes it impossible to save B and so is not a case of failing to care enough for B, in this case the special bond with B requires not making it impossible to save B. That is part of having a special bond, and to break special bonds of care I have with another is to fail to care enough for their pursuit of happiness which includes this bond as part of their standard of satisfaction. Thus it would be wrong to save C. More generally when there are special bonds of trust it is wrong to be neutral as to whether to help the person one has the bond with or in the same way help another one doesn't have the bond with. Suppose I promise to help B paint his room. Then it is wrong to help C paint his room rather than helping B. Even if in this case the bond is not part of B's standard of satisfaction—still breaking the general trust of keeping special bonds demotes the conditions of people pursuing happiness. Returning to the case of saving B, even if it is wrong not to save B isn't it still the case that I fail to care enough for C? Since I have no special bond with C I do not have to care enough for him to make it possible to save him. I don't now have to make it possible to save a starving person in a distant country. Caring enough for another doesn't mean making it possible to care for them if making it possible costs too much to my pursuit of happiness. In this case if I truly have a bond with B then it costs me too much for me to make it possible to save C by failing to save B. The fundamental principle is not that it is wrong to fail to care enough *equally* for the pursuit of others. It allows that caring more for the pursuit of some is consistent with caring less but still enough for the pursuit of others.

The evaluation of an act is one thing; the evaluation of the motive is another. Following Williams (1985) it would call the bond I have with my wife into question if I went through any general moral evaluation of what is required in the situation before I saved her. Evaluating the act this way would express to her that my care for her is lacking emotionally. If the bond is there then going through the evaluation of the act would misrepresent the strength of the bond. In this manner my motive "should be" just to save her without evaluating the act. This is analogous, I suggest, to conversational implicature. If I say "He didn't beat his wife today" my statement is true but can also be evaluated as not the statement to make for what it incorrectly seems to imply. This further evaluation comes in after the evaluation for truth. If I make a false statement it is outright not the statement to be made independent of what else it seems to imply. Similarly the evaluation of my motive comes in after the evaluation of the act. In the case of saving my wife the only way the act can fail to be required is if it is wrong in that it is required not to do it. Suppose I fail to apply the Heimlich maneuver to C in which case his liver can be transplanted into my wife to save her, and suppose that this act is wrong. Then I shouldn't do it for whatever motive, whether the motive is that I hate C and so take the opportunity to let him die or the motive is that I love my wife. Just as "badly" stating that he didn't beat his wife today doesn't call into question truth as the basic standard for evaluating statements, so too "badly" saving my wife because it is required doesn't call into question morality as being the basic standard for evaluating actions. It might be problematic if the evaluation of the act is inconsistent with the "proper" motive. But the evaluation according to the fundamental principle in the case where I love my wife is in part that it isn't wrong to fail to save C because it costs me too much to make it possible to do so; an evaluation that is perfectly consistent with the nature of the bond. If I don't really love her anymore a different evaluation pertains along the lines of favoring saving her for the "promise" the bond still is until properly broken.

Consider next the case where B and C are my two adult children and I can save only one (a variant of Sophie's choice). My special bond with B requires not making it impossible to save him by saving C and reverse-wise my special bond with C requires not making it impossible to save him by saving B. Whoever I save I fail to care enough for the pursuit of the other. There is no way I can avoid doing wrong.

The issue of caring for the welfare of those in poverty, the hungry, the sick, and all others who lack the wherewithal to pursue happiness was considered in Chapter 4. The result recall according to the rationale of caring enough for others was that it was a failure to care enough only to fail to do my part in contributing to socio-political arrangements for caring for the welfare of others. This point applies to the special most serious cases of saving the very lives of others starving to death or in the midst of a deadly epidemic, and so on. It is not wrong then to fail to save lives in all ways that it is possible to do so. The fundamental principle is a principle of the "sanctity" of pursuing happiness; not per se a principle of the sanctity of life. It does not imply that killing is always wrong no matter what, or that saving lives takes precedence over all other things. In a sense it is a principle of the "sanctity" of uniquely human life. We shall see below that this doesn't imply only human life has moral standing.

(iii)

We consider next cases of inflicting bodily harm. If I injure another by breaking their foot I interfere with their bodily conditions for pursuing happiness. It closes off considering options such as running marathons or doing ballet. This is so whether or not I am found out to be the one who inflicted the injury. The rationale for its being wrong that it goes against my happiness is the same whether I am found out or not. Their foot may or may not properly heal over time but in any case I at least tamper with their pursuit of happiness in opening up the possibility that it might not heal. This is like the case of causing a crack on a valuable vase. It may or may not be that it can be restored but in any case in thus tampering with it I am failing to respect it. Any time I do bodily damage I tamper in this way with the person's pursuit. This is to hedge my commitment to the open nature of standards of satisfaction and so it goes against any self-fulfilling satisfaction.

None of this is to say that the harm of bodily damage for a person is just its interfering with their pursuit of happiness. It is surely intrinsically a harm not to be able to walk around when one has a broken leg. Just as the intrinsic value of a work of art doesn't depend on its connection to what is right or wrong so the intrinsic dis-value of a broken leg doesn't depend on moral issues. Morality rather presupposes a field of harms (or values) adjudicating when doing that harm or failing to help alleviate it is or isn't wrong. It isn't morality which first defines what the harms are or in what intrinsic regard they are harms. Suppose I fail to amputate a fellow climber's gangrenous foot because cutting off a foot is such a terrible harm. That is not the reason it is wrong since in fact it isn't wrong. If my neighbor keeps walking on my grass on the other hand and I cut off his foot that is still not the reason that the act is wrong—that it is a terrible harm is the reason only that it is a *terrible* wrong. One might say that its being a harm that is not necessary for preventing greater harm is the reason it is wrong. That depends however on being able to grade harms. On my view they cannot be graded independently of how they figure into the pursuit of happiness so if this is the reason, it is not inconsistent with our view that the wrongness of actions is not the intrinsic harm of the action but rather how that harm relates to the pursuit of happiness.

Taking away another's full and free use of their body or even tampering with it fails to respect their pursuit of happiness. To kidnap someone is a clear case of taking away their free use of their body. There is no such thing as this having no lasting consequences once they are freed. During that time their considerations are clearly burdened and skewed by less than optimal circumstances with at least some likelihood that the considerations they would have had if they had not been kidnapped are lost forever. To interfere with the overall *progression* of another's optimal considering interferes with or tampers with their pursuit of happiness, and kidnapping stops this progression in its tracks. Of course kidnapping has other lasting consequences, for example to the person's sense of security. In this way it is not only a bodily harm but an emotional harm as well, which is a further way it fails to respect another's pursuit of happiness. Rape can be characterized as a particularly brutal kind of kidnapping. One's free use of one's body is violated, there is danger of great bodily harm, and there are lasting consequences not only to the person's sense of security, but to their entire emotional well-being. Again it may seem shallow or minimizing to say rape is wrong for failing to respect the victim's pursuit of happiness, but firstly their pursuit of happiness is not something that exists alongside other facets of them. In failing to respect their pursuit I am failing to respect the "deepest" part of them. Secondly this is a devastating failure in how much and in how many ways it damages their pursuit. Thirdly the devastation is in part because of how intrinsically horrible as an occurrence considered in itself the rape is.

If we think of private property functioning as an extension of our bodies as far as pursuing happiness is concerned then stealing becomes a case of inflicting extended bodily harm. Consider a person's clothing. It keeps him warm and so works in effect as an adjunct of the temperature-controlling mechanism of his body. A person's food is an "external" reserve of energy extending his body's storage of fat. The body as something functional versus something merely anatomical is not enclosed within the skin. To harm this functional body interferes with a person's pursuit of happiness. Stealing food or clothing then is inflicting bodily harm like amputating a leg is, although the stolen items are replaceable "body parts." Similar remarks apply to a person's tools such as hammers, plows, bows and arrows. They extend the scope of what a person can bodily do so that to steal them is to interfere with his extended bodily functionality. What I can get other people to do and provide by my money makes that money a sort of all-purpose tool for extending the powers of my body. Simply by handing over a piece of paper I can get a house built—surely an extension of the power of my bodily movements. This leaves the issue of what is or isn't private property. Although my leg is mine "naturally" it isn't true that a house is mine naturally. Even if I squat in it and work on it, it doesn't become mine perhaps in part because unlike my legs it is replaceable. For something to belong to a person is for him to have free and unfettered use of it according to general agreement as to what is required for such use. What that agreement is may be different in different cultures. That there is some such agreement by which each can expect to have exclusive use is crucial to the pursuit of happiness. For me to steal from someone is a violation of trust they have with me as to how we will each behave— which is a failure to respect the pursuit of happiness which depends on such trust. The difference is that the violation of trust in the case of stealing is dependent to some extent on "conventional" agreement whereas the violation of trust in killing or maiming another is not. There aren't alternative agreements to allow killing blond people on Tuesdays that can serve the pursuit of happiness.

Stealing money from a rich person as the only way to feed my starving wife or to get her a life-saving operation doesn't undermine the general trust by which we all have free use of money in pursuing happiness. The reason is that it is a *rare* emergency. In such a rare emergency it is wrong for the rich person not to give up some money just as it is wrong of me not to give up eating my salad to get up and apply the Heimlich maneuver. It goes against the rich person's own caring enough for the pursuit of others to fail to give up money in such a case and so against his own pursuit of happiness. He fails to give himself over to the open-ness of standards by failing to protect a train of considering to be otherwise lost. Since he is not pursuing happiness by keeping his money I do not fail to respect his pursuit of happiness by taking the money. This is different than continually stealing from him to save as many starving people as possible. His caring *enough* for others' pursuit to be consistent with his open-mindedness doesn't require that he give up his own pursuit altogether. Issues of general income redistribution are to be handled as all welfare issues—by organized divided responsibility such as graduated income taxes.

Suppose I take some money from someone but I calculate that the chances are very small that this act of stealing will become public and so violate trust, and that the chances are also very small that the stolen part of his fortune will ever be missed in his pursuit of happiness. For this calculation to work the chances of others chipping further away at his fortune will also have to be small. I am still tampering with his pursuit by doing what might make it vulnerable to damage and so still failing to respect his pursuit which according to the fundamental principle is wrong. The issue this case raises is how such stealing goes against my happiness? Because the chances of the stealing actually contributing to any damage to considering on his part are small and there is value in my achieving my goal G by stealing, it seems to follow that the greatest utility is to go for G and so promote my happiness. However achieving G *by itself* has no flat-out value whatsoever. Only if G's achievement is something I can claim as fulfilling to me as a reasoning being does it contribute to my happiness and so have any value. Hence the greatest utility is not to steal. Still I don't just gain G. I gain retrospective considerations regarding G as part of a standard of satisfaction, and that has value. Thus against the small chance of losing his considerations there is the greater chance of gaining my considerations. If such utility calculations are a norm of reason that I can give myself over to in devising standards of satisfaction, then the expected gain of considerations regarding G has value as being a gain I can claim as a reasoning being. My gaining *my* considerations, however, cannot be a part of a norm of reason that I give myself over to. A norm is supposed to be that against which *my* considerations hold up or not. It makes no sense for my considerings and my retrospective re-considerings to be part of the norm that these considerings are supposed to measure up to. Hence to give myself over to utility calculations that factor in my considerations is not to fully give myself over to any norm of reason. The only norm I can give myself over to as a reasoning being then is one which precludes tampering with others' considerations however small the likelihood of its leading to the loss of those considerations. Any considerations I gain by such tampering I gain at the cost of failing to give myself over to a norm for coming to standards of satisfaction, and so have no value as contributing to my happiness. Since stealing in the case at issue does tamper it goes against my happiness.

(iv)

We consider next harms to the considering or reasoning mind such as manipulating, deceiving, lying and breaking promises. To manipulate another's thinking for one's own purposes by pressuring them threatening them or charming them is to make one's own thinking at least part of the source of their considerations. This is to fail to respect their considering and so their pursuit of happiness. It is also clearly the polar opposite of my being open-minded to do so and so goes against my own happiness. For some reason Skinner (1971) classifies appealing to someone's reason as a case of mild control or manipulation of them. To offer someone reasons or considerations may very well redirect their considering but it does so via their considering of those reasons and so accepting or rejecting them, which doesn't supplant their considering with my own. More generally the attempt by some group to control the free use of reason by others whether institutionalized as political tyranny or less formally as social pressure to think certain ways goes against the happiness of the members of the group. This is Rousseau's point that the master, the one who controls, is as much a slave as the slave, the one who is controlled. The master has abandoned his own open-minded reason even if he thinks he is controlling for the good of the slave. He is taking his idea of the good to be definitive or at least more correct than other ideas of the good. The controlled group is in circumstances analogous to groups of people lacking welfare such as the impoverished in that conditions for their pursuing happiness are lacking. As in the welfare case for me to care enough for the pursuit of others doesn't require that I fight tyranny at extreme cost to myself but only that I do my part in the divided responsibility of all to improve circumstances. I do not care enough for the pursuit of others if I simply ignore tyrannical control.

The pursuit of happiness involves being apprised of the facts. Some facts appear to be more significant in this regard than others. If I tell you falsely that there is a car for sale down the block and you go there this is not very likely perhaps to be damaging to your overall pursuit of happiness. On the other hand to falsely tell you that there are no job prospects in Cleveland because for some reason I don't want you to move there is major enough to count as damaging. Since none of us are in a favorable position to ascertain all facts that may be significant it is central to the pursuit of happiness to be able to rely on others as to the facts. Even "small" lies that on their own might not rise to the level of damaging count as tampering by weakening and possibly contributing to the undermining of reliance on each other for the facts. Lying even in small matters then is a failure to respect others' pursuit of happiness. If the police come to the door asking for the whereabouts of an innocent person so they can torture him and I lie when I say that I don't know, this lie is no disrespect for the pursuit of happiness of the police since any pursuit of theirs which involves failing to respect the pursuit of the innocent person is not a pursuit of happiness at all. Not only is it not wrong to lie to them but supposing that the danger to me is not immediate and great it would be wrong not to lie—a failure to care enough for the pursuit of happiness of the innocent person. If I am a moral person then perhaps my having to lie should bother me even if it would be wrong not to. Lying so to speak goes against the grain of who I am and what I am used to as a moral person. It is just one of the inevitable consequences of other people doing wrong that it forces others in this way to go against the grain of their moral nature.

If I break a promise to someone then I am disappointing an expectation I gave them which they rely on in considering what to do. This clearly damages that particular considering of theirs. As in the case of lying, breaking the promise say to meet someone for coffee at 3 o'clock might not be significant enough to damage or even tamper with his considering regarding his standard of satisfaction for his life. There are however promises significant enough in this regard, such as an employer promising a promotion if I do my job well over the next year, and so breaking even "small" promises that in their own right aren't significant damages or tampers with the general reliance on induced expectations of others' behavior involved in pursuing happiness.

This understanding of breaking promises (Scanlon 1998) seems to be called into question by cases in which one person has no faith in a second person's promise. They have then no expectations which stand to be disappointed by the promise being broken. A promise however is like a mutual contract. It may not seem like a mutual contract since the promisor "gets" nothing. However if I make a promise I have some reason for doing so. The employer's promise of a promotion is to keep me in the firm, quiet my complaints or whatever. My promise to meet you for coffee at 3 o'clock is to show you I care about you, to get the latest news about a mutual friend and so on. Contracts in general require some reasonable expectation that and how the terms of it will be filled. If I loan you money which you agree to pay back in a month then if I know you are destitute with no likely source of funds coming in there is no loan since a loan requires a meeting of the minds as to whether and how it will be repaid. Similarly if I have no reasonable expectation you will keep the promise there is no contract made. The illocutionary force in Austin's sense of the promise is merely to "give you" to expect compliance—that you actually expect compliance being rather part of the perlocutionary effect. This seems right to me but morally irrelevant as to whether a genuine contract has been made. If a person is so unreliable that his utterances of promising mean nothing to people who know him, then the person does not tamper with the others' pursuit of happiness in failing to keep the promise since the person is already excluded from general issues of trust in such utterances. Nor I believe is it wrong for the person to fail to behave in accord with his promise-utterance. It is worse than that—the person doesn't have the standing (Scanlon 1998) to do wrong. Less stringent cases of giving others expectations such as expressing an intention to do something are similar to promising in regard to failing to respect the pursuit of others. The expression of an intention carries with it some hedge that one might not be able to do so for some reason and so give others less strict or more tentative expectations. If these intentions are significant in a major way to the others' pursuit of happiness then not carrying them out damages the others' pursuit and so is wrong. If they are minor then not carrying them out tampers with the general reliance of the person on others' expressions of intention and so is wrong. The difference from promising is in degree of likely damage or likely tampering since the person's considerations based on the expectations that the expression of intention induces already partly take into account the greater chance of the intention not being carried out. What holds for breaking promises holds as well for breaking any contractual agreements. A special case of the latter is cheating on an exam. By taking the exam one has contracted to perform in accord with certain rules and cheating violates the contract.

If I promise to meet you for coffee at 3 o'clock but along the way I stop to give emergency aid to an accident victim thus breaking my promise I do not tamper with your general reliance on promises once I explain the circumstances to you since such emergencies are rare. On the other hand if instead of meeting you I go to a soup kitchen to help serve lunches then I do tamper even after explaining to you. I or anyone else can always break promises this way. If I fail to meet you because all of a sudden I received an appointment for an important job interview then again such circumstances are significant and rare and so I do not tamper with a general reliance on promises. A general reliance on induced expectations is an important condition under which each of us is able to pursue happiness. Our pursuits often depend on being able to rely not only on how other people generally will behave in certain general ways, such as not running red lights, but on others particularly or specifically behaving in certain specific ways. To tamper with this latter reliance then is to tamper with conditions suitable for pursuing happiness and so is both wrong and goes against my own happiness. However absolute unyielding reliance on the keeping of promises is not the "optimal" condition for each of us to pursue happiness. Rather something along the lines of rare-and-highly-significant circumstances allowing for failure to keep promises is "optimal." Hence I do not degrade or tamper with the optimal conditions for the pursuit of happiness by

breaking promises in such circumstances once I explain myself to the person
I made the promise to.

(v)

Besides bodily harms and harms to the reflective considering mind there
is infliction of what I will call conative harms such as disturbing a person's
self-confidence, self-esteem or self-worth, and emotional harms such as making someone feel sad, anxious, humiliated, fearful. These classes of harms are
connected to each other psychologically in all sorts of ways and any of them
can be harmful to the body as when depression makes a person sick and to
the considering mind as when loss of confidence distorts and limits one's considerations. Reverse-wise harm to the body can bring with it fearfulness and
loss of confidence and being manipulated can bring with it emotional pain
such as sorrow or anxiety. This is just to say that it is the whole human psyche
and the whole human organism that is the basic object of harm. It is as well the
whole human being that is involved in the pursuit of happiness. That pursuit is
not isolable from any of these harms to various parts of the body or the psyche.

Disturbing a person's confidence by belittling them, bullying them, dispar-
aging their projects, failing to encourage them, and so on induces conditions
that are unfavorable to the pursuit of happiness and so tampers with that
pursuit. For example carrying out one's projects to realize one's standard
of satisfaction may be hindered by a lack of confidence induced by being
ridiculed. Further the standards one holds may be up-ended and abandoned
not by cogent considerations but by being disparaged—thus blocking any
further considerations of those standards and leaving a person unsettled as to
what their happiness involves. By the fundamental principle infliction of conative harms in thus disrespecting another's pursuit of happiness is morally
wrong. They clearly as well go against my own happiness. In harming another's
carrying out his projects I at least tamper with if not outright damage retrospective considering on his part and in influencing another's standards by
factors other than his consideration of them I at least tamper with if not
outright damage prospective considerations. In either case I cannot claim to
give myself over to open minded-ness regarding my standard of satisfaction.
These points apply as well to failing to care enough for another's conative
"health" such as failing to encourage them.

To make a person feel sad or humiliated or anxious is to tamper with their
emotional temperament or nature. If, for example, I contribute to making
them a more anxious person then their pursuit of happiness is diminished in

that this may distort their considerations, may block them from carrying out their considerations and leave them unsatisfied with how their lives are going even if they realize their standard of satisfaction. Being satisfied recall involves emotional contentment and their anxious nature may preclude this. According to the fundamental principle then it is morally wrong to make another feel bad. Following Mill however it is not wrong to make another feel offended, horrified, troubled, bothered or upset by how I pursue my happiness, by what my standard of satisfaction is. Their emotional nature in this regard is already inconsistent with a supposed pursuit of happiness on their part in that their emotional contentment and so their happiness depends on my not pursuing happiness in certain ways, and so depends on their losing my considerations. The only way they can be emotionally content is being closed-minded and so happiness which involves open-minded contentment cannot be what they are pursuing until they alter their emotional condition. Since they are not pursuing happiness I do not fail to respect their pursuit by the offense I may cause.

It is similarly wrong to fail to care enough for others' emotional nature by failing to alleviate their anxiety, sadness, etc. Since both the infliction of emotional harm and the failure to care for the emotional condition of another involve understanding the emotional nature of the other, it follows that it is wrong to fail to try to understand others emotionally. Since part of this involves trying to empathize with their condition it is morally wrong to divorce oneself emotionally from other people. Further such divorce goes against my happiness not only because it may lead to a failure to respect or care enough for others' emotional nature and so their pursuit, but because it is a failure to grasp what the emotional possibilities are for my happiness. My happiness involves emotional contentment. I have to understand what sort of contentment I am capable of. I cannot claim a standard of satisfaction to be well-considered if I have better reasons for a different one that fails to appeal to me because of my emotional make-up unless I assess that make-up itself. If it is my fearful or wanton emotional nature alone that "selects" one standard over another as a standard for satisfaction that includes emotional contentment, then I cannot claim that standard as belonging to me as a reasoning being unless and until I consider the issue of altering my emotional nature. I have then to understand what my emotional nature is, how it affects the standards I come to and what the possibilities are for altering it before I can truly claim to be satisfied with how my life is going according to my standard of satisfaction. In short the possibilities regarding my emotional nature itself must be considered as one key part of considering standards of satisfaction. But now to understand what emotional possibilities there may be for me involves to a large extent discerning what is emotionally achievable by others. Hence to divorce myself emotionally from others may limit me in my standard of satisfaction by closing me off to other standards which might bring emotional contentment if only I had understood that altering my emotional condition is possible in certain ways. In sum the open-ness to emotional possibilities is part and parcel of the open-ness of standards of satisfaction. Hence being closed off to others' emotional lives goes against my standard being an open-minded one and so against my being happy.

That emotional inter-connection (empathy exchange) is essential to the pursuit of happiness can be seen by comparison with the example of the sociopath who cannot feel empathy for others. This person can feel joy, calm, exuberance and a whole range of emotions which constitute emotional contentment. Others' altruistic feelings of sympathy, love or joy at other people's success, however, is not something the sociopath can connect to. They are not emotional possibilities for him. Hence any standard of satisfaction with how his life is going cannot include altruistic values concerning the well-being of others. His emotional make up is not such that his contentment is sensitive to altruistic values. The best he can do is to have such values as part of his standard of satisfaction to the extent that he thinks of them in relation to his selfish contentment. He knows for example as if to care for others to avoid sanctions, as if to care for a friend to have resources for his own goals, and so on. He doesn't then value others but values making as if he values others. His emotional possibilities as he sees them limit what values go into his standard of satisfaction. Only egoistic conceptions of happiness are possible for him and so he is not open to the full open-nature of standards of satisfaction.

Since satisfaction includes emotional contentment, in talking about the open-ness of standards of satisfaction we are talking about standards for beings such as us with a range of emotional possibilities. We are not talking about sheer intellectual considering, nor considering for beings with alternative possibilities for emotional contentment. The sociopath by his emotional limitations in effect makes egoistic standards *definitive for him*. For the ordinary person to divorce himself from others' emotional natures would be in effect to limit himself to reduced emotional possibilities making a restricted range of standards definitive for him. This voluntary sociopathy goes against being committed to the full open-ness of standards and so it goes against happiness.

The place of emotional open-ness in the reasonable adoption of standards of satisfaction leads to the important conclusion that failing to care for animals being happy in, if not with, their lives is wrong according to the fundamental principle of morality. There is overlap between the emotional and conative nature of animals and human beings, as well as a clarity in animals not found in human beings. This makes understanding that nature in various circumstances an understanding of our emotional possibilities that goes beyond what we get from each other. There is a kind of steadfastness and patience in dogs or a kind of emotional presentation of grief in elephants at the death of one of their own that in its purity is not to be found in humans whose conative and emotional characters are so intertwined with abstract thinking and reasoning. To walk by the road and come face to face with a deer that for a brief period meets you eye to eye with all the emotions to be seen its eyes and posture is a kind of emotional enlightenment impossible to express but real. We are similar enough emotionally to see in animals emotional possibilities for us while different enough to see those possibilities in them in a way we can't see those possibilities in each other. Nor is it the case that these are only species-wide conative-emotional profiles without significant individual differences due to circumstances and genetic variation. To fail to respect and care enough for the contentment of an animal in its life is to lose this opening of emotional possibilities for other persons as well as for me and so is a failure to respect and care enough for the pursuit of happiness of others. It is thus morally wrong according to the fundamental principle to needlessly harm an animal's contentment or to fail to care enough to promote it.

It seems that there is some kind of species-chauvinism or lack of caring for the animal's own sake in our account of our relation to animals. However on this account it is morally required to be kind, protective and supporting to animals for the sake of their contentment, not because it suits our purposes or makes us feel good. That it is morally required in that it is inherent to our human pursuit of happiness still makes it seem as if animals have worth or value only in relation to us. In one sense of worth or value this is true. An animal's contentment has no worth or value for it any more than a painting's beauty has value for the painting. Animals cannot find their contentment to be worthwhile in considering or reflecting upon it any more than a painting can find its beauty worthwhile in reflecting upon it. The animal, unlike a painting, can value in the sense of be attracted to kindness or finding food but not the contentment that comes with it. The fact that on our account we value kindness to the animal for the sake of its contentment but do not value that contentment for the value it has for the animal is not species-chauvinism, but just the fact that there is no such thing as the value it has for the animal to be valued by us. As in Chapter 5 to say we value the animal's contentment in that it is part of our final good, part of what it is for us to be happy, does not mean that we don't value it when considered or contemplated just in its own right. It means rather that any flat-out value it has is that it is part of our final good. To think that an animal's contentment should have flat-out value apart from this significance in relation to our final good is to think of flat-out value as an objective inert property of things. Who should that contentment have flat-out value to but us—since it has no flat-out value to the animal?

One might still say that according to the definition of wrong and the fundamental principle I have only an indirect moral relationship to animals that is in place only because of my moral relationship to other people. This I claim is an artifice of how the definition and the fundamental principle are formulated. Once being kind to animals is part of what it is for me to be happy we can reformulate the definition as stating that an act is wrong if it fails to respect or care enough for the pursuit of happiness of others *animals included*, without losing the justification of avoiding wrong in terms of what it is for me to be happy. Of course what it means to respect and care for the pursuit of happiness of animals is their pursuit of being content *in* their lives not *with* their lives. So reformulated my moral relationship to animals is direct and my moral relationship to other persons is not complete without it.

A supposed defect of accounts of what is morally wrong which make respect and care for each other as persons central is that they fail to encompass moral wrongdoing in relation to beings who aren't persons. We see now that basically because of the central place of emotional contentment in our account that the fundamental principle encompasses animals. Further in several ways it encompasses small children who are not yet persons; who are not yet beings capable of pursuing being happy *with* how their lives are going. Firstly emotional interaction with small children opens up and extends emotional possibilities in ways somewhat like interaction with animals. Hence respect and care for their emotional contentment in their lives by which such possibilities are opened up is integral to respect and care for the pursuit of happiness of other persons. Failure to respect and care for the happiness of children *in* their lives is thus morally wrong according to our principle. Secondly it was claimed in Chapter 5 that respect and care for the enterprise of pursuing happiness, a respect and care integral to any person's happiness, involves regard for future generations. That regard includes preparing children to enter the enterprise. They are like the novices in the analogy to the enterprise of pursuing chess excellence who must be taught and nurtured to enter into it by those who care for the enterprise. As in the chess case this is a matter of divided responsibility according to some social arrangement which doesn't undermine the pursuit of chess excellence by those already in the enterprise. For the most part the social arrangement for the enterprise of happiness is that children be prepared to enter it by parents. For a parent to fail to do what is necessary for preparing a child is *morally* wrong according to our fundamental principles since it fails to respect and care for others' pursuit of happiness.

In this chapter we have outlined various ways in which the fundamental principle of morality has concrete meaning for a range of harms and needs that are the context of human existence. Equivalently we have outlined what it is to respect and care for the cooperative enterprise of pursuing happiness in various dimensions in which we are liable to harms and to needs. What R.M. Adams (2006;85) says of cooperative enterprises that in

> situations in which one cooperates with others to make a product...one is expected to care about the product in a way that is not easily or obviously reducible to caring about the welfare of the individuals affected.

holds as well for the cooperative enterprise whose product is the pursuit of happiness. At a general level caring for the enterprise is caring for the "welfare" (the pursuit of happiness) of each of the individuals affected. However at a more concrete level caring for the enterprise is not reducible to behaving in regard to each individual in a way that can be isolated from other individuals. Many difficult moral and socio-political issues that have not been settled in this chapter concern just this connection between individuals and the enterprise. What has been "settled" rather is how to behave in regard to other individuals in idealized situations in which we specifically disregard complicating factors that arise "in the field" (in the actual unfolding of our lives). This is analogous to seeing what a scientific theory comes to by what the consequences are for experimental situations that we design to be isolated from complicating factors that arise in the actual unfolding of nature. Further what has been "settled" are certain laws of morality that follow from the moral theory. One such law for example is that it is morally wrong not only to harm but even to tamper with the pursuit of others. Another law is that if it is wrong to do x then it is so whether one is found out or not. A third law is that it is wrong to put a price on the worth of another's pursuit because of the lexical priority of considering standards of satisfaction over pursuing specific goals. A fourth law is that it is wrong to put another's pursuit up for grabs based on utility calculations because of the incomparable and so inestimable worth of each person in relation to one or more other persons. A fifth law is that it is wrong to divorce oneself from and fail to care for the emotional well-being of other people, children, and animals. Like some scientific theories, like legal theories and like political theories what it is to set out the content of a moral theory is not to settle all issues in its realm but rather to set out how it works in a broad range of idealized situations and what general laws it implies.

CHAPTER 7

Other Accounts of Morality

(i)

Our account of morality strongly overlaps Korsgaard's account (1996). Her account begins with the idea that we set or construct ends and the capacity to do so is the ground or basis of all values. In constructing ends we do not conform in any way to true ends that exist outside or apart from the constructing. We do not set ends in accord with antecedently existing values. The very idea of an objective value will have to be what is essential to or universal *within* the practice of setting ends. If we elaborate on this idea of setting ends to include how the ends we set fit with others into a system of ends for our lives, then her idea of a person setting ends is equivalent to our idea of a person having a standard for his life to be going well. One adopts a standard because he thinks its realization will be satisfying. Although the standard is not responsible to some objectively existing standard or system of ends that is antecedent to the setting of ends, it is responsible to its realization making us or leaving us satisfied with how our lives are going. Otherwise we adopt ends to no point other than to realize them whether or not we can endorse and emotionally embrace the realization, which makes the adoption arbitrary. Given this we can equate Korsgaard's capacity to set ends with the capacity to adopt standards for being satisfied with how our lives are going, in the sense of being satisfied set out in Chapter 1. As argued in Chapter 2 it is in terms of this capacity that anything has flat-out value. Something has flat-out value to the extent that it contributes to being satisfied with how our lives are going in a way that we can claim as our own This matches Korsgaard's claim that the capacity to set ends is the ground or basis of all values, and it is consistent with things such as friendship and art having intrinsic value that belongs to them independent of fitting into a system of ends.

Korsgaard's first attempt to ground morality depends simply on the fact that setting ends is the ground of all flat-out value. She claims that I must value my capacity to set ends in that it is the basis of all values and if I value this capacity in myself I must value it in others. We can add that to value the capacity in others is to treat it deferentially with respect and care. Further, since valuing this capacity is the basis of anything having value I cannot value anything above this capacity in others or in a way inconsistent with valuing this capacity in others. This implies the lexical priority of valuing the capacity in others over any personal projects or goals of mine. In sum respect and care for others' capacity to set and realize standards for being satisfied is a constraint on my being able to flat-out value anything. This in turn constitutes a justification of morality; i.e., a justification of restricting one's actual ends by respect and care for others' capacity to set ends.

This first attempt of Korsgaard's is problematic because it isn't quite the capacity to set ends that grounds all value but rather the proper exercise of that capacity. If my constructing of ends is defective then the values the capacity to construct ends makes possible would seem to be defective as well. The fact that there are no values apart from the constructing activity doesn't imply that some constructions aren't better or worse than others. It doesn't even preclude that all constructions except one are defective exercises of the capacity. Suppose that a person sets as their end to develop his intellect above all else and holds that this is the only non-defective exercise of the capacity to set ends. Then it is not incumbent upon him to value this capacity in himself or others except when the exercise of this capacity leads to developing one's intellect as one's end. Thus any failure to respect or care for people's ends other than developing the intellect is not a failure on this person's part to value his (proper exercise of the) capacity to set ends. This would lead to a justification of a fundamental principle of morality allowing disregard for those who lack "proper" ends.

Even if I don't think that my exercise of the capacity is the only non-defective one I may think that I exercise the capacity far better than many other people. Why should I value all exercises of the capacity equally? I do still value perhaps others having the capacity, but only because it enables them to exercise it in ways that I, in using the capacity, value. On this way of thinking since I value the capacity for certain of its exercises, then I value it in others by getting them by hook or by crook to exercise it more in line with the way I do. If we hold that any exercise of the capacity has worth enough to be valued then perhaps it follows that I must value the capacity in others. That any exercise has worth enough to be valued however is not something that follows from the fact that the capacity is the source or condition of all values.

Korsgaard's first attempt to ground morality is a failure but her second attempt (1996;131–136) I claim is a success. An end is valuable just in so far as I have reasons for adopting it. If out of the blue I endorse something as my end and hold to it except if out of the blue I give it up to endorse a second end then the endorsement is estranged from me as a reasoning being—it fails to be something I can own as a reasoning being. Korsgaard, following Wittgenstein, argues that reasons must be public. I must recognize others' reasons for *their* ends as reasons for ends. It cannot be that I have a reason for *my* ends that is

private in the sense that it is a reason *only* for being my end which makes no
demand on others (Darwall; 2007) as reasoning beings to at least consider
in adopting their ends. Reverse-wise another's reasons aren't private to them.
A reason for their ends makes a demand on me to at least consider it as a
reason for adopting that end. Reasons are public or shareable in that if something is a reason it belongs to any reasoning being to consider it and hence to
"treat it" as a reason pro or con. Equivalently reasons are not private in the
sense that only I have reasons (a sort of solipsism regarding reasons), Others
have reasons that cannot be set aside as if these reasons don't exist. Reasons
are public in that we all share what are reasons.

As a reasoning being however I am not just after reasons for my ends but
good reasons for them. It is not coming up with any old reasons for an end that
will do for me to claim the end as belonging to me as a reasoning being. Suppose
that I have definitive or conclusive reasons for adopting certain ends. They are
not conclusive specifically for *my* adopting ends as this would make conclusively good reasons private. Then others have only what they think are good
reasons for not adopting these certain ends-they can't be good reasons since to
have conclusive reasons is to have reasons which preclude opposing reasons
being good ones. The "demand" of others' reasons on me to at least consider is
no longer in effect since they are no longer good reasons at all. It is not incumbent on the mathematician as a reasoning being to consider others' reasons for
holding that it is possible to square the circle once he has definitive reasons
that it cannot be done. In such a case I need not and indeed should not value
or respect what others take to be reasons.

If I have definitive or conclusive reasons for adopting certain ends then the
public or shared nature of reasons requires only that I value those others who
share these ends. Of course Korsgaard holds that there aren't such conclusive
reasons. My point is that this fact is a pivotal premise in her second attempt
to justify valuing all others. Once it is accepted that there are no conclusive
reasons then the point about the public or share-able nature of reasons for
ends or for systems of ends (standards of satisfaction) is that reasons are not
restricted to reasons that I can come up with. Hence as a reasoning being
I must value or give myself over to whatever further reasons there may be pro
or con for my standard of satisfaction. This includes reasons that others have
for their standards and so I must value or give myself over to their pursuit of
happiness within which prospective and retrospective reasons arise. Not only
must I value their setting of ends but I must value their retaining, abandoning,
or modifying ends in the face of their realization which gives rise to reasons
that aren't anticipated prospectively. What I give myself over to as a reasoning being I claim is not the public or share-able nature of good reasons which

by itself would allow that I have conclusive reasons. Rather I give myself over to what makes my reasons good reasons *when there is no conclusive settling of the matter.*

Even in this circumstance what I precisely give myself over to is still not the public or share-able nature of others' good reasons. I could do that by blocking others from having those reasons. In blocking those reasons there aren't any public, share-able reasons of theirs I need recognize as *also* making a demand on me to consider. I precisely give myself over to there being further reasons to consider and so, a fortiori, to others coming up with such reasons. Wittgenstein's point about the public nature of language was that rules or norms must be such as to allow for failure. The norm for good reasons then cannot be that whatever I come up with as good reasons are so. I have to subject myself or keep myself open to pertinent reasons that I don't come up with. Thus since others' reasons are pertinent reasons the norm involves having regard not for just their reasons, but for their coming up with reasons. Properly understood the role of publicity is secondary to the nature of what a norm is. If, thinking along Korsgaard's lines, we give full force to Wittgenstein's point and if we give sufficient emphasis to there being no conclusive reasons for ends (for standards of satisfaction) then Korsgaard's second attempt successfully establishes that to claim ends as my own as a reasoning being justifies valuing all others' setting of ends.

For Korsgaard my practical identity or my self-identification as a friend say is in my giving myself over in how I am and how I act toward someone to a standard or norm of friendship. My identity as a member of a club is giving myself in how I am and act toward others in the club to the norms of club membership. My practical identity or self-identification as a person is giving myself over in how I am and how I act to the norms or standards of setting ends. These norms for Korsgaard include valuing others who give themselves over to the norms or standards of setting ends. Hence for her my practical identity as a person entails valuing in how I act the practical identity of others as persons. Since it is in terms of my practical identity as a person that anything has value for me it follows that valuing the practical identity of others is likewise that in terms of which anything has value for me. Equivalently valuing others as persons takes precedence over all other values. If to value something is to respect and care for it then respecting and caring for others as persons takes precedence over anything else that has value for me. Since this is the core of a justification of morality, for Korsgaard then it is our practical identity that is the core of a justification of morality.

One's practical identity as a person in Korsgaard's sense is essential to happiness on our conception of what it is to be happy. One cannot be satisfied with how one's life is going in a self-fulfilling way without giving oneself over to the norm for setting and holding to or revising a system of ends that constitutes one's standard for being satisfied. Without giving oneself over to the norms by which can own the standard as a reasoning being one cannot claim any emotional contentment in or endorsements of one's way of living and so cannot be happy with how one's life is going. This connection of Korsgaard's idea of practical identity to happiness is important for the justification of morality in the following way. If there can be happiness apart from my practical identity as a person then the fact that the latter involves respect and care for the practical identity of others still leaves it open that my happiness may conflict with such care and respect, and what justifies abandoning my happiness for my practical identity as a person? Because Korsgaard's conception of practical identity is essential to happiness (on our conception) this question doesn't arise. Even if the terminology of being *happy* with how one's life is going doesn't figure centrally in Korsgaard's account, the fact of it does and in a way basically equivalent to how it figures in our account. This is not just a terminological point however since an explicit defense of happiness as involving practical identity as a person is necessary for a complete justification of morality. Without such a defense the justification is too "formalistic" in that practical identity concerns only one's system of ends having a reasonable form apart from what that means for happiness. Further, not making explicit the role of emotional viability,the possibility of emotional contentment aligning with one's ends, part of the norm for setting ends would sever one's own practical identity as a person from valuing other persons' emotional conditions as well as the emotional contentment of animals and children leaving us with a defense of morality that is too "rationalistic." My point is that the work done in Part One is a necessary preliminary for Korsgaard's justification of morality to avoid the semblance of being formalistic and rationalistic.

(ii)

The criticisms of a justification of morality being formalistic and rationalistic are of course the criticisms often made of Kant's justification. Although they don't hold up against Korsgaard I claim that they do hold up against Kant and they do so precisely because Kant's conception of happiness severs it from what Korsgaard calls our practical identity. For Kant the idea of happiness is an indeterminate idea of maximizing the satisfaction of desires. There is no issue of whether or not the desires are worthwhile or valuable ones to have. This doesn't mean that all desires are equally important-some may be stronger than others. What it does mean is that all desires with their strengths are given to us by nature. Any setting of ends *as far as happiness goes* is a matter of how to act so as to maximize desire satisfaction. In particular there is no setting of non-instrumental ends in Korsgaard's sense. In our terms we don't consider whether and how the satisfaction of desires is endorsable and meaningful in contributing to a way of life we can be satisfied with. As far as happiness goes any endorsement is set or fixed by the overall balance of satisfaction of desires. On Kant's view there is no such thing as on balance having one's desires satisfied while yet failing to be emotionally content unless one is "naturally" defective in one's emotional constitution. Overall Kant's conception of happiness is what we called in Chapter 1 being happy (content) *in one's life the way animals can be.*

On Kant's view a person can be happy without being autonomous. His ends aren't set or adopted by him in a way that he can claim to have full authorship over them since any ends are at the service of desires that he doesn't set or author. For this reason happiness simply in its own right is something foreign to me as an autonomous being. It is something estranged from what I as an autonomous being can claim as self-fulfilling. Happiness then has at most emotional value. It has no value in relation to my autonomous nature. As far as my autonomous nature goes it is alien in the way, for example, that the satisfaction of desires or emotional contentment might be alien to someone who distances himself from being in his life and wonders why any of it is meaningful or significant. Wiggins (2006;127) says against Kant:

> an ordinary carefully considered, reflectively ratified desire is not an alien force.

Presuming that part of the careful consideration is whether to set satisfaction of the desire as an end and that this consideration is not just in terms of how it balances with other desires, then Kant holds that there is no careful consideration or reflective ratification and so that all desires are alien forces or heteronomous.

Kant it seems holds a basically Humean view of the role of reason in happiness. Hume's view is based on his claim that reason by itself cannot motivate. Since ends must motivate reason cannot set ends. Kant actually denies this as a general thesis since for him pure reason by itself in the form of giving oneself over to a law one authorizes can motivate or can be practical. Hume's thesis cannot be the basis of Kant's view of happiness. In any case it seems to me that reasoned conceptions or thoughts can motivate. Consider someone who observes a person riding a bicycle. What they observe makes it seem appealing to them to ride a bicycle and so they are at least somewhat motivated to do so. Further observation of aspects there are to riding a bicycle and consistency with the person's given emotional set may give the initial appeal full force. The given emotional set is not necessarily a system of natural desires to be satisfied; it can be what other activities or things seem appealing or not all of which is in place as with the appeal of bike riding due to previous observations of characteristics of the activities or things. If experience can motivate then it seems so too can depictions of experiences in thought of, say, what it would be like to fly to the moon. If in regard to riding a bicycle further detailed observation by which certain aspects become salient can strengthen the appeal, then it seems that further detailed thoughts, by elaborating and making otherwise hidden aspects salient, can likewise strengthen the initial appeal of the thought of doing something or going for something. But elaborating and making factors salient in one's depiction in thought is just providing reasons for the appeal. In this manner it seems that reasons can motivate just by their nature as reasons without sitting there inertly until desires come along or not to strengthen the appeal.

It is true that happiness is "hostage" to emotional contentment in a way that morality isn't. If I am not emotionally content in my life even though it is going in a way that accords with my reasoned ends (my standard of satisfaction) then those ends *perhaps* need revising. Reason may be completely on the side of Van Gogh's continued painting and for all that may be a failure as far as happiness goes. Reason doesn't guarantee emotional contentment. In *this* sense reason is not fully autonomous in regard to happiness. My reason is not the full author of my happiness. In the case of morality it may be as well that avoiding wrong fails to bring emotional contentment, but in this case there is no revising of what is right or wrong. In regard to morality then reason seems self-contained in a way that it isn't in regard to happiness. But for Kant morality too in its way is "hostage" to a certain sort of emotional condition, namely, feelings of respect for the moral law which feelings are not guaranteed by reason. The difference then between the case of happiness and the case of morality is that in the former case the ends aren't fixed as definitive and so are subject to modification, replacement, and so on. This however is not a difference between autonomy and heteronomy of reason unless one holds that the autonomy of reason exists only in provable ends.

In sum on Kant's understanding happiness is heteronomous though he doesn't give any good reasons for that understanding and nor do I think there are any. The only end for Kant then that is set by autonomous practical reason is conformity to universal law. Whatever else, what I simply as a reasoning being can give myself over to as a standard by which my reasoning nature is fulfilled is what I can deem as a standard for all reasoning beings. Thus if I am to claim the maxim of my action as a reasoning being I must deem it at the same time a universal law—a standard for all reasoning beings. Kant's first formulation of the law is in the form of a second-person address—act in terms of what *you* can will as a universal law. If it is somehow dependent on your will in particular however it is hardly a standard you submit to as a reasoning being. I think Kant used this form of address to mark that the standard is to be used as a test for the individual in determining what is or isn't right to do. One runs the test of seeing whether the maxim of one's action can be at the same time willed as a universal law. The second-person address, that is, simply emphasizes the deliberative standpoint not any person relative character in the willing. The sense of the first formulation then is that what I give myself over to in my nature as a reasoning being is a universal law that any other person in his reasoning nature also gives himself over to. This leads in turn to the formulation of the categorical imperative in terms of humanity. What it is to treat another as an end and not merely as a means is to respect their reasoning nature. This nature is totally nothing other than that they submit themselves to the very same universal law I submit myself to. But then Kant's view of the fundamental principle of morality is a version of the contractualist one that an act is wrong if its maxim violates a law or principle of prohibition that everyone agrees to. This isn't quite how Kant puts it. Rather his formulation is that an act is not wrong if its maxim is consistent with a universal law of permission that everyone else can will. However if the act is not consistent with willing it as a universal law, then I cannot will that everyone be permitted to do it. But, as far as right and wrong go what is not permitted to everyone is not permitted to anyone. Therefore I must will a universal law forbidding the action. In other words if I cannot will stealing as a universal law of permission then I must will not stealing as a universal law of prohibition. The latter is just the usual contractualist formulation. Kant's formulation of the fundamental principle of morality in terms of autonomy (the kingdom of ends) just emphasizes that the standard I submit myself to as a reasoning being I myself authorize as a reasoning being. I give myself over or submit myself to it in that it fulfills me as a reasoning being. The portrayal of a kingdom of ends then is not, as with Korsgaard, that of a kingdom in which each sets their own specific ends for their lives while respecting all others in their setting of specific ends. Rather it is a portrayal of a "contractual" kingdom in which each limits their own individual naturally given end of maximizing desires by what others as well agree to as a limitation on their individual naturally given ends.

I shall return to contractualism below. For now the issue is how Kant's contractualist view fits together with his conception of happiness in his justification of morality. Kant's contractualist principle is justified in terms of autonomy. If I violate the contract I violate governing my actions in a way that I can authorize or claim in accord with my reasoning nature. Equivalently the action cannot fulfill me as a reasoning being that is the source of its own specific standard of satisfaction since the contract is the *only* standard reason gives to itself. Further it is only my reasoning nature that can be autonomous in the sense of being its own standard. Our desires may in a sense be standards for acting but our desiring nature doesn't give itself its own standards for desiring. Morality then takes precedence over happiness (desire-satisfaction) in that only by submitting our happiness to morality are we autonomous beings; beings who can claim what they do as belonging to them by their own authorization. But note that happiness remains heteronomous even when subjected to limitation by morality. If particular desires achieved in certain ways violate morality they are eo ipso dis-avowed by my autonomous nature. This doesn't imply however that desires achieved in certain ways that conform to morality *thereby* can be endorsed (avowed) as belonging to my autonomous nature. By allowing desires that are foreign to my reasoning nature in that they have not come from it, I don't thereby make them any less foreign (heteronomous). If the desires make no sense when I think about what is valuable in achieving them, then they continue to make no sense when I think it is permissible to achieve them so far as my authorization by reason is concerned. In terms of emotional contentment suppose a manic person in a continued condition alternating between bliss, exuberance, joy, etc. dis-owns his contentment as divorced from anything he can hold to be valuable in what he is doing or how he is living, If he conforms what he does to the categorical imperative he can own his morality perhaps, but his emotional contentment remains divorced from any positive value he can see in it.

In sum the "cost" of Kant's justification of morality via the autonomy of universal law over the heteronomy of happiness is that I cannot fully own how my life is going. This I claim supports the charges of formalism and rationalism against Kant. Reason is valuable only or purely according to its *form* of universal law not according to its protecting or promoting anything valuable (desire-satisfaction). Desire-satisfaction simply gives us something on which to impose universal law or the form of reason. Our *rational* nature is severed from supporting any value in our particular pursuits. It has no role in our devising our *own* values by which emotional contentment or desire satisfaction is meaningful to us. In thus ascribing value to reason only in virtue of its form and denying value to anything but reason Kant's defense of morality can be charged with being too formalistic and rationalistic. He makes moral value takes precedence over all other values by in effect *denying there are any other values.* Once he has demoted happiness to sheer desire-satisfaction or sheer emotional contentment, and so to its being something that is foreign or estranged to our authorship (heteronomous), there is no way to resuscitate it. For this reason Kant's including happiness alongside morality as part of the summum-bonum makes no sense. My desire satisfaction is not a good for me if I cannot claim it or own it.

The picture I have drawn of Kant's justification of morality seems to be called into question by what he calls imperfect duties to others. This includes basically doing what I can to help others in need and so fostering to some extent the desire-satisfaction and so the happiness of others. If the happiness of others thus has moral value then apparently it does have value that can be claimed by autonomous reason. However what belongs to autonomous reason for Kant is the *restriction* on *my* desire satisfaction by helping others. This doesn't make their desire-satisfaction or mine any less heteronomous. If their desires or mine couldn't be antecedently claimed as worthwhile based on considerations, they can't be so claimed simply because restrictions on them can be claimed to be worthwhile (autonomous).

The picture I have drawn of Kant's views seems also to be called into question by what he calls imperfect duties to oneself, including the duty to exercise and develop one's natural talents. Kant's defense of such duties is based in part on some sort of natural teleology. But now if developing my talents is a value I can claim as belonging to me as a reasoning being in that it fits or accords with a natural teleology, then my acceding to developing my talents is autonomous, not merely a matter of desire-satisfaction. This however cannot be Kant's understanding of the role of teleology, for suppose that the principle of universal willing forbids a maxim of stealing and suppose that stealing promotes the development of my talents. Then there is a conflict *within* autonomous reason and I cannot say that morality takes precedence over developing my talents because only the former realizes me as an autonomous being. Kant simply cannot allow adoption by reason of *any* end such as developing talents whose adoption is not based on universal willing without threatening his justification of morality. The question then becomes in what way natural teleology has a role for Kant only in terms of universal willing? Suppose my maxim is to forgo developing my talents in order to satisfy my desire to loaf on a beach. As a universal law this would imply that all may forgo developing talents to satisfy other desires. Why can't I will this law? It seems that without anyone developing talents for hunting, gathering, amusing others, etc. my desires cannot be fulfilled. There would be little food to eat, little amusement to be gotten from others and there I would be bored and starving on the beach. The inability to will it as a universal law has nothing to do with any intrinsic worth of developing talents. It has to do rather with the fact that failure to develop talents undercuts how we are designed individually and socially to maximize desire satisfaction. My maxim by itself, apart from consistency with universal willing, to loaf on the beach doesn't conflict with any natural teleology—I could satisfy my desire to loaf on the beach letting it to others to exercise and develop the talents required to underlie desire-satisfaction. I must adopt developing my talents then as a *limitation* on my maximally satisfying desires exactly as I must adopt refraining from lying and stealing. Other than conforming to universal law there is nothing worthwhile to my developing my talents, since there is nothing worthwhile to the desire satisfaction that such development is designed for. This makes Kant's imperfect duties to oneself consistent with his justification of morality, but again at the cost of that justification implying that I cannot own how my life is going, I can only own restricting how it is going.

As opposed to Korsgaard's understanding of Kant not only doesn't Kant have an idea of setting ends by considerations of their worth as contributing to our lives, but such an idea is inconsistent with Kant's justification of morality. It seems to me that Korsgaard's notion of setting ends is not derived from Kant but is best looked at as a criticism of Kant. This leaves the question of what happens to contractualism as a justification of morality when one, as one should, allows an autonomy within happiness itself; i.e., when one allows reasonable considerations of a standard for satisfaction with how one's life is going. Before turning to this I finish the discussion of Kant with a couple of points about his moral philosophy in relation to the first and third Critiques.

In the first Critique what the understanding brings forth from itself are the logical forms of judgment which for Kant are empty unless schematized (mediated) by space and time which organizes experiences. Only so do they have application to what can be given in experience. Without this application experience remains blind. It remains foreign or estranged from who we are as thinking beings. Kant charged his predecessors, notably Leibniz, with empty rationalism and empty formalism for the failure to thus connect what pure theoretical reason brings forth to the apparently heterogeneous deliverances of experience. Despite Kant's love of architectonic he fails to apply this structure to pure practical reason. Practical reason brings forth from itself the form of universal law. In the practical realm maxims (what to do) play a role analogous to the deliverances of experience in the theoretical realm. Instead of holding this pure rational form of universal law is empty without being schematized (mediated) in terms of a principle that organizes maxims, he directly applies this form to our maxims. My contention is that this failure to mediate leaves the pure form of practical reason empty just as the failure to mediate would leave the pure forms of theoretical reason empty. Kant's universalization principle is empty in that it is indeterminate in its application until it is settled how to formulate maxims. I may not be able to will a maxim to steal for the sake of attaining goods as a universal law but I may be able to will a maxim of stealing for the sake of promoting art as a universal law. In Hare's (1963) terminology I am an art "fanatic" willing even to be stolen from for art's sake. It won't do to say that only the more general formulation of the maxim can be law-like, for the art fanatic exactly denies that his formulation is just a special case of the semantically more general one. On our account there is something that "organizes" maxims so that there is always a favored formulation. Since the purpose within any maxim has any flat-out value only from its contributing to our happiness, it is the formulation in terms of contributing to happiness that is the favored formulation for any maxim. The maxim to steal for art's sake *as potentially contributing to my happiness* cannot be willed as a universal law without inconsistency since on our account it permits people to interfere with others' pursuit which undercuts their claiming any value to the promotion of art as part of their happiness. Kant might say that he too can organize maxims to give a favored formulation in terms of his conception of happiness as maximizing desire-satisfaction, so that, for example the maxim to steal for art's sake *as potentially contributing to the maximization of desire satisfaction* cannot be willed as a universal law. However it isn't clear why this maxim cannot be willed as a law if my desire for the promotion of art is greater than desires to be secure in my personal goods. Kant in effect applies his universalization principle to the "animal" will, or to that part of the human will that is shared by animals. This makes his principle empty in regard to the human will, whose organizing principle is being happy *with* one's life, not being happy by having desires satisfied *in* one's life. Once the application is mediated by the human will then if there is a provable standard of satisfaction I can will promoting it by whatever means as a universal law. I can be a "fanatic" about it in Hare's terms. If there is no provable standard then I can only will what is consistent with open-mindedness as a universal law. Kant's failure to apply his pure form of practical reason (willing universal law) to the organizing principle of the human will leaves him open to the same charge of empty rationalism and empty formalism he makes against his predecessors in the theoretical realm. Kant himself is sensitive to the supposed dis-analogy between practical and theoretical reason. He claims explicitly that unlike the theoretical realm, it better be that practical reason by itself can be pure *and non-empty* if there is to be morality at all. Any subjection of practical reason to happiness he thinks would undercut the categorical nature of morality. This however is only true if universal law is a mere means to happiness, not if it is part of what is to be happy.

In the third Critique Kant gives an account of aesthetic judgment that can be carried over in all its important aspects to an account of happiness involving reason's authorization of emotional contentment. An aesthetic judgment is neither a judgment of taste (the Mona Lisa gives me pleasure) nor a judgment subject to proof by observed characteristics of the object independent of the pleasure taken in considering those characteristics. These considerations turn my being merely pleased into appreciating in that I aesthetically "own" the pleasure. Aesthetic judgments unlike judgments of taste are objective in that they call for agreement, not in the sense of proof by looking at the object but in the sense of exchanging considerations so that each of our appreciations are part of an inter-subjective enterprise of common understanding as to what might or might not be what there is to appreciate. These considerations are not derived from what pleases us. If positive they give aesthetic value to pleasure and if negative they withhold such value. Kant would have done well I suggest to give an account of happiness more along the lines of his account of aesthetic appreciation in the third Critique, making "appreciating" how our lives are going the basic notion rather than being just pleased in satisfying desires.

(iii)

We consider now how contractualism as a fundamental principle of morality relates to our account in terms of the pursuit of happiness. The general contractualist definition is that an act is wrong if it violates a law that everyone agrees to, so that its fundamental moral principle is to avoid violating such laws. I set aside Hobbes' version of contractualism because he provides no justification for why I shouldn't violate the law when doing so is to my advantage and so no justification for avoiding wrong-doing as opposed to merely seeming to avoid wrong-doing. The only thing that is advantageous for Hobbes is having the security against harm by others to get what I want or to fulfill my desires. There is no advantage to keeping to the law when violating it gives me a good chance of getting more of what I want without losing security.

For Rousseau and for Kant the laws that everyone agrees to are similarly laws that secure or promote each person's desires but the justification of keeping to the laws is that only in doing so do I fulfill myself as a reasoning being. This justification holds whether or not my violation is found out by others. Rousseau (1968;65) says that by submission to the general will, a person acquires

moral freedom which alone makes man master of himself, for to be gov-
erned by appetite alone is slavery, while obedience to a law one prescribes
to oneself is freedom.

By freedom Rousseau means autonomy which is the authorship of action
by reason. For Rousseau all grounds of our action other than submission to
universal law are driven by appetite since any other grounds are no more than
a matter of figuring out how to satisfy desires or needs. For Rousseau as for
Kant happiness as desire satisfaction is heteronomous without any involve-
ment of autonomous reason. For Rousseau as for Kant the justification of the
fundamental principle of morality, to act only in a way consistent with what
everyone can agree to as a way of acting, is that only in being moral does one
realize one's autonomy. This is a justification not just of morality having worth
or value but of its having predominant worth or value over all else. Because of
the heteronomy of happiness as appetite driven satisfying desires has no real
value I can claim as belonging to me.

For Scanlon (1998) the justification of submission to living by standards of
behaving that no one can reasonably reject is that it gives us a certain standing
in relation to others we don't otherwise have. To fail to submit estranges or
isolates a person from others in regard to his reasons for acting or how he lives
his life. For Scanlon submission to standards has this value for those who care
to justify themselves to others. On Wallace's (2006) reading of Scanlon having
this standing in relation to others can be a reasonable component of our lives
going well even when it goes against other interests. If this is Scanlon's position
then he has no justification of morality as a predominant value that must take
precedence over all other values. I contend that without settling the issue of
what happiness is contractualism cannot justify any fundamental principle of
morality.

First in relation to Rousseau and Kant, once we consider that being happy
with how one's life is going involves having considerations or reasons for the
standard by which one is satisfied, then apparently happiness is an expression
of autonomy. I am the author of what my being happy involves or consists in.
But now if the considered standard includes manipulating others for the sake
of my artistic endeavors if I have to, then my autonomy as the author of what
is valuable in my life conflicts with submitting myself to universal law that
we all can agree to. Given that both of these are expressions of autonomous
reason we are left with a conflict *within* being autonomous without as yet any
standard by which autonomous reason can settle the conflict. I either abandon
my use of reason in establishing good reasons for valuing ends or I abandon my
submission to reasons consistent with what others can sanction as being good

reasons. Until it can be shown that autonomous reason must resolve the conflict by abandoning or altering artistic endeavors when they can only be kept by manipulating others, there is no justification of submission to universal law (morality) as predominant over other authorized values. One might say that one could always find good reasons for other endeavors, but this leaves it still that my best reasons are for valuing artistic endeavor no matter the manipulation involved.

There is no way to resolve this conflict except to show there is no conflict at all. On our account any reasons I have for artistic endeavors can be claimed by me as good reasons only if I give myself over to the open nature of standards of satisfaction for my life, including standards that contain artistic endeavor. But this means I must give myself over to the considerations of others. Whatever the good reasons there are for the intrinsic value of artistic endeavor there can be no flat out good reasons for pursuing art that undercut being satisfied in a self-fulfilling way with how my life is going. Even if manipulating or otherwise disregarding others contributes to the realization of the intrinsic worth of my painting by stealing to get better paints, by killing to get a good cadaver model, etc., the "conflict" between the intrinsic value of art and regard for others is not a conflict within autonomous reason since only as consistent with regard for others are reasons for valuing artistic endeavor flat-out good reasons – reasons I can claim as self-fulfilling to my reasoning nature.

Once it is shown that regard for others takes precedence over all other reasons it follows that submission to universal law likewise takes precedence. The fundamental universal law that everyone has to agree to is respect and care for the pursuit of happiness of others. It is submission to this law by which anyone has authorship over his life and so by which anyone can claim satisfaction with his life as belonging to him. Let us say that the principle of submission to universal law is a *formal* principle in the sense that it doesn't say what those laws are. My contention is that submission to such a formal principle can be justified as predominant over all other uses of reason in our lives only because the basic universal law has the content of respect and care enough for the pursuit of happiness of others. This is the only universal law submission to which takes precedence over all other reasons for having ends or goals in life. It is submission to this universal law in particular, not the sheer formal submission to universal law, which is the justification of morality. Submission to any other universal laws which are not specifications of this law are simply not justifiable as predominant.

Turning now to Scanlon unlike Kant and Rousseau he holds that reason sets all sorts of ends and authorizes all sorts of values and so is not limited to reasoning about means to maximizing desires. Therefore his universal laws (kinds of actions) that no one can reject are not laws each person accepts as consistent with or involved in maximizing desires—what Scanlon calls welfare contractualism. This sets Scanlon's view apart not only from Hobbes but from Rousseau and Kant as well. Scanlon offers no principle by which the value of submission to universal law as having thereby a certain standing in relation to others takes precedence over other values that might conflict with it. If there are reasons for valuing artistic endeavor even when it requires manipulation this would seem to set up an irreconcilable conflict between moral value (having standing in relation to others) and artistic value. Even if we forgo a demand for absolute moral predominance there remains a problem concerning the value *at all* of having standing in relation to all others. Consider a group of people such as Wall Street bankers and investors who value making deals, growing money, and so on even as against the interests of the rest of us. They lose standing in a relation of justification to the rest of us but not necessarily with each other. They are all "in" on the enterprise and may each submit themselves to rules that others on the inside cannot reject—even if these rules are cut-throat in regard to each other. This seems to reconcile two values of winning at the Wall Street game and standing in a mutual relation of justification with others—just not *all* others. Unless Scanlon can show why being in this relation to others in a particular community has less value than being in this relation to all others it seems that moral value in his sense can always be trumped (abandoned at no cost) by submission to laws of a particular community. Those in the Wall Street community would find no value in submitting to laws the rest of us cannot accept. To them we are less than stellar people whose failure to accede to their laws expresses our inability to live the life they value. The same point holds for those of a particular religious community, of a particular cultural heritage, etc. Even if losing all relations of mutual justification would be a severe loss, losing this relation just to outsiders seems not to be. If so then Scanlon's view fails to give even a partial justification of universal moral law against communitarian morality according to which there are only "thick" moral laws which express shared but not universal values. This includes unfortunately communities that share values that involve oppressing outsiders such as the community of slave-holders in the pre-civil-war south. For communities to be subject to universal inter-communal laws in order to get along with each other just re-introduces a Hobbes-like contractualism at a communal level subject to all the usual problems of why submit when one, or one's community, can get away with not submitting either by brute power or by merely appearing to submit. Rousseau and Kant don't have this communitarian problem since for them submission to universal law is definitive of reason and so of autonomy. The relation of mutual justification is valuable for them only as a submission to reason and reason for them is not hostage to communal values.

On our account each person submits to the universal law of regard for other persons' pursuit of happiness because that submission is constitutive of what it is for each person to be happy. Since anything has flat-out value for a person only as contributing to his happiness any value inconsistent with submission to this universal law cannot be flat-out valuable. It can be intrinsically valuable considered in its own right but not valuable all things considered and so not valuable in the sense of a reason for setting it as an end to act upon. Scanlon resists bringing the plurality of values that people can have under a unifying system of contributing to well-being or happiness. On my view such value pluralism holds only of intrinsic value not flat-out value. We adjudicate the plurality of things we find of value so as to fit together into some system determining to what extent if any we set the realization of each of those values as ends to guide our behavior. We do so according to what we hold is a way of living that we can be satisfied with. As in Part One the latter is not an "extra" over-arching value but rather the "point" or "success-condition" of behaving to realize values. This unification into a system doesn't violate value pluralism as regards intrinsic value nor does it make being satisfied with how our lives are going an extra reason over and above our systematizing of our reasons for valuing various things. I believe this is sufficient to avoid Scanlon's rejection of a notion of well-being or happiness figuring centrally into issues of submission to universal law. Once we have this notion and once we have the open nature of any systematizing into a standard of satisfaction our account goes through. The fundamental universal law that no one can reject is regard for others' pursuit and any other universal laws, such as don't manipulate for your artistic endeavors, are specifications of this fundamental law. Unless the communitarian can prove the particular shared values as the one true standard of satisfaction his submission to laws that are less than what everyone can accept in inconsistent with his claiming as a reasoning being any satisfaction with how his life is going in realizing his shared values.

Contractualism is less a justification of morality than it is a constraint on what can count as a moral law if there are any. If morality is to be a universal demand on everyone and a demand everyone submits to of their own accord as opposed to being forced to, then a moral law must be a law that everyone can agree to and agree to submit to. Contractualism then is a requirement that moral laws be justifiable to all who are capable of morality. It is not itself a justification since by itself it leaves it open whether there is such a thing as moral laws. This conception of contractualism overlaps Habermas' (1990) moral discourse theory. For Habermas a moral rule is justified if its general observance could be jointly accepted by all without coercion in a reasonable discourse. I take this to mean that a rule is justified as being a moral rule rather than some other kind if it can be so accepted. The justification of any specific moral rule or principle is not that it can be thus accepted, but what in virtue of which (the reason why) it commands acceptance. Scanlon's contractualism as well can be taken this way. His further point that there is value in or if there are moral rules is tantamount to Habermas' claiming that there is value in the kind of discourse that leads to or defends the existence of such rules. None of this shows that there are such rules or that their material justification *is* that they cannot be rejected by anyone. I would add that to be a moral rule requires it be jointly accepted by all as predominant and to be strictly observed; not observed only in general or for the most part. The appeal of the contractualist's constraint on what can be a moral law is that when I demand submission to it by any other person I do so not in a coercive way but in a way that holds them responsible for what they themselves can take responsibility for. It seems unjustified to hold someone responsible for failing to submit to a law that I cannot justify and so convince them is a law they should accept. Without the convincing I am left with either coercion or giving up the demand for compliance. The latter would turn moral standards into something each of us can take or leave.

Returning to Rousseau and Kant one last time they too hold that contractualism (submission to universal law) is definitive of morality. For Rousseau all justice, all right and wrong exists only under the general will and for Kant the categorical nature definitive of morality can only be realized if conformity to law itself is what makes for a moral law. Where they go wrong I believe is in holding that this constraint on what it is to be a moral law can by itself both *directly* establish the existence of such laws and also their justification. For Kant as for Rousseau all issues of how to act pertain to maximizing the satisfaction of natural desires that are universal (=happiness as an apodictic end). It is also a universal fact that anyone's satisfying desires requires we each behave in ways that don't stultify each other satisfying desires. This is Rousseau's point that the general will "harmonizes" the happiness of all, and Kant's point that what we subject to universalizability are maxims expressing our natural ends or purposes. Laws expressing these ways of behaving then are therefore laws that all with the same apodictic end can accept. Finally submission to such laws is justified for all in so far as it constitutes each person's autonomous nature. This is Rousseau's point that submission to the general will makes each of us subject to reason rather than appetite and Kant's point that submission to law that we ourselves will is autonomy. Korsgaard and Scanlon in holding that reason sets ends or authorizes a plurality of values that can be different for different people undercut *both* elements of the Kant-Rousseau view. What has to be brought to universal law is no longer satisfaction of desires common to all but values and standards of what can satisfy us in life that are not universally fixed by nature and which may involve values that not all of us pursue. Even if there are laws that we each behave in certain ways under which we can each pursue our values (and so laws we can all accept) strict submission to such laws cannot be justified by a supposed heteronomy (appetite-driven nature) of everything else other than submission to law. Nor can it be justified by any common values. What this calls into question is whether submission to universal law exists at all; viz., whether there is such a thing as morality— a question which contractualism itself can no longer answer, but which Korsgaard's account can.

(iv)

On our account the nature of happiness is central to the justification of morality. This would seem to align it with what is called eudaimonistic ethics, the view deriving from Aristotle that once it is settled what it is to flourish in one's life (to be happy, to live well) and what virtues are constitutive of such flourishing one has given all the account of "morality" that can or needs to be given. Eudaimonistic ethics is called hard virtue-ethics by Russell (2009). It involves practical wisdom and an ethical outlook of how to live based on human nature. For Annas (1995) it involves an account of how virtue relates to the person's overall flourishing. What is evident on the surface however is the radical difference between our account and eudaimonistic ethics. In Aristotle there is no talk of moral laws or of a fundamental principle of morality. Nor is there any talk of individual autonomy, of endorsement of one's life, or of authorizing standards all of which on our account fundamentally underlie moral laws. I want to argue that the radical differences are due to a shift away from Aristotle's notion of reason as *apprehending* a principle of reasonableness in the natural unfolding of things us included, to our notion of reason as *constructing* self-authorized principles. I contend that this shift should not be regarded as an abandonment of eudaimonistic ethics but rather as what that ethics becomes once reason is held to be self-authorizing. There is a deep unity between our account and Aristotle's that is as significant as the equally deep differences—a unity that was lost, for example, by Rousseau and Kant in their understanding of the role of self-authenticating reason. I begin by elaborating the Aristotelian view and then turn to how our view can be regarded as a modification of his in terms of self-authorizing reason.

For Aristotle happiness or flourishing is practicing the skill of living well. Just as the carpenter flourishes in his carpentry if he is skillful in the various dimensions of carpentry (choosing materials, cutting pieces, connecting pieces) so too the person flourishes in his life if he is skillful in the various dimensions of living well (work, social relations, contemplation). The overall point of what the skill of carpentry is for determines what being skillful in the activities of carpentry comes to. In the case of living there is no overall point in the sense of what the skill of living is for since for Aristotle living well or happiness is not for the sake of anything else; it is that which all else is for the sake of. Rather for Aristotle it is immanently in living well that one comes to see what living well comes to. There is an immanent principle to human existence by which its unfolding is reasonable (integrated, unified). This is just a special case of reason governing all that naturally exists. What this principle is for plants, for atoms, for human existence is shown in the unimpeded activities or "goings on" of plants, particles, our lives. Activity that is impeded (stultified, frustrated, disorderly) masks rather than reveals the immanent reason that governs things. There is no external teleology or purpose—just the immanent principle which gives reasonableness to the phenomena. If you like nature everywhere authorizes itself as to the principle or reason that governs it. Applied to us what the principle of living well comes to is immanent within the unimpeded progression of living going on or happening. Thus practical wisdom is not a matter of setting the right standards or ends. It is a matter of *discerning* or apprehending the principle or rationale of living in or by acting in unimpeded ways. (For Aristotle unimpeded activity for sentient creatures is equivalent to activity one takes pleasure in, has no trouble with, etc.). Just as the smooth (unimpeded) unfolding of the solar system indicates the true principle of its existence so too the smooth unfolding of our lives is what indicates the true principle of reason that governs it. Aristotelians must give something like this account of a natural immanent standard governing our lives if they are to prosecute the analogy between living well and other skills, since any skill involves there being some point to it if there is to be excellence in practicing the skill.

It is important to note that carpentry is a social skill. It is practiced by many and based on a certain kind of solidarity among practitioners. Each learns from the others' practice and there is no antithetical opposition in skillful practice even if each has their own individual practice. Plato makes this point about musicianship in Book I of the Republic. We can emphasize this social nature of a skill by calling it a craft. Likewise then there is the craft of happiness or living well. Both in regard to cooperative "projects" like friendship or individual projects like developing athletic ability there is a certain solidarity by which each learns from others' practice so that the craft (unimpeded friendship, unimpeded athletic development) is improved and perfected. Since we find or discern the principle of our existence in actual unimpeded activity, such solidarity is essential to our discerning our happiness. This solidarity is not a matter of shared *values* that each person sets but a matter of participating in a common craft. This relationship of solidarity in a common craft of happiness has its counterpart in our account according to which pursuing happiness is an enterprise we each participate in.

Since it is in the practice of the craft of living well (in unimpeded ways) that the principle or point of living (and so what living well comes to) is apprehended, it follows that any rules of practical wisdom (what to aim for) are generalizations gleaned from the practice of those whose lives are overall smooth and unimpeded and so happy. Activities or ways of being that contribute to the overall smooth activity of living are thus the source of any rules of practical wisdom. But then having and exercising traits or propensities for such activities is more fundamental than any rules or standards for acting well. Defining a virtue now as a trait for acting in a way that contributes to the overall smooth activity of living (happiness), the fundamental tenet of virtue theory follows; viz., virtues and their exercise are basic to any rules or standards of acting well. Russell (2009;92) says,

> To avoid parochialism one must look somewhere to explain why one trait is virtuous or admirable, while another is not.

Defining a virtue as a trait for acting in a way that contributes to happiness exactly explains its being an admirable trait – one to aspire to have. Further each virtue is measured or standardized in relation to overall virtuous practice; the smooth unfolding of living within which the principle or point of the craft of living is apprehended. All traits are virtues then only in relation to practical wisdom that apprehends in overall virtuous practice what it is to live well. If one's traits are for acting which fails the measure of practical wisdom then they are not virtues. Too much courage and one is foolhardy; too little and one is cowardly. In this manner practical wisdom gives the measure by which a trait is of the right proportion (is in the mean) to be a virtue.

We turn now to specifically moral virtues. In the case of carpentry there are virtues pertaining to various specific dimensions of the craft (carving wood well, picking out materials well), virtues pertaining to being in solidarity with others who practice the craft (generosity in sharing one's skill, respect for others' skill) and all-purpose virtues pertaining to having any of these other virtues (diligence, determination). In the case of living well likewise there are virtues pertaining to specific dimensions of the craft. For example in regard to the dimension of social relations there are virtues such as being friendly, witty, loyal, courteous, etc. There are virtues as well pertaining to being in solidarity with others that include being generous, honest, and trustworthy, etc., and there are all-purpose virtues (temperance, courage). The specifically moral virtues I contend are those that pertain to being in solidarity with others.

A carpenter's solidarity is with other carpenters generally, not just with those whose projects are similar or those he is familiar with or those who belong to the same tradition. Further solidarity with the craft involves tutelage of others (novices) entering the craft. Following Plato again solidarity involves not harming but benefiting others in the practice of the craft. Applying this to the craft of living well the scope of the virtues that constitute solidarity extends to all those who practice the craft whether strangers or foreigners and to all who can be brought into the craft. It isn't limited only to those who practice the craft within a certain tradition. On this understanding Aristotelian ethics is cosmopolitan not communitarian. Solidarity in this craft likewise is a matter of not harming but benefiting others in the practice of the craft. (In the terminology of the account in Part One it is respecting and caring for others in the practice of pursuing happiness.)

Just as there are no rules for living well that don't derive from or summarize the practice of living well, since only in practice is the smooth unimpeded nature of activity discerned that reveals the natural principle or reason of our existence, so too there are no rules for solidarity with others as regards living well (rules for harm and benefit) that don't derive from or summarize the practice of living well in solidarity since only in practice is the unimpeded or smooth nature of the activity discerned. Any solidarity with others that is not unimpeded and smooth (part of the overall smooth, unimpeded character of living) does not reveal the natural reasonableness that governs our lives. Because of this it follows that being morally virtuous is not a matter of conformity to a fundamental law or principle that *imposes* on practice what being morally virtuous is. No law can be set up to determine what the unimpeded exercise of solidarity is, any more than a law can be "imposed" on the interactions of atoms to determine what their unimpeded interaction is and so what the principle governing such interaction is. Any law has to be found out in the unimpeded interaction. Specific moral virtues such as honesty, fidelity to one's word, fairness in one's dealings and so on then are not a matter of conforming to specifications of a fundamental principle that we impose on practice. What specific moral virtues come to is determined within the practice of being overall morally virtuous.

A virtue theory of morality then will hold that specific moral virtues are components of being morally virtuous, that being morally virtuous is being in solidarity with others who practice the craft of living well, and that what this comes to us determined only in the practicing of the craft itself. Since what the principle of living well, not just how to "achieve" it, is apprehended in the practice of others as well as one's own, therefore solidarity with others who practice the craft is internal to each person's apprehension of what happiness is. Hence being morally virtuous, and having the particular moral virtues that contribute to it, is internal to each person's practical wisdom (his apprehension of what to go for or aim at). In this manner a virtue theory of morality is a justification of being morally virtuous, and a justification in which any moral laws or rules of right action are secondary to moral practice. Annas (1995;444) says,

> In some modern discussions the turn...to virtue has been accompanied by the rejection of the very idea of a moral *theory* at all. Concentration on character and virtue has often gone with the rejection of any aspiration to systematize ethical thinking into a single structure,

and holds that this is not the understanding of virtues in Aristotle or the ancients. I am claiming as well that the turn to virtue should not be accompanied by a rejection of the aspiration to *justify* morality. What sets Aristotelian ethics apart from our account is that the justification is in moral virtues contributing to solidarity in the craft of living well which leaves those virtues to be determined only by exercising that very craft. This justification doesn't need and indeed precludes a theory of right action that is antecedent to being in unimpeded solidarity with others.

I have tried to set out how an Aristotelian-like ethics (hard virtue theory) is a justification of being morally virtuous. It should be clear that there are significant parallels between this account and ours. For Aristotle the craft of living well like all crafts involves solidarity with others in order for each to discern by the practice of the craft in others what unimpeded activities are possible. This solidarity, again as with all crafts involves not harming but benefiting the exercise of the craft by others. On our account the enterprise of pursuing happiness involves solidarity with others who partake in the enterprise in order for each to claim the satisfaction with activity of living as belonging to them as reasoning beings. This solidarity involves respecting and caring enough for the participation in the enterprise of others. For Aristotle happiness is unimpeded activity that exhibits and so apprehends the immanent reason of our existence; the principle according to which the unfolding of our nature flows. For us too happiness is "unimpeded" (satisfying) activity where part of its being unimpeded is that we can claim it as belonging to us as reasoning beings. For Aristotle unimpeded activity fulfills that by which our nature has an immanent principle of reasonableness to it, whereas for us unimpeded activity is *self*-fulfilling to us as reason*ing* beings. This latter requires that we have standards for satisfaction that we can claim as reasoning beings. These standards may or may not pan out in practice so they are not norms or rules which by themselves determine satisfaction (unimpeded activity). But nor are they summaries of what activities are found to be unimpeded in practice. It is not the case that anything that "satisfies" us in practice thereby has a claim on us as reasonable. It is reason which sets up what it can or cannot claim or find self-fulfilling. We are not "passive" Nous apprehending the "active" Nous governing our nature. We are instead the active Nous in setting ourselves standards that we can then as passive either find to be satisfying in practice or not. The difference then as regards happiness is not that for Aristotle finding out what living well comes to is determined in practice whereas for us it is determined simply by recipes or rules. Rather for us what is to be found out (what living well comes to) is whether in practice our rule or standard for what we require of ourselves in order to be happy or in order to own any satisfaction is realized or not. For us part of the craft of living well is devising standards or setting ends that we can claim as belonging to us as reasoning beings. In a word what Aristotle misses is that *autonomous* reason is part of our nature—part of what it is to live as a human being.

The consequence of this difference as regards morality is that solidarity with others if it is to be a component of living well must likewise be claimed or authorized as belonging to a standard for being satisfied with our lives that can be self-fulfilling. Not harming, but benefiting (or respecting and caring for) the practice by others of the craft (enterprise) of living well (pursuing happiness) must conform to a law that reason gives itself over to. Hence the requirement of a fundamental principle or law of morality (solidarity) that reason demands of itself. Further it cannot be a law that undercuts or conflicts with the setting of personal standards that can be owned by reason if it is to be a standard of solidarity with others in the enterprise of setting such standards. It has to be then a law that all other components of personal standards conform to if they are to be claimed by reason. The fundamental principle of morality therefore has to be justified to reason as an over-riding or predominating principle of pursuing happiness or of living well. Likewise specific aspects of solidarity must themselves be laws (maxims) that reason gives itself over to. Only what specifies or derives from the fundamental principle can be a non-harming or a benefiting that reason can claim as its own. In this manner a solidarity that we can claim as belonging to us, and so consistent with how we live being something we can likewise claim, requires a theory of right action; viz. specific laws or rules of right versus wrong. For solidarity to be discerned (as with Aristotle) by what activities of solidarity run smoothly in practice would be a heteronomy of reason—something reason doesn't demand of itself according to its nature as giving itself norms. Thus a moral theory must be a theory of principles through and through—not a theory of virtues that principles follow from as summaries of the practice of smoothly living in solidarity. Only with such a moral theory are the traits in people by which they conform smoothly to such principles (the moral virtues) traits that can be claimed by us as reasoning beings as worth having. An honest person conforms smoothly to a moral principle of truth-telling. It is his authorization of the principle which males the unimpeded conformity a trait he can own as a reasoning being. Virtue theory then is not a substitute for moral laws and principles determining right and wrong practice—it is rather a theory of what we need to become to realize those laws smoothly in our lives. The failure of smooth realization, although it is threat to emotional contentment in life without which there is no happiness, doesn't by itself overturn the laws or add to the laws that reason gives to itself according to its nature as reason. If telling the truth is so frustrating and upsetting because one lacks the courage to do so and if this frustration is pervasive in living in solidarity with others, then the one who still does tell the truth (to be aligned with his reason) is like the artist who still paints (to be aligned with what he values in thought) though it makes him emotionally miserable. Clearly then developing the virtues is central to our pursuit of happiness. In this sense Aristotle is right that happiness involves activity in accord with virtue.

The contrast we have just drawn between our account and Aristotle's can stand as our critique of Aristotle's ethics and of hard virtue theory in general; viz. our nature is not to discern in practice what our nature (and so our living well) is, but rather to authorize by reason what our nature needs to be. This critique applies as well to any theory which denies moral principles and laws as fundamental, such as pure virtue theory (Slote 2001) and care theory (Noddings 1984). If we understand communitarian theories as basing morality on the smooth practice of values embedded in a cultural community or a tradition, so that our nature is to discern in practice what our cultural or tradition-belonging nature is, then the critique stands as well against communitarian theories. If we understand communitarian theories as holding the ultimate authorization of moral rules or standards is within a culture or tradition, our objection has all along been that the fundamental community is that of all who live a human life; a life in pursuit of well-considered satisfaction one can claim as one's own.

PART 3

Freedom

∵

CHAPTER 8

Freedom, Deliberation, and the Self

The goal of Part Three is to show that a certain conception of freedom is demanded by our account of happiness as self-fulfilling satisfaction with how our lives are going. Only beings that are free according to this conception of freedom have the capacity to act in a way consistent with achieving such happiness and therefore only beings who are free in this sense have the capacity to pursue happiness. In this chapter it is claimed that our actions being subject to we ourselves determining them in accord with reasonable deliberation is necessary for pursuing happiness and for we ourselves being held morally responsible. In Chapter 9 it is claimed that this is not sufficient unless this determination by ourselves is original or ultimate in regard to what we will call inter-subjective availability. This leads to the conception of freedom as an original and ultimate power by deliberatively determining one's actions to make that deliberative action itself inter-subjectively available. It is this conception of what may be called availability-freedom that is required for the capacity to pursue happiness and for it being we ourselves that are ultimately to be held morally responsible.

In Part Two we claimed that our account of happiness in Part One justifies the nature of morality in the sense that it justifies a fundamental principle of morality. In this Part Three the claim is that our account of happiness justifies the reality of moral freedom and ultimate moral responsibility. This would complete the justification of morality as something real and fundamental in our lives.

(i)

The first two sections of this chapter set out what is basically a compatibilist component to freedom and responsibility and do not involve anything fundamentally new. It isn't until the third section where we introduce a version of what is called agent-causation as required for the capacity to pursue happiness that what we have to say goes beyond ground that has been well covered by others.

If a person is pursuing happiness then his actions are determined in accord with (are at least partly in terms of) his open-minded standard for being satisfied with how his life is going. There are many choices in a person's life that are neutral with respect to his standard. Going to the fair or staying home may each be perfectly consistent with what one wants out of life. In such cases the action is not determined by one's standard. Further factors are involved in determining how one acts. Nevertheless if one is pursuing happiness even such choices and so how one acts are determined *in accord with* one's standard. One's standard, though not the full cause, is a controlling cause. If a person is explicitly considering his standard in determining how to act, then he is considering and so deliberating about how it is flat-out valuable to act. In such a case the person's action is determined in accord with his reasonable deliberation about values. One may act without explicitly deliberating at all or without one's explicit deliberation reaching all the way unto what one's acting means for one's life. Conformity or consistency with one's standard must nevertheless go into determining a person's action if he is indeed pursuing happiness. We can say that a person has a standing intention to determine his actions to be in accord with his standard. This is a standing intention to deliberate if needed to ensure his action is in accord with his standard and, if needed, to ensure his deliberation conforms to the standard (to ensure considerations about whether the action conforms are brought up and are decisive). This standing intention is just the person's commitment to his standard of satisfaction. The standing intention to determine his actions to be in accord with his standard includes the intention to consider and make apparent, if needed, what his standard is.

If a person's actions are to be determined in accord with the norm of reason then his standing intention must be must be to determine his actions to be in accord with this norm. In relation to morality (which is part of the norm of reason) this means he has a standing intention to deliberate if needed to ensure his action is moral and if needed to ensure his deliberation itself conforms to morality (to ensure moral considerations are brought up and are decisive). This standing intention is the person's commitment to acting morally and is essential to his commitment to acting in accord with the norm of reason. In relation to developing and having a standard of satisfaction for his life this means he has a standing intention to deliberate if needed about his standard and revise it or not according to circumstances of how things are going in his life and what considerations he gets from others. This together with his commitment to morality constitutes his commitment to the norm of reason. His commitment to acting morally makes him open to such circumstances and his commitment in relation to having and developing a standard of satisfaction is his use of such circumstances for making his standard well-considered.

A person pursues happiness only if he has a standing intention to determine his actions in accord with the norm of reason that is in fact effective. A person has the *capacity* to pursue happiness then only if he has a standing intention that can be effective if it works well. In the case of morality this means that his actions are *subject to* being determined in accord with morality whether or not they are in fact determined in accord with it. By being subject-to I mean he could have refrained from doing wrong if he had deliberated as opposed to acting impulsively, or if he had deliberated better (giving moral considerations due weight to be decisive and effective in acting) and he could have done either if he had exercised better control over whether to deliberate or not or over deliberating well or not; i.e., if his standing intention had worked effectively. But this is just to say that he acts freely in regard to doing wrong or refraining. We can say then that a person's being morally free is necessary for his having the capacity to pursue happiness. In relation to developing standards of satisfaction, having a standing intention that can be effective if it works well means that his actions are subject to being determined in accord with a well-considered standard of satisfaction whether or not they are in fact in accord. This means that he could have acted in accord with his well-considered standard if he had deliberated instead of acting impulsively, or if he had deliberated better (giving considerations of what his standard is due weight to be decisive and effective in acting), or if he had deliberated about his standard and revised it or not when circumstances had in fact called for it; i.e., if his standing intention to act in accord with a well-considered standard had worked effectively. But this is just to say that he acts freely in regard to the prudential value of his actions. We can say that a person's being prudentially free is necessary for his having the capacity to pursue happiness. Of course being morally free is part of being prudentially free, but we single it out since our basic concern is with moral freedom and moral responsibility. Being prudentially and morally free together constitutes the person being free in determining his life as conforming or not to the pursuit of happiness (determining his life to go in a way that is consistent or not with his ever being happy with how it is going). This I claim is the core of being free in a specifically human sense. Put another way, for a person to act freely in this sense is for their actions to be subject to being determined in accord with their well-considered system of values where having a well-considered system of values includes (necessarily) having moral values.

A person has a diminished capacity to pursue happiness if his standing intention cannot be fully effective, and the extent to which the capacity is diminished is the extent to which it cannot be fully effective. A person who cannot resist certain temptations has such a diminished capacity. A compulsive hand washer who disowns this compulsion as no part of his standard of satisfaction but does it anyway has such diminished capacity. Even if his standing intention to determine his actions to be in accord with his standard of satisfaction is working as well as it can (he calls up all the resources he has for controlling his actions) he still doesn't act in accord with his standard. A person with a full capacity would only fail because he failed to call up all the resources he had. Diminished capacity goes exactly with diminished freedom to act morally or not or to act prudentially or not in one's life.

If a person's standing intention in regard to morality is fully effective then the person has good (and in one sense perfect) moral character. He always ensures his actions are determined in accord with morality. If his standing intention in regard to morality can be fully effective but isn't then he has defective moral character in one way or another but also the capacity for that defect to be removed. That capacity we shall see is realizable by inputs from the person himself or from others that hold the person responsible for his defective character so that if he indeed takes up the responsibility the defect gets removed. Even if he doesn't take up the responsibility he could have if the inputs had been effective. In either case the person has the capacity to take responsibility for his defective moral character. Not only are a kleptomaniac's actions not subject to being determined in accord with morality, he has besides no capacity to take up responsibility for the defect and thereby remove it so long as he remains a kleptomaniac. We can say therefore that if a person has a capacity for pursuing happiness then it must be that his actions are subject to being determined in accord with morality *and further* his character is subject to the removal of defects. This means that he is free not only in regard to how he acts but also in regard to taking up responsibility for what his character is like. This latter I claim is also part of what it is to be free in the specifically human sense. Similar remarks hold in relation to prudential character, such things as whether the person in general gives in to certain temptations, whether he is too quick to abandon his values, etc.

Freedom is a capacity or power that can be exercised well or not. This implies that it can fail to be exercised well even when the power to exercise it well still exists. In particular even if the power is not interfered with it can still fail of its own accord. Otherwise all failures would be cases of interference and so not failures that could be attributed to the person. There must then be a distinction between failures that derive from the power itself versus those that derive from its being interfered with. The power or capacity of an automobile to run is in place even if there is not enough gas for it to run because all the parts required for running are in place as they need to be. It is just lacking an input of energy. The power is in place as well if it doesn't run smoothly but sputters along due to a lack of enough transference of energy from one component to another. Neither of these are cases of interfering with the power as when a perfectly well-running car is chained to a tow-truck. If we talk of freedom as a mechanism in place in the organism by which it has the power then the distinction between failures due to the mechanism and those due to interference is a distinction between inputs of energy having to be added somewhere in the mechanism or system on the one hand and the mechanism or system having to be left to itself to unfold or operate on the other. This admittedly vague characterization of the distinction is all the understanding of the identity conditions of a mechanism or power being in place despite failure to operate as it should that is required for attributing failures to it versus attributing failures to interference with it, or not attributing failures either to it or to interference with it for its not being in place at all.

If a person is to pursue happiness then his standard of satisfaction needs to be sensitive to how it reasonably developed in the course of his life, what his previous standards were, the reasons (pre and post considerations) it has shifted, and so on. Otherwise his standard is closed off from his previous reasoning which diminishes his present reasonableness about his standard. In short what makes his present standard reasonable depends to a large extent on how it reasonably developed in his life. Since being happy requires one's standard be something one can claim as a reasoning being and one's past development is an important source of reasons pro and con it follows that one cannot be happy in closing oneself off to the development of one's standard. But now someone is not pursuing happiness if they do what is inconsistent with what it is to be happy. Hence there is an essential historical or biographical component to pursuing happiness. For one to pursue happiness requires thus that one's actions be determined in accord with reasonable deliberation (about values) that is open to one's own past reasonable deliberations about value. For one to have the capacity to pursue happiness requires one's actions be subject to such historically sensitive reasonable deliberation. In deriving freedom from what is involved in the capacity to pursue happiness we get that this same historical component pertains to freedom as well. Wiggins (2006;114) makes this point when he says that a free agent's

> biography unfolds...intelligibly...in that each new action or episode constitutes...a further specification of what the man has by now *become*.

If part of what the man has by now become includes what his biography of what to go for in life has been then we get this historical constraint on being free (Fischer 1995 and Mele 1995). Being subject to this constraint implies that a certain further counterfactual holds of a free person; namely, if they had thought about where have been in their lives they might have now acted differently.

If a person acts freely he has the capacity to determine his actions to be in accord with the norm of reason. To the extent that he exercises the capacity well he is acting autonomously – in accord with his own nature as a reasonable being. But the extent to which he exercises the capacity well is also the extent to which he is in fact pursuing happiness and so a person is pursuing happiness to the extent that he acts autonomously. Autonomy is not one value among others in life (Fischer 2006). In terms of Part One acting autonomously has flat out value and acting out of anything else one values has flat out value only to the extent that one acts autonomously. It follows that only a person who determines his actions to be in accord with morality (care and respect for the pursuit of others) can be acting autonomously since morality is an essential component of the norm of reason.

The result so far is that freedom in the sense of one's actions and character being subject to the norm of reason is necessary for the capacity of pursuing happiness though it turns out that such freedom is not sufficient. Our basic goal in developing a conception of freedom that is sufficient is to justify our ultimately deserving to be held responsible for failing to conform to the standard of morality. Because of this the subsequent discussions of freedom and responsibility for the most part emphasize moral freedom in particular as opposed to prudential freedom. Further the focus will be on cases where deliberation is indeed called for. In such cases determining one's actions to be in accord with the norm of reason is equivalent to determining one's actions to be in accord with reasonable deliberation which involves determining one's deliberation, if needed, to be in accord with the norm of reason. It is such cases involving explicit deliberation that are the usual focus of discussions of moral freedom and moral responsibility.

(ii)

We consider next how notions about responsibility such as holding one another responsible and taking responsibility connect to the capacity to pursue happiness. As with the notions of freedom and autonomy what we now set out is an idea of responsibility that is necessary but not yet sufficient for the pursuit of happiness. Unlike the notion of freedom holding responsible and taking responsibility is a social or inter-personal activity and so the capacity for these things is a capacity for engaging in this activity. For Scanlon (1998;280) holding each other responsible is part of being a "participant in a system of co-deliberation." For Smilansky (2002;496) it involves "membership in a Community of Responsibility in which most people have the required control."

Further holding each other responsible pertains to failures in the exercise of freedom or at least to how the exercise might have proceeded better. It is a normative notion then in relation to the good (Wolf 1990). The task is to explicate these ideas in terms of the pursuit of happiness.

The pursuit of happiness involves two components—that individuals deliberate about values reasonably and that their deliberations are effective in leading to action. The former is required for coming up with or having reasonable standards of satisfaction while the latter is required for realizing them (and so potentially being happy, or else reasonably modifying those standards by post-considerations of how they pan out). Though a simplification, the effectiveness component is basically a matter of trying hard enough to effect the choice that deliberation comes up with. To further simplify (following Mele 1995) I presume that such trying is for the most part making one's reasons for the choice salient (attending to them some more), talking oneself through as to the importance of those reasons, and so on, so that the execution is effected by further thinking. This leaves aside trying to make sure one's limbs move properly (=attending to the acting itself).

The responsibility-exchange of one person holding another responsible who then takes responsibility is an exchange that *holds up* the pursuit of happiness due to some regard as to how it might or must go better. Thus if a person B offers a consideration as to a person A's values, B is putting a hold on A's pursuit by indicating how it might go better. This is a case of holding things up in regard to the prudential component of pursuing happiness. If B offers a condemnation of A for a supposed moral failing on A's part then if B is correct this puts a hold on A's pursuit by indicating how it must go better. When these hold ups are taken and dealt with by A then the exchange is over and the pursuit of both A and B continues on. The source of the holdup is always some supposed defect in either A's deliberations or in A's effectiveness in pushing them through to action.

At the first stage B holds A to an accounting of A's action; as to whether it was determined by his reasons or not, if so what the reasons were and if not where the failure was (did A fail to try hard enough or was he interfered with?). In terms of the accounting B can then indicate how things could or might have gone better. In doing so B holds A *responsible to* what B has indicated. For example, if B indicates "You might have acted better if you had thought of such and such considerations against your values" then B holds A responsible to consider these considerations—maybe to accept them or maybe not. If A indeed does now assess these new considerations then he has taken up (discharged) his responsibility to what B has held him to, which is we note a responsibility of A to his own pursuit of happiness. On the other hand if

B indicates "You might have acted better if you had tried harder to resist your temptation to steal from C by focusing on what it does to C" A takes up or discharges the responsibility he has been held to by, say, on his own repairing what has been done (returning to C what he took or in some other way making reparation). Note that in either case of taking up responsibility, prudential or moral, A must in effect now be *capable* of doing what he didn't just do. In the prudential case he must be capable of now determining his action in accord with newly available considerations. In the moral case he must be now capable of trying hard enough to resist the same temptation to have what he stole by on his own returning the item to C. Only so is A capable of taking up the responsibility that B has held him to. But now capabilities (capacities, mechanisms) don't shift from moment to moment. If A is now capable of doing it then he was capable just before when he didn't do it. Whether a capacity is exercised well or not may be fleeting or transitory, but not whether it is in place. What B does in effect is to provide an input into A (in the form of better reasons for deciding or better ways of effecting a decision) designed to repair or improve the workings of a capacity already in place in A – somewhat like putting higher octane gasoline into a car to make it run better. It follows then that if A is capable of taking responsibility then we was capable of having done otherwise or better; i.e., A could have determined his action in accord with B's prudential reasons if he had thought of them, or could have avoided stealing from C if he had tried harder by focusing. But this latter is just to say that A was subject to determining his action in accord with moral reasons. In sum A is capable of taking up responsibility for stealing from C only if he was morally free in stealing from C. It is this steadiness of the power of freedom that gives substance to the difference between B's holding A responsible (You could have done better if...) and B's merely making an assessment as to what would have been better (It would have been better if you had not stolen from C). The sheer assessment pertains as well to a helpless kleptomaniac and hoarder (Fischer 2006;210). Once A has discharged the responsibility the pursuit of happiness that was held up can continue on for both of them.

So far the claim has been that A is to be held responsible only for freely stealing C's purse since otherwise A cannot take up responsibility to return it. But does A specifically deserve to be held responsible for the repair? A, like everyone else, benefits from the repair being made since potential reasons that have been closed off by the theft are to some extent opened back up. Thus the repair contributes to everyone's pursuit of reasonable standards of satisfaction. But how does A specifically benefit so that he specifically is to be held responsible for the repair? In freely stealing the purse it is A specifically who fails to be committed to open-mindedness. A not only closes off potential

reasons for everyone he besides is defective in giving himself over to reasonably pursuing happiness. In holding A responsible then B is holding A to at
least begin to repair his commitment to open-mindedness. A deserves to be
held responsible then not in the sense that he deserves punishment, but in the
sense that holding him responsible shows respect and care for his pursuit of
happiness (his participation in the enterprise). In other terminology A in doing
what is wrong shows defective moral character and in freely doing what is
wrong A has repairable moral character. Since having good moral character in
the sense of not being liable to do what is wrong is essential to A's pursuing
happiness, holding him responsible to repair it doesn't punish A. It is what
he specifically as a participant in the enterprise deserves; what benefits him
specifically beyond what benefits all in having the theft repaired.

It follows from the account that only a person capable of determining his
actions in accord with morally reasonable and effective deliberation can
be held responsible, which is to say that only a person who is morally free is
subject to being held responsible and discharging that responsibility. To be
capable of determining his actions this way moral reasons or considerations
must both be understandable to the person in order to be available to him for
his deliberation and also capable of being decisive for choice and effective in
executing choice if focused on well enough. This is to say that the conditions
for moral responsibility are that the person must be able to both understand
moral reasons and care enough about them (Wallace 2006). On this account
the system of co-deliberation (Scanlon 1998) carried out by holding each other
morally responsible is a co-deliberation based on promoting the enterprise of
pursuing happiness. It is not a merely formal exchange of justifying our actions
to one another for the sake of such mutual justification itself. We "owe it to
each other" to hold each other morally (and prudentially) responsible and
to take up responsibility, since failing to do so fails to respect and care enough
for each other's pursuit of happiness. The "Community of Responsibility"
(Smilansky 2002) within which holding each other responsible and taking up
responsibility occurs is just those who are capable of pursuing happiness and
that capability (the "required control" of members) is that one acts freely.

The sketch we have given of holding-responsible pertains to making things
better as far as the pursuit of happiness goes (offering new reasons for consideration, repairing damage done by wrong-doing), and pertains as well to making people's character better as far as the pursuit of happiness goes (offering
ways and chances to improve their character, repair their character, etc.).
This again pertains to people who are capable of improving or repairing their
character; people who have the capacity by reasonable and effective deliberation on one or several occasions to do better in subsequently determining their

actions in accord with reasonable deliberation. The issue of whether they can ultimately be held responsible for exercising that capacity to change will have to wait until we come to issues of ultimate responsibility in Chapter 9.

Holding each other responsible often involves emotional attitudes (Wolf 2011 and Wallace 2011) such as indignation, resentment, etc. Some philosophers (Pereboom 2001) hold that we don't lose out in abandoning any aspect of holding each other responsible that calls for or underlies these reactive attitudes. Even if we set aside the emotional component however the *reactive* nature of holding responsible that seeks repair or restoration not just future improvement is central to the pursuit of happiness. To the extent that this in turn requires freedom therefore as against Pereboom we do lose out in abandoning elements of our practice that presuppose freedom. Pereboom might be claiming that these emotional attitudes are apt only if we have ultimate freedom or responsibility. In Chapter 9 I will claim that having ultimate responsibility is likewise essential for the pursuit of happiness.

The connection between freedom and being held responsible is called into question by causal over-determination of the kind Frankfurt (1969) discusses. Suppose that I have my finger on the trigger of a gun deciding whether to pull it and so shoot Mary, and suppose that if I am tending to decide not to that would cause an intervener to force me to decide to press my finger and so shoot Mary. If without intervention I decide to pull the trigger I am clearly to be held responsible for the harm despite the fact that I couldn't have avoided the harm by deciding differently. It is true that I could have avoided responsibility by tending toward deciding not to, and it is true that I could even be said to thus have avoided *my* shooting Mary (making the intervener do it), but I still cannot have avoided the harm by deciding not to. I am still held responsible for what I had no power to avoid. The Frankfurt intervener apparently severs the connection between what I am held responsible for (avoiding the harm) and what I was free to do (avoid the harm).

Though I am clearly to be held responsible for shooting Mary, the question is what fault of mine am I being held responsible for? Where, that is, is the hold-up of the pursuit of happiness that calls for repair? In this example the fault is in my moral character, in my just going ahead and deliberating in a way that doesn't even tend against doing wrong. If I had better moral character I would have produced reasons that go towards swaying me against shooting Mary, and supposedly I could have had better moral character if I had previously in my life thought or deliberated about and resolved thereby to be alert to moral reasons. Thus I am being held responsible for what I as a free agent could have avoided. This is only a "flicker" of freedom on the occasion of the intervener being present in that even with good character I couldn't have avoided the harm and avoiding harm is the whole point of having good moral character. Still by repairing the damage I at least begin to repair my bad character. Being held responsible for bad moral character however makes sense only because in general, even if not on that occasion, having good moral character is effective in avoiding harm. If so then an intervener on a single occasion eliminates the connection between being held responsible and being able to avoid harm, but only because in general that connection still obtains. We are being held responsible on that occasion for what in general enables avoiding doing harm. If the presence of the intervener were pervasive then the general connection between having good moral character and avoiding harm would be broken. In such circumstances holding each other responsible for bad moral character would have no significance or point. It's not as if moral character itself is priceless or valuable in its own right when it has nothing to do with avoiding wrong. In terms of the pursuit of happiness, in such a world being held responsible for moral character would have nothing to do with either damage to the enterprise or one's own specific commitment to open-mindedness. The loss of reasons that shooting Mary engenders is going to happen anyway. Since I can't now or ever avoid loss of reasons by having good moral character, it is no longer relevant to being open-minded and being committed to open-mindedness in my pursuits. I no longer deserve to be held responsible for my character as it is no longer due to me as a participant in the pursuit of happiness. In such a world then where our moral-reasons-sensitive mechanism is "locked in" holding each other responsible for harm would be empty and otiose. Roughly, bad moral character would no longer be a fault, a place where there is a hold-up, in the enterprise of pursuing happiness. In sum the *connection* between what harm we could have avoided and what we are to be held responsible for is merely relaxed, not eliminated with a single-occasion intervener and the connection holds up (in the sense that both go by the boards) with a pervasive intervener.

A case intermediate between a singular and pervasive intervener is a world in which the intervener is always present when the initial harm is done but then removes himself when it comes to repairing the harm. Thus after I take Mary's purse I am still to be held responsible *when* I don't return it because I could have returned it if I had deliberated better – in a way effective for returning it. In this world I am held responsible for failing to repair harm, not for doing it in the first place, since the hold-up doesn't occur until I fail to repair it. Again the connection is maintained between what I am held responsible for and what I could have done otherwise. Such a scope of holding each other responsible wouldn't be empty or otiose, but it would make morality and moral freedom not a matter of doing harm or not, but a matter of repairing harm or not. Suppose someone in this world had bad moral character in the sense that he is liable to deliberate straight off to do harm (versus coming up with reasons that tend against it and so causing an intervention) but that he also had good moral character in the sense that he is liable to repairing harms that ensue from him. Such a person would have all the good moral character that is required in such a world to promote the enterprise of pursuing happiness such as it is in that world. Since there is no defect in him in deliberating straight off to do harm he doesn't specifically deserve to be held responsible for it. There is nothing in him to be made better by holding him responsible and so holding him responsible isn't a matter of any due respect or care for him. The only connection between doing the harm and he specifically being called on to repair it is the practical one that he happens to be around most of the time to repair the harms he does. Unlike in our world he wouldn't be held responsible for repairing the harm after first being held responsible for doing it. No hold up calling for repair and so for holding responsible exists until after he fails to make the repair and so that is what he is being held responsible for.

The lesson of the Frankfurt intervener is not that there is a disconnect between what we are held responsible for (avoiding harm) and what we are free to do (avoid harm), but rather that circumstances of the world, in particular whether it is "out to get us" by thwarting our ability to avoid harm, determine the scope if any of the connected practice of being held responsible only for what one could have done better by deliberating reasonably and effectively. The Frankfurt case as I have presented it doesn't require prediction of the person's decision only how he is tending in his decision and so it applies as well to the connection between being held responsible and libertarian freedom, whether or not that incorporates agent-causation. Suppose that my deliberating is not determined as to a decision until the decision occurs (=indeterminism). It still must be that whether a decision to do wrong happens is made more or less likely according to the reasons that go into the deliberation. Otherwise the deliberation has nothing to do with reasons, and that would not be a case of being free at all. The intervener then can step in if he discerns that reasons are making it likely that the decision will be to not do wrong. If in deliberating I actually indeterministically decide to do wrong without such contra-indicating reasons arising then I am responsible for the harm even though I couldn't have avoided it. The best I could have done is come up with contra-tending reasons forcing the intervener to intervene. In this case just as in the deterministic case I show bad moral character for not forcing the intervention and so can be held responsible for the harm but again only because in general good moral character is effective in avoiding harm. Similarly if an agent is the cause of his decision then he causes it via reasons for it. If not then agent-causation has nothing to do with reasons and so is irrelevant for acting freely. The intervener then can again step in if he discerns the agent considering reasons against doing wrong and force the agent to consider bad reasons so that he causes a bad decision and acts. If the agent causes a decision to do wrong without considering reasons for not doing wrong and then acts he is responsible for the harm even though he couldn't have avoided it. Once the intervener is possible, all we have said about the lesson of Frankfurt cases applies as well to the connection between responsibility and libertarian (agent-causal or not) freedom. For the rest of this work I presume we are living in a world without the pervasive presence of an intervener.

(iii)

So far the claim has been that the capacity to pursue happiness requires that one's actions be subject to determination in accord with reasonable deliberation (ultimately about values). This version of a compatibilist conception of freedom though necessary is not sufficient for the capacity to pursue happiness. It needs to be extended in two ways in order to be sufficient. The first to be considered in this section is that it requires the self or the agent to be the cause of the determination. It requires that is that our actions be subject to determination in accord with reasonable deliberation by the self. The self must be capable of being the cause of reasonable deliberating (the legislative will) and of effecting its result for acting (the executive will). The second extension to be discussed in Chapter 9 is that the self must in a certain regard be the originating or ultimate cause in relation to deliberative action. The compatibilist conception requires these controversial extensions if freedom is to be adequate to the capacity to pursue happiness.

It was claimed in Part One that being happy with how one's life is going requires that one be satisfied with how it is going in a self-fulfilling way, which requires that one is not just satisfied but that one *gives oneself over* to the standard of satisfaction which one does by its being in accord with the norm of reason that one gives oneself over to. If a standing intention together with deliberations that it determines to be in accord with the norm were all nothing more than what takes place in me or exists in me (if they were sub-personal occurrences and conditions) then what goes on in me would be given over to the norm but I *myself* would not thereby be giving *myself* over to the norm. Inside me there would be the workings of a mechanism being given over to a master mechanism for controlling the workings to go well. That such a mechanism or capacity exists in me is not yet giving myself over to the norm of reason. Hence I wouldn't be fulfilled-rather a capacity that exists within me would be fulfilled by working well. But then *I as a reasonable being* would not be satisfied with how my life is going in a self-fulfilling way. Instead a capacity in me would make the satisfaction with my life to be a reasonable one. The reasoning nature in me would be fulfilled but I myself would not be. But for me to be happy with how my life is going requires that I be satisfied in a way that fulfills *me* with how my life is going.

The standing intention is to ensure that the deliberations are given over to the norm of reason. If the deliberations emerged or came from me and the standing intention was identifiable with me myself, then and only then would it be that I myself ensure that my deliberations are given over to the norm of reason. Only then would it be that I myself, as being identifiable with the standing intention, give myself as a deliberating being over to the norm of reason. Hence to be happy with how one's life is going the self I am has to be the cause of the deliberations and the standing intention has to be identifiable with who or what that self is. In other terms, there must be agent-causation by an agent that embeds the norm of reason within what it is.

If I am not the cause of the deliberations and the standing intention is not what I am then there is no such thing as being happy and so no such thing as the capacity to pursue happiness. The capacity to pursue happiness then requires not just that my actions are subject to being determined by reasonable deliberation, but that they are subject to being determined by deliberation *that I myself cause and I, being who I am*, determine to be reasonable. This augmented conception of freedom then is an extension of our previous conception that is necessary for the capacity to pursue happiness. This leaves us with the issue of how the self can cause deliberations (agent-causation) and how the self can within itself be a standing intention. To deal with this issue we first have to consider what the self is.

To this end suppose that I am playing chess and deciding how to next move and that prior to coming up with the thought of a particular move to consider I have a sense or inkling of figuring what thoughts to come up with. I feel as yet unsettled as to what to consider or think about and then I feel a first thought of a move emerging from that unsettledness. Let us say that a first thought of a move emerges as a conscious imagining of making that move. Let us further say that the unsettled figuring from which it comes is the brain transitioning between *incipient* inchoate productions of imaginings before any full imagining comes to fruition. Because I feel or discern this unsettledness we can say that this brain transitioning exists at the interface between the part of brain processing that is unconscious and the part that is conscious, or is the initial entrance of brain processing into consciousness. Much of what underlies the formation of a thought may not be conscious. My point is that part of it is conscious *before* I am conscious of a first thought of a move. I am not just conscious of the thought but of the thought emerging from a condition of dynamic unsettledness that is itself present in consciousness. The first thought may call up other thoughts as to the consequences of that move so that I consciously imagine what other moves might follow from that move. It may do so either with or without further intermediate unsettledness as to what the consequences are. In either case what emerges from the unsettled dynamic action are reasons for or against the move (thoughts of consequences). It may be the case that the first thought is held to until I discern those consequential thoughts to be decisive, which is to discern the complete settling of the brain processing from any further transitioning to come up with further thoughts or reasons. It may rather be the case that the first thought and the line of thinking that comes with it is abandoned or taken over by the episode continuing as before to a thought of a second move to make. The point is that in the deliberation I am not just conscious of a sequence of thoughts and reasons giving way or not to other thought and reasons. I am conscious of all this emerging from a sustained condition of inchoate dynamic processing that is also present in consciousness. There is one more point to be made. The dynamic processing can be present in consciousness even without any thought emerging. Consider the chess player sitting there until a first option comes to him. He doesn't sit there absent mindedly waiting, but consciously discerns struggling to come up with an option. It may start to come up but fail remaining so to speak not on the tip of his tongue but on the tip of his thinking. The separation in consciousness between that from which thoughts emerge and any thoughts emerging is clear in this case of sheer consciousness of unsettledness.

What we can say of this discerned dynamic processing, this transition prefiguring thoughts arising is that it is that from which thoughts emerge, that which holds to thoughts for further reasons to emerge, that which releases thoughts by transitioning to other thoughts to consider. In a word it is that to which the emerging of thought belongs. *But now the conscious thinking self or the conscious subject of thinking (the self or subject as it is present in consciousness) is just that (in consciousness) to which the arising of thoughts belongs.* The dynamic processing therefore *is* the conscious thinking self or the conscious subject. Hence the conscious self is not an entity—it is a dynamic processing. The entity is the person or the organism. For Sartre (1957) the ego is that entity to which consciousness belongs. Sartre characterizes it as transcendent to distinguish it from the self that is present in conscious which for Sartre is not an entity at all. Similarly, Kant in the *Paralogisms* allows that a subject (the I-think) not just thoughts are revealed in the cogito – but denies that it is an entity or substance that is revealed.

What I am claiming is that people are or are capable of being in a dynamical condition of being a conscious self (of being a self that is present in conscious-ness). They are not always in this condition not even when they are conscious since they can be so engrossed that there is no inchoate processing discerned. However most of the time the conscious person has a sense or discernment as to whether activating this condition is called for (a sense that things are progressing smoothly—not needing any figuring in order to think what to do). In such cases all the causal determining is carried on unconsciously and routinely. It is when care and attention are needed that the brain-processing extends into conscious processing. When it does the person is active in being a self or subject. Otherwise for the most part he is only capable of being active as a subject if needed. It is no more the case that there are two entities involved (the person and the self) than two entities are involved in Mary being a policewoman. Sometimes Mary is in an active condition of being a police-woman. In arresting someone or patrolling she acts from her policing-capabil-ities. This could be semantically expressed by saying "Mary, the policewoman, arrested the subject." The noun in apposition doesn't refer to a second entity, but is rather a sortal of the kind of "source" from which various actions of hers come (those due to her status as a policewoman). Analogously, in saying that Mary *herself* decided what to cook the noun in apposition doesn't refer to a second entity, but is rather a sortal of the kind of source from which various actions of hers come (those due to her consciously coming to a decision if need be).

One might claim all this is just a functionalist, causal-role account of the self. This would miss the point however that the causal role is as it is evident to con-sciousness, so that it is a phenomenological "functionalism." All that is present in consciousness I claim, including thoughts and being a subject of thoughts, has quality (Melnick 2011). It feels a certain way, as a struggle, as unsettledness, as emerging from unsettledness, to be the conscious subject. Phenomenological functionalism then may replace an entity-self in favor of a causal role but unlike usual functionalist accounts it doesn't replace qualia with causal role.

The ultimate basis of mistakenly thinking that the conscious self is an entity lies I believe in a mistake about consciousness. The subject is not that to which processes have to come in order to be conscious. The subject is not that which makes things conscious by lighting them up as they are enveloped in it or by enveloping them as within a "searchlight." Sartre again is right that there is no such subject making for consciousness. There is only "Nothingness"-i.e., as discerned nothing *makes for* consciousness. Consciousness is a field that allows for modifications or perturbations that can exist without any such subject at all. This is the case for example when I am conscious of my overall bodily condition without any focal point from which there is any being enveloped or enveloping—there is just the overall evenly dispersed conscious relaxation, tension, etc. It is not the case that there is this inert emanating reality which just lights things up, but doesn't act or do anything to light them up other than just being what it is. If there were such a subject of consciousness it would be tempting to think of it as an entity. But there is no such subject not even of observational consciousness. The subject that observes is something present in the observational consciousness as an unsettledness as to where to look, what to focus on, etc.—again a dynamic processing from which in part visual percepts emerge. It is true that the concentration of consciousness (attention) of the chess player can be on his unsettled struggling to come up with a thought. This concentration then with the emergence of the thought as an imagining of the move emanates out toward the chess board. This is just to say that the self is present in a conscious field that has a certain distribution of concentration or attention. It is not to say this distribution is created by variations in the intensity of a searchlight. According to this account the brain turning consciousness on and off is one thing: brain-figuring "entering into" what is turned on is another. This leaves it open as to what it is for the brain to turn on a conscious field which is just the problem of consciousness. The point now is just that the conscious thinking subject is a dynamical processing present in consciousness from which thoughts emerge, not an a-dynamical source, a source simply by just being, of the consciousness of thoughts.

So far an account has been offered of what it is for a person, say, Mary to be conscious of having thoughts emerge from being a self. To complete the account we need to explain what it is for her to be conscious of thoughts emerging from being *her*self personally. Return for a moment to the chess player. The chess player knows in a non-occurrent sense what is or isn't relevant to playing chess – making a move publicly is relevant, singing while making a move is not. It is the inchoately discerned occurrence of this knowing that is his sense of the context in which he is thinking about moves. The brain-processing which underlies his thinking of moves somehow encodes this context. Otherwise he would be deliberating about what song to sing. Hence it is a contextualized brain-processing. His sense of the context is just the inchoate discernment at the "entrance" to consciousness of the dynamic unsettledness *with its context*. The player then has a sense not just of being a self from which thoughts emerge, but of being a chess-playing self from which they emerge. It is the discerned contextualized dynamic processing that is the presence in consciousness not just of a self but of a chess-player self.

We need to ask now what the context is of Mary being the person she is as far as having deliberative thoughts is concerned. The context I suggest is being public and being biographical. By being public I mean that presenting thoughts to others and engaging with them is overall relevant, and by being biographical I mean that when and how thinking in terms of where one is in one's history is overall relevant. Mary knows in a non-occurrent sense when and how it is relevant to present her deliberations in a public and biographical way. It is the inchoately discerned occurrence of this knowing that is her sense of the context of thoughts emerging. This occurrence is the contextualized brain processing that she discerns as unsettledness *with that contextualization.* She has a sense then not just of being a self or a thinking subject from which thoughts emerge but of being *herself*—a being that is perhaps to be made public and has a biography that is perhaps to be retrieved. She has a sense, that is, of being the thinking subject she, a public and historical person, is. It is the discerned contextualized dynamic processing therefore that is the presence not just of a self, but of herself personally in consciousness.

It is not the case that the context of having thoughts, even deliberative thoughts, is always public and biographical If I am day-dreaming a fantasy existence and in that mode deliberate about how I will take over the kingdom I still have a sense of being a self from which thoughts emerge since though day-dreaming there is a real inchoate unsettledness in these very difficult deliberations. The context is neither public nor biographical. Exchanging my fantasy thoughts with other persons is not relevant, and nor is retrieving my biographical history. The inchoate unsettledness is not contextualized in these ways and so I have no sense of *my*self personally from which thoughts emerge. In the day dreaming I have no sense of being one self publically among others. P. Strawson's (1959) claim that there is no consciousness of self without the contrasting idea of other selves is false in the fantasy mode. Heidegger's claim (1962) that even concealing oneself from others is still a defective mode of being with others is likewise false of this fantasy mode. This "de-contextualization' of the self from public and biographical relevance is possible, but it is also not the mode in which the pursuit of happiness or being held responsible for morally violating it is possible.

Since the self on our account is not an entity, the self's determining or causing a deliberation is not a matter of substance causation (causation just and only just by being a thing). Instead it is a matter of a discerned dynamic process causing other events, which is an ordinary kind of natural causation. One may object that what is really wanted by agent-causal theorists is causation by the self as an entity, and so our account is an impoverished account on the cheap of self-determination. However causation of deliberation by the self is wanted in the first place surely because one wants conscious causation of deliberating by the person. Suppose Mary the entity (the person, agent) caused the sequence of conscious thoughts-with-reasons that constituted a deliberative episode but that she caused it unconsciously. How would that give her any causal control over her deliberation? Suppose Mary the entity consciously observed thoughts formulated as sentences emerging from her ears (those entities). How would this make the deliberating more up to her than if it were caused by some foreign machine? If one says that Mary isn't conscious of those thoughts emerging from her ears emerging from *herself,* then it is Mary as she is a self present in consciousness that matters—not whether that is consciousness of an entity or not.

Returning now to the way the self determines deliberations consider again the example of playing chess. When I am being fully deliberative as when it is difficult to decide what move to make, the first thought of an option doesn't just happen to me, it comes from my unsettledness as to what might be an option to think about. This unsettledness is the dynamic brain-processing at the entrance to consciousness that we identified with my being present in consciousness. The reasons for or against the option don't arise easily but emerge as a settling of further processing. After several reasons, the processing switches to an unsettledness as to a second option or it closes off that further processing. The former case is my discernment of myself abandoning the first option by struggling to call up another until it emerges, while the latter is my consciousness of myself deciding on that first option. If not decisive the deliberating continues to emerge as a settling on what a second option might be, etc., until finally settling on reasons for an option being decisive by the processing ceasing to figure for any further thoughts to arise. The deliberation, of course needn't be as linear as we have made it out to be. For example previously abandoned options might be called up and become decisive later on when reasons for subsequent options are unfavorable. Whether linear or not, deliberating is not a matter of thoughts and reasons for those thoughts arising until there is decisiveness, with consciousness of all that being simply observation "lighting it all up." Rather it is a matter of thoughts and reasons emerging from the conscious self until that self is settled on a decisive option. Note in this case of studied deliberation that the self is a sustaining presence as an ongoing source or cause of the deliberation. It isn't a matter of thoughts and reason happening and the self entering in only in determining their being strong enough for being decisive. That I don't decide which reasons arise for consideration doesn't imply that I don't determine which reasons to consider. The processing which is my presence in consciousness is inchoate as to the "steps" it is going through before a first thought emerges. The self doesn't cause itself to produce those reasons as opposed to others by a still further self (discerned dynamic processing). As Kane (1996;29–30) puts it,

> ...because one does not control or determine which of a set of outcomes [reasons] is going to occur before it occurs [it does not follow] that one does not control or determine which of them occur *when* it occurs.

This leaves the worry that the self doesn't have any ultimate control of deliberating the way it does and so is not truly free; an issue to be considered in the next chapter.

The case we have described is a case of studied deliberation. If the move to make is a straightforward familiar one the brain-processing-settling-on-it is something stored needing only to be called up not gone through again. What seems straightforward however is not always so and hence it is judicious that it reach the interface between consciousness and unconsciousness discerned as a bare inkling of not having to struggle to settle.

So far we have described the determination by the self of the legislative will—the will as coming to a decision as to what to do. The self however remains a sustaining presence causally determining as well the executive will—the will as effecting a decision unto action. If the person is in action mode the settling into decisiveness of reasons is a settling as well on an immediate intention. By action mode I mean the deliberation is in regard to what to now do, not in regard to what might be a good thing to do later or sometime or other or if one had it all to do over again. In action mode the dynamic processing is connected to motor readiness. Let us say that this motor readiness extends to the full body pathway for acting only not with the energy to actually act. If the person holds on to his decisiveness we presume that "pumps" enough energy so that he actually acts making thereby his decisiveness effective. His action then isn't just determined in accord with effective deliberation that occurs in him; it is determined in accord with effective deliberation that emerges from him in being a conscious subject or in being his presence in consciousness.

The standing intention throughout the deliberation, recall, is to ensure its reasonableness by activating controls to that end if needed. The activation consists of reflections upon how the deliberation might be going wrong and what might correct it. For example I might think or say to myself that I need to cool off and not be in such a rush or that I need to remember how I tend not to consider long-term consequences, etc. If I were deliberating out loud and another person were helping me to get it right this would be the kind of reflecting upon my deliberation that he might do. These reflective thoughts emerge from the standing intention. The standing intention itself is a feature of the

dynamic processing from which the deliberation emerges. It is an encompassing or framing feature of the processing like the safety-control mechanism of a
machine is an encompassing feature of the overall workings of the machine.
It is inchoately discerned as a sense of whether the deliberation is going well or
needs guidance. As such it is a feature of the dynamic processing that *is* the
presence of the self in consciousness. It is then an aspect, indeed a framing
or encompassing aspect of the self built into what the self is. Hence it is the
person *himself* in being that dynamic processing that works to ensure the
deliberation that emerges from him (from he himself) is determined in accord
with the norm of reason. But then the person himself, in being that dynamic
processing, works or tries to *gives himself* (as subject of deliberative thoughts)
over to the norm of reason that is embedded in who he himself is. If the standing intention is effective, if it works, then the person himself in fact gives himself over to the norm of reason. By doing so he *fulfills* himself as the reasoning
being he (the standing intention with the norm embedded) is. Self-fulfillment
then is literally a case of realizing or fulfilling an intention. This is the self-
fulfillment that is required for the possibility of being happy and hence for the
capacity to pursue happiness.

The extension of the conception of freedom that is needed for the capacity
to pursue happiness has been validated. This extension recall is that a person
acts freely if his actions are subject to being determined by deliberations that
he himself causes and that *he himself* determines to be reasonable. If a person's
actions are in fact so in accord then he acts autonomously. Note that the self in
this conception of freedom has to be the personal self – a public and biographical presence in consciousness, since the norm according to which deliberations are reasonable involves the overall relevance of exchanging considerations
with others as to how each other's lives are going. A dynamic processing that
isn't contextualized this way as in day-dreaming will not be capable of determining deliberations in accord with the norm of open-mindedness, and in day
dreaming indeed there is no commitment to the norm of moral or prudential
reason. The autonomous person over time will successfully effect his deliberations in accord with the norm of reasonableness which is just what it means for
him to *give himself over to* the norm of reasonableness. The non-autonomous
but still free person will fail to completely give himself over to the norm. Since
open-mindedness as usual entails deliberating in accord with moral reasons of
care and respect for others being decisive, the autonomous person over time
gives himself over to the predominance of moral reasons.

In discussing what freedom and autonomy are Frankfurt (1982) emphasizes
the importance of identifying ourselves with second-order desires and Watson
(1982) of identifying ourselves with values. It seems to me rather that we

identify ourselves with the norm of reason by which we hold or abandon prudential values and by which we keep our lives in line with our values (moral values included), and it further seems to me that we "can" identify with the norm because in fact the norm is literally embedded as an encompassing feature of who we ourselves are. The identification is not something we make or something that we perform—it is something we find we are.

An enriched conception of being held responsible goes with this extension of the conception of freedom. In holding someone responsible we characterize the fault in a way designed to indicate how things could have gone better. This leads to the conditional form "You could have avoided...if you had..." as the expression of the ascription of responsibility. Further in ascribing responsibility there is the locus or target of the ascription which goes with what the source of the fault or of the hold-up was in the pursuit of happiness. For example if I am a kleptomaniac the source is not me but some defect that operates in me. In such a case the source is not the person but something sub-personal and we don't hold the person responsible. If the person is just an organism in which faulty processes occur then the locus of ascribing responsibility is something in the person but not the person *himself*. In our previous discussion of responsibility the locus was a process of a deliberation effecting action. It is only if the source of the fault is the person himself however that it is the person, not what occurs in him, who is addressed as the source in holding-responsible. What I claim is that given our conception of what the person himself is (viz., the person present in consciousness as himself) it follows that the person himself can be held responsible if he himself is the source of the fault. We consider two examples to show indeed that the person himself is the source. The first is to show that he himself failed to think hard enough and the second to show that he himself failed to try hard enough.

Suppose the person is deliberating about whether to steal and eat Mary's sandwich and finds moral reasons decisive and so forms an intent. This much we have argued all emerges from the presence of himself in consciousness. Suppose now that a desire to have the sandwich arises or occurs in him, say from a vivid memory arising of how good that kind of sandwich tastes, and that this desire retracts or withdraws the intent (the motor readiness to avoid taking the sandwich) by unsettling him. It causes that is the dynamic processing from which deliberating emerges to lose hold of the intent (release the motor readiness) by instigating a thought (how good the sandwich tastes) that returns the processing back instead to unsettled transitioning mode from which thoughts emerge. Because the desire disturbs his acting morally by in effect being a new reason that comes upon him we can call it a Scanlon-desire (1998). All this happens to him. It doesn't emerge from the unsettled dynamic processing that he is—it resets it. We are back again then with the determination of a new decisiveness. Suppose the new reason is found decisive and he takes her sandwich. The source of the fault is in the dynamic processing failing to remain unsettled until thoughts of moral reasons re-emerge saliently enough to be settled on as decisive. But this is to say that the source is in the processing that is his presence as himself in consciousness. The fault then is in he himself not considering moral reasons well enough—not holding off so as to bring them back up. Equivalently, the fault is in the person himself not thinking hard, well, or long enough in the presence of counter-desire. The ascription of responsibility would be that if he had held off and thought harder he could have avoided wrong and the locus of the fault and so the target of the ascription is the person *himself* (the contextualized standing intention he is failing to work properly).

The example just described is a case of acting against one's better judgment or verdict by deciding against one's better judgment (the original decisiveness) and is a weakness of the legislative will. Our second example is a case of acting against one's better judgment not by deciding against it but by being ineffective in prosecuting it (a weakness of the executive will). Again suppose the person has decided not to take Mary's sandwich and has formed an intent. Suppose again that a desire for it arises in him but this time it retracts or withdraws his intent by diverting motor readiness along a different path, the path for snatching the sandwich. Whereas in the first example he discerns being tempted to take the sandwich in this case he feels drawn to take it. Because the desire doesn't disturb his acting morally by being a new reason that instigates returning the processing to not-yet-decided mode, we can call it a non-Scanlon desire. The source of the fault is that the diversion of motor readiness wasn't countered by re-settling on the original decisiveness thereby diverting motor readiness back along the original path and then holding steady to that decisiveness (to "pump' or infuse enough energy to ensue in action). But this is again to say that the source of the fault is in the processing that is his presence as himself in consciousness. The fault is that he didn't try hard enough or make enough of an effort (he didn't re-settle and hold steady) to resist the desire. The ascription of responsibility would be that he could have avoided wrong if he had tried harder not to let his desire take over, and the locus or target of the ascription is indeed the person himself.

A person who does wrong can be held responsible for failing to deliberate at all on the occasion. It is no excuse for taking Mary's sandwich that it was done completely on impulse. The question is how can the person himself be thus held responsible when on the occasion he himself was not consciously present (there was no discernible dynamic processing going on)? This case parallels to an extent the case of holding a drunk person himself responsible for hitting a pedestrian with his car although at the time he is "not himself." It was the person himself previously who decided to drink. Part of the deliberative character of a moral person is that he checks his impulses by moral considerations. Equivalently impulses to do what is wrong call up in him his being present as himself to keep from acting on them. In other words part of good moral character is to know when to become present in consciousness as the cause of deliberating. In the case at hand then we are holding the person responsible for bad moral character. Suppose that the source of that character is his previous failure to think hard and well enough of the need to check his impulses and how he could be reminded to do so. At this source he himself is present in consciousness and so it is the person himself who is to be held responsible for doing wrong on the later occasion by not being present. This leaves open issues of whether and in what sense we ourselves are *ultimately* responsible for our moral character—issues to which we now turn.

CHAPTER 9

Freedom, Ultimate Power, and Ultimate Responsibility

So far the claim has been that the capacity to pursue happiness requires the capacity for a person himself to determine his actions in accord with reasonable and effective deliberation. This makes the person himself the source of his deliberative action but leaves open whether and in what regard the capacity to pursue happiness requires a person to be an ultimate or original source—the issue so forcefully pressed by Kane (1996). The contention of this chapter is that there is a kind of ultimacy required for the capacity to pursue happiness. For reasons that will become clear I call it inter-subjective—availability ultimacy versus intrinsic-existence ultimacy. The contention is that by adding such ultimacy to the conception of freedom we get a conception of inter-subjective freedom that is both necessary and sufficient for the capacity to pursue happiness. In (i) I set out what this conception is that is required for pursuing happiness and claim that it is sufficient for our ultimately deserving to be held responsible for our actions and our character. In (ii) I defend the status of this freedom as being something real in the nature of things, and that the sense of ultimately deserving to be held responsible that goes with it, as opposed to the sense that goes with existence ultimacy, is the only significant one.

(i)

Suppose I am acting in a play that calls for my character to deliberate for the audience at various points. As I go through the deliberations I already know what they are – the reasons that come forth, when reasons become decisive, and if and how that decisiveness is effective for action. In a sense I, the actor, am estranged from these deliberations I go through. I don't look *to* myself to deliberate I look *at* myself deliberating. If I am really getting into the part and not reciting automatically from rote these deliberations indeed emerge from me myself, the presence of the self I am in consciousness, but not from my full self, my full presence in consciousness. The latter includes knowing the outcome and the deliberating remains something foreign to and unclaimed by that self. It follows that I cannot fully claim the deliberative action as my own or as belonging to me. The estrangement is not due to my knowledge that

© KONINKLIJKE BRILL NV, LEIDEN, 2014 | DOI 10.1163/9789004283213_010

it is only a part I am playing. It doesn't hold for example if I am in an impro-visational play where the characters make up their part without a script. In that case I don't look at myself deliberating I look to myself and so there is no estrangement. The estrangement that comes with being in either sort of play has to do with emotional seriousness. I can withdraw from the anger and the tragic sadness and just walk away in the middle of the performance. The particular estrangement when the script is known is that the deliberating doesn't emerge from that component of my presence in consciousness that just regards it.

Suppose now that the deliberations of the scripted character as he pursues happiness in the play are in accord with norms of reason in being open-minded to other characters' reasons and conforming to moral reasons. I then look *at* myself giving myself over to the norms. I remain estranged and so I do not fully give myself over to the norms since it is not my full self that gives itself over to them in deliberating. It follows that any self-fulfillment of one's reasoning self that comes from giving oneself over to the norms of reason doesn't fulfill me when I know the script. This self-fulfillment of reason is foreign to or fails to reach to the knowing part of myself, the knowing part of my presence in con-sciousness that is dissociated from the giving-over-to part. This same estrange-ment would hold in real life even if I am not playing a character so long as I know what the "script" of my deliberatings is prior to or apart from actually producing the deliberations.

The characterization of happiness in Part One was that the satisfaction with my life be something I could fully claim as belonging to me; something that was deeply, all the way through self-fulfilling, not just fulfilling, say, to my emotional nature where such fulfillment by itself remains something foreign to or estranged from me. It was there presumed that claiming something as belonging to what I could claim as a reasoning being would make it all-the-way-through self-fulfilling since, supposedly I am not estranged from myself as a reasoning being. But now we see that a further level of estrangement, and so failure to claim as my own, would exist if I antecedently know what the script is of my deliberatings. It follows then that it is essential for what it is to be happy (viz., to be all-the-way-through self-fulfilled) that one doesn't know what one's delib-erations are prior to going through them and making them happen.

Suppose finally that knowledge is available but I just don't avail myself of it. In this case there would still be this "could-avail" part of me, the part resisting knowing, which holds off any self-fulfillment from being complete—a fulfill-ment reaching deeply to my full self. Failing to avail and so "seeming" self-fulfilled would be like the dogmatist who fails to avail himself of reasons against his standard when he knows there are such reasons. His dogmatism doesn't deeply fulfill the dogmatic self that he is if it has to be kept up by him this way. It follows that it is essential to being happy that knowledge of how I deliberate is not available antecedent to or independent of my deliberating. If I do not in my pursuits fully own my standard of satisfaction by my deliberating according to norms of reason, then any satisfaction I may have or achieve is not fully owned. Hence for my pursuit to be a pursuit consistent with what it is to be happy requires that I by my deliberative action am the ultimate or original source of the *availability of knowing* what that deliberative action is. This I claim is all the ultimacy that is necessary for the pursuit of happiness. In particular the pursuit does not require that I by my deliberative action am the ultimate or original source of the existence of that deliberative action itself. Even if I am not the ultimate source in that sense, there is nothing in that fact by which I can do anything except look *to* myself in deliberating if the knowledge of what the source beyond me is simply not available.

As far as the pursuit of happiness is concerned it is not enough that a person be subject to or capable of he himself determining his behavior in accord with reasonable and effective deliberation. It has to also be the case that *by doing so* he himself is the ultimate or original source of the possibility of knowing the deliberative action that determines the behavior. In being the ultimate source of the possibility of knowing his deliberative action each person by his own deliberative actions is also the ultimate source of the availability of knowing those actions for all others. If knowledge were *available* to others beforehand then it would be *available* beforehand to him as well. We can say therefore that each person by deliberatively acting is the ultimate source of the inter-subjective availability as far as knowing is concerned of his deliberative actions. But now it is the inter-subjective availability of deliberative action by which the action is open to others' reasons and so is subject to the norm of reason that requires open-mindedness. It follows then that if each person by his deliberative actions is the ultimate source of the inter-subjective availability of those actions then he is also by his deliberative actions the ultimate source of his giving himself over to reason by his actions and hence an ultimate source of his self-fulfillment as a reasoning being in so acting. To be deeply or completely self-fulfilled without estrangement in one's deliberatively acting is at the same time by so acting to be an ultimate source of being fulfilled as a reasoning being, and both of these together are necessary for what it is to be happy.

One may object that ultimacy as to availability is trivial since it is true of any phenomenon in nature that is not predictable that it is only by its happening that it is inter-subjectively available as far as knowing it to happen goes. A particular parrot in Australia turning its head to the left at a particular moment is by its action the ultimate source of any of us being able to know it to happen. The point however is not the unique or special nature of being un-predictable, but rather what this unpredictability effects. The reality of my deliberative actions being a pursuit of happiness does depend on the availability of knowing by us, or on inter-subjective availability. Without that these deliberative actions cannot be open-minded. Thus being the ultimate source of inter-subjective availability is being an ultimate source of the reality of pursuing happiness which exists with and by such availability. If it is by and only by my deliberative actions that the inter-subjective availability of knowing them exists, then it is only by them that my deliberative actions *are real as* a pursuit of happiness, and this can hardly be called trivial.

Freedom involves not just a capacity for determination by oneself of one's deliberative action, but a capacity that in some sense is original or ultimate. We have now set out what sense of ultimacy is required and sufficient for pursuing happiness – ultimacy as to inter-subjective availability of knowing, not ultimacy as to existence or happening. Extending our account of freedom as determination by the self with this sense of ultimacy we get as the definition of freedom that is necessary and sufficient for the capacity to pursue happiness the following:

(1)   A person acts freely if his action is subject to being determined by deliberations that he himself causes and determines to be reasonable whereby his deliberatively acting (whether reasonably and effectively or not) he is the original source of the inter-subjective availability of his deliberative action.

The definition incorporates the fact that if it is not predictable what a person's deliberation is then it is not predictable whether it is reasonable and effective or not. I call such freedom in (i) inter-subjective-availability freedom and sometimes availability freedom for short and sometimes inter-subjective freedom for short to contrast it with freedom that incorporates ultimacy in regard to the existence of the deliberative action itself as follows:

(2)   A person acts freely if his action is subject to being determined by deliberations that he himself causes and determines to be reasonable and (whether his deliberative action is reasonable and effective or not) he is the original source of his deliberative action existing (happening).

I call such freedom in (2) intrinsic-existence freedom and sometimes existence freedom for short and sometimes intrinsic freedom for short since it pertains to how his actions exist apart from how they are for him or any other subject. It is inter-subjective freedom that is necessary and sufficient for (indeed is equivalent to) the capacity to pursue happiness. Intrinsic freedom is not necessary for inter-subjective freedom. For example if determinism is true intrinsic freedom doesn't exist but availability freedom remains so long as our deliberative actions are unpredictable. Both are conceptions of freedom that involve the person having an ultimate power; they diverge as to whether this is an ultimate power for availability or existence. The addition of originality or ultimacy in the conception of freedom in (1) brings with it an incorporation of ultimacy as to holding each other responsible. Previously we claimed that the person himself is to be held responsible for his faulty deliberative action because he himself is the source of that action and the target or locus for being held responsible is the source of the fault. If a person acts freely in the sense of availability freedom then if his deliberative action is faulty he himself by so acting is the original source of the entry of the fault into the enterprise of the pursuit of happiness. Nothing in the course of events prior to his so acting makes that fault discernible or available for his being held responsible. That it was already determined that the fault would happen is beside the point. It is only when faults are discernible that anyone can be held responsible. If there were some particular occurrences previous to his action which enabled us to know the fault would arise, then we could hold their occurring responsible for the fault which puts the pursuit of happiness on hold. But if he acts freely as in (1) there are no such previous occurrences. It follows that it is the person himself by his deliberative action that is originally and ultimately to be held responsible. He is the ultimate locus for being held responsible (whether he is in fact held responsible or not). The point is not that he is to be held responsible for originally making the fault available. He is still being held responsible for the fault itself since that is what holds up the pursuit and needs to be rectified. The point rather is there is nothing previous to his deliberative action to target as the source of his fault.

This sense of a person's being originally to be held responsible by his free faulty deliberative action does not require that he categorically could have done otherwise. As in our previous discussions it is only the capacity to have done differently or better that is called upon in holding the person responsible to rectify the fault in the moral case or to consider further reasons in the prudential case. As in our previous discussions the objection that he isn't "really" or "validly" to be held originally responsible since he couldn't flat-out categorically have done otherwise would only work if his being held responsible would be unfair or undeserved if he couldn't have done otherwise. However not only isn't it unfair or undeserved, but it would be unfair not to hold him responsible.

It would disrespect his pursuit of happiness. If deserving to be held responsible for faulty deliberative action is secured simply by my being a member of the enterprise of pursuing happiness the question is how ultimacy in any sense matters for desert. What has always driven the idea that ultimate responsibility is significant is that only so is a person "truly," "really," "deeply" deserving of being held responsible.

Suppose then that I am held responsible and I take up the responsibility by rectifying the fault and that I know all along that this exchange is going to happen in this exact way—again as if I am performing a scripted play. Then I am estranged from the exchange. The source of the fault is the deliberating self-not the self that looks at all this happening. Hence I am not deeply or fully at fault. Since the target that is held responsible is the source of the fault which again is not my full or complete self, I am not deeply or fully held responsible by others. Nor am I deeply or fully charged to take up the responsibility since it isn't my full self that is to be the source of rectifying or doing better. Furthermore, predictability estranges me from complete self-fulfillment altogether. Because it does, what goes by the name of the pursuit of happiness would only be a pursuit of incomplete, shallow self-fulfillment. Hence there is nothing to be deeply held responsible for since the fault only damages the pursuit of shallow self-fulfillment. My being held responsible, that is, is not something that I *deeply* deserve since it doesn't respect and care for my pursuit of happiness (deep self-fulfillment), but only "respects" my "pursuit" of a shallow and estranged fulfillment. In this manner the fact that I by my deliberative actions am the ultimate source of the availability to myself and others of these actions is essential for my being deeply, fully deserving of being held responsible.

The conception of freedom in (1) is a version of compatibilism since it is consistent with determinism being true. Unlike other versions of compatibilism it takes the issue of whether we are ultimately responsible to be a decisive one. It is this issue (Kane 1996) which drives the incompatibilist libertarian conception of freedom in (2). The libertarian is correct that there is no genuine freedom and responsibility without ultimacy but that properly understood the only ultimacy relevant to genuine desert is in regard to availability, not existence, an ultimacy that can be incorporated by a version of compatibilism.

Turning now to the issue of character, a person's moral character is not just how he tends to act under various conditions but how he tends to deliberatively act—to reason, decide, and effect decisions either generally or under certain conditions. It includes whether he tends to consider moral reasons in deciding how to act, whether he makes them salient enough to be decisive, whether he uses his imagination, whether he is alert to his weaknesses, whether he gets himself to try hard enough to resist them and so on. All this constitutes the nature of his commitment to morality. It is the person himself by his deliberative actions over time who originally makes his moral character inter-subjectively available. We cannot predict what the character of his particular deliberative actions will be-what reasons will emerge with what force, etc. and so we cannot predict what the general features are of his deliberative actions. The only way of knowing his moral character is by generalizing from his ongoing series of deliberative actions. Hence he himself by those actions is the ultimate source of the inter-subjective availability of his character. If we think of character as a disposition of the person then so far as inter-subjective availability is concerned it is a thin or sheer disposition; a disposition apart from the underlying structure and processing by which the disposition exists or is explained. We don't know it by what underlies it but only by its manifestations. Without hyperbole it can be said with Sartre that so far as being inter-subjectively available goes the person creates his character out of nothing but his own free deliberative actions, which is a case of existence preceding essence. This pertains to everything about his character including how flexible or rigid the person tends to be, since everything about his moral character is to be found only in the series of his free deliberative actions. Because it is the person *himself* who deliberatively acts it follows that as far as inter-subjective availability is concerned it is the person himself that is the source of his character. This doesn't mean that the person has to first be character-less in his deliberatively acting in order to fully originate the availability of his moral character. That might be the case for a power to originally determine the existence of his character. If so, then such a power is impossible since any deliberative action has to already have some character or other—good or bad reasons were considered, etc. A person being the source implies only that the person in deliberatively acting always with some character doesn't determine the availability of his general character until he deliberatively acts over time.

If a person has availability-freedom then his deliberative action isn't predictable. Hence even if his character that is so far available is of a certain sort that doesn't settle, in the sense of make available, what his next deliberative action will be or what the series of his future deliberative actions will be. This is true even if the underlying brain-processing that is the basis of his dispositional character is deterministic. It follows then that so far as inter-subjective availability goes a person's character so far never settles how he will deliberatively act and never settles what his deliberative action will be in the future. It is only the person's subsequent deliberative actions that determine whether his character changes or not. The person himself then by his free actions has ultimate power to settle whether his available character will change. In this sense Sartre is correct—the person's free deliberative actions are not fixed or settled by his character—he can, by his choices, alter his character (another case of existence preceding essence). If a person acts with availability freedom, then the kinds of predictions we make based on his past free deliberative actions are only as to what is probable or likely. The availability of such predictions doesn't estrange us as does the availability of the script in performing a play because they still leave us looking *to ourselves* in deliberatively acting. The prediction leave open that knowing how I have been in the past can influence me now not to continue that way. It is these kinds of predictions that we ordinarily make of one another's character in everyday life when we regard each other as being free as opposed to being unable to reasonably deliberate and effect decisions. Even if determinism is true anything more than such predictions is not to be gotten by scientific explanation. The complexity of the relevant factors again precludes the prediction of individual deliberative actions even with past character added.

A sort of original or ultimate responsibility for our moral character goes with the authority over our own character that goes with availability-freedom. As in Chapter 8, we don't just hold people responsible for doing wrong. We hold them responsible as well for having bad moral character, for generally giving into temptation too easily, not considering carefully enough the moral implications of what they do, for not deliberating in the first place when needed to avoid acting impulsively, etc. Bad moral character puts a hold on the enterprise of pursuing happiness as a threat likely sooner or later to lead to damage even if on the occasion the person did no harm because he was lucky or because someone intervened. In holding a person responsible for a particular wrong action we provide an input of how things could have gone better so that he can take-up responsibility for repairing it by incorporating that input (Chapter 8). Thus we say "You might have avoided stealing if you had considered how hurtful it is to Mary." Similarly in holding a person responsible for a defect in his moral character we provide him an input so that he can take up responsibility for removing the defect from his character by incorporating that input. To improve moral character is to make the standing intention by which deliberative action is controlled (Chapter 8) more effective, either by making it more likely to activate when needed or by making it more likely to be effective when activated. The inputs then are directed toward the person's standing intention in one of these ways. Assuming that the person already has a standing intention to bring up considerations against egoistic reasons the input might be – "You could have avoided stealing if you hadn't been so quick as to fail to consider how hurtful it is to Mary." This input, supposedly, makes the standing intention the person already has more likely to activate and thereby to improve his moral character by removing a defective component. Alternatively the input might be – "You could have avoided stealing if you had really imagined how hurtful it is to Mary." This input, supposedly, makes the standing intention the person has to bring up non-egoistic reasons more likely to be effective when it is activated.

If a person is acting freely then his doing wrong is a matter of there being *some* defect or other in his controlling capacity to determine his actions to be in accord with reasonable deliberation. Simply taking up responsibility and repairing the damage of his wrong action at least begins to repair that defect as well. Hence in holding a person responsible for his wrong action we are in this way always as well holding him responsible for a defect in his moral character. It is for this reason that the person who does wrong is *specifically* the one to be held responsible for repairing the damage. It is his pursuit of happiness in particular that needs repair as far as character goes. Anyone else might repair the damage of the wrong act, but it is only by his repairing it that the further damage of his defective character likewise at least begins to be repaired.

As in Chapter 8 for a person to be held responsible for his character he must have the capacity to take up that responsibility to repair the defect. It isn't the input which first gives him that capacity. An entire complex capacity isn't instituted by being told how to do better. Hence he must already have had the capacity in order to be held responsible. But now that capacity is just the capacity to develop the resources for controlling his deliberative actions which (as in Chapter 8) is part of what it is for him to be free. Hence only a person who is free can be held responsible for his character.

The locus or target of holding a person responsible for defective character is the source of the defect. But that (as in Chapter 8) is the person himself as a presence in consciousness over time. Hence it is the person *himself* that is to be held responsible. It should be clear further that the person deserves to be held responsible for his defective character since being so promotes his pursuit of happiness. It removes the damage to his commitment to acting in accord with the norm of morality and so the norm of open-mindedness.

Finally now the person himself is the original or ultimate available source of his faulty character. Since in so far as inter-subjective availability is concerned his character is a thin disposition of his determined only by its manifestations in previous faulty deliberative actions, the ultimate source in relation to holding responsible is the person himself over time. We conclude then that it is the person himself that is ultimately held responsible or is the ultimate target of being held responsible. Of course this is true only if the person is free and it applies only to his deliberative character. It doesn't apply for example to his emotional character. There may be nothing at all about his deliberative action which determines that character. It may be that no matter how carefully he has been in his deliberative action he could not have altered his passionate nature. If he is free however his could have had a deliberative character which didn't give in to that nature, and so he ultimately is to be held responsible for his characteristic failing of letting his passionate nature get the best of him. If that nature is overwhelming in the way the passion of the compulsive hand-washer is for washing his hands, then he is not capable of resisting that nature by better deliberative action and so is not free and hence is not held responsible for his deliberative character in that regard at all. This is not the case for the highly passionate person for whom it was only harder to be the ultimate source of good moral character. To be the ultimate source of good moral character then doesn't require either being the ultimate source of whether one is free or not or the ultimate source of how difficult it is to exercise one's freedom. Each of these is a matter of good fortune – a gift of our genetic make-up and upbringing.

Following the discussion above of being held responsible for particular deliberative actions, since it is the person's full and complete self, not an estranged part, that is the source of his moral character the person himself fully and completely is held responsible for his moral character. Finally since what he is held responsible for is repairing a defect in his pursuit of deep, rather than shallow or estranged self-fulfillment, the person himself fully and deeply deserves to be held responsible; it is due to him fully and deeply, not due to an estranged part of him. Thus if a person is inter-subjectively free it follows that he himself by his free deliberative actions is and deserves to be held responsible for faulty moral character, and this is true whether or not he is the ultimate source of the existence of his deliberative actions.

(ii)

We consider now whether the inter-subjective freedom that has been claimed to be necessary and sufficient for the capacity to pursue happiness is something that belongs to the true nature of reality or something that exists only in relation to ignorance, merely as a practical necessity, or merely from a phenomenological perspective. We consider these three contrasting characterizations in turn. This issue turns mostly on what it means to belong to the true nature of reality. It arises particularly for inter-subjective freedom since intrinsic freedom if it exists clearly belongs to the nature of things defined as it is apart from any relation to our knowledge, to our practical pursuits, or to a phenomenological point of view.

Spinoza says that we *think* we are free because we are aware of our deliberations, choices, and efforts but not aware of the causes. Taking him to mean by
this that we are unaware of what causes our deliberations rather than unaware
that they are caused, it follows that for Spinoza the ignorance of what causes
our deliberative action is not part of being free but only what makes us think
that we are free when we really aren't. Inter-subjective availability freedom
for Spinoza then would only be a case of thinking we are free. Note that the
ignorance involved is not a matter of failing to know what we can know.
Knowing the causes in order to predict deliberative action is unavailable to us;
we lack the capacity to know the deliberative action prior to its occurring.
Watson (2004;214) says,

> Indeed it is hard to see how a designer could determine a creature's
> thought and action without designing a whole world.

His point equally applies to predicting. To be able to predict whether and how
John will deliberatively act next Tuesday requires knowing what brain processing that underlies such action will then occur which in turn requires knowing
what his circumstances have been and will be, what inputs to that processing
there have been and will be, and how these inputs figure into that processing.
We have to predict pretty much John's whole world. This requires predicting
whether or not he will meet Mary who will give him some information or
encouragement and so in part we have to be able to predict Mary's world as
well making Watson's point applicable to predicting. We can no more predict
the deliberative process unto action that John goes through than we can predict the creative process a deliberate as opposed to spontaneous painter goes
through unto the production of his painting. The free person's deliberative
action might not be as artistically creative in what goes into it and what product (behavior) it ensues in, but there is a lifetime of details of experience, inputs
by life and by others, and developmental features of brain-processing that goes
into deliberative action making it complex enough not to be predictable.

The conception of inter-subjective availability freedom in effect then is that
we are free relative to the non-omniscient beings that we are. For Spinoza the
true nature of reality is as it is grasped by omniscience. This is just part of his
rationalism. Hence for Spinoza our inter-subjective freedom would not be part
of the true nature of things. Setting aside this over-zealous rationalism, what
can still be said is that the conception of availability freedom is that it is something relative to the kind of beings we are. Hence it is no part of the true nature
of things which pertains to how they are intrinsically apart from any relation to
how we happen to be. However, our being the kind of beings that we are and

certain things being so only relative to that is altogether itself something intrinsically so and hence part of the intrinsic nature of things. What is true is that there could be a kind of being in relation to which we by our deliberative action would not be the ultimate source of the availability to him of that action.; e.g., an omniscient deity. This would show that our freedom was not absolute in the sense of something that exists relative to all possible beings, not that it doesn't belong to the true nature of things. Even the omniscient being would admit that we in relation to ourselves are free. The fact that if we were each omniscient there would be no inter-subjective freedom doesn't imply that our freedom isn't part of the true nature of things any more than the fact that if we were each omnipotent beings there would be no immoveable mountains implies that immoveable mountains are no part of reality.

There is an ambiguity in the idea that the true nature of things exists in how things are to an omniscient being. Omniscience might mean having a complete theory of things from which all causal laws can be derived or it might mean in addition knowing enough of the circumstances and initial conditions to be able to predict everything. The former means that everything is explicable while the latter means that everything is predictable. It is only the former I claim that is pertinent to the true nature of things. The latter pertains to the nature of the being that has such a theory. The true nature of reality is only how it is to an omniscient being in the former sense. It would be the same whether or not there is or could be an omniscient being in the latter sense. Our conception of inter-subjective freedom allows that everything be explicable and so even the complete theory of things that explains the entire causal nature of things would leave such freedom intact. It is false that inter-subjective freedom is relative to something less than the true nature of things.

Any conception of freedom will have it be something that exists from or within a practical point of view. Not every conception however makes it something existing only from such a point of view. The contention that we act under the idea of freedom for example allows at least that it exists only in idea, not as part of the true nature of things. This is not the status of inter-subjective freedom. In particular the conception of inter-subjective conception is not that we act under the idea that we originate the existence of our actions; viz. under the idea that we are intrinsically free. We can know full well for example after a person by deliberatively acting has made that deliberative action available that he couldn't have done otherwise than that, that it was determined that he would so act that very way and so thereby make that very action available. Our conception of freedom doesn't require acting as if determinism weren't true. Rather we in fact find ourselves unable to avail ourselves of a person's deliberative action except by their so acting. Further there is no dis-harmony between the practical and the theoretical point of view. The latter is the "point of view' of explaining or understanding the nature of reality, not per se of Laplacean prediction. We miss nothing of the theoretical point of view by failing to be able to predict everything. We think we understand the nature of how each leaf in the world moves about in the wind without being able to predict it. It is compatible with our conception of inter-subjective freedom that it be as explicable as any other phenomenon.

Nor is the thrust of inter-subjective freedom that we *must inevitably* deliberatively act under the idea of freedom, thus justifying it independent of whether it is something real or not. Indeed (contra Kapitan 1986) I denied that we must deliberate under the idea of inter-subjective freedom when I talked of performing the deliberative actions called for by a script. The point was that I couldn't so deliberate without a certain estrangement from myself. What is true is that our "practical" relation to one another would be drastically altered if we could predict each other's deliberative actions. We would each be like books (biographies) to one another and to ourselves in that we each could shift back and forth along the stages of each other's lives as well as our own in the way in which we can shift back and forth between the pages of a book, rather than knowing each other only as or when we live and deliberate. It would all be like a gigantic play with each of us knowing everyone else's part. We wouldn't fully engage each other or ourselves in the course of living for being able to circumvent such in-course engagement by "reading off" each other's script at any point past or future. It is hard to fathom what this would really be like, but the defense of inter-subjective freedom is not that we must act under the idea of such freedom because we can't fathom acting how it would be without it. Whether we can fathom it or not is irrelevant to the fact that we are inter-subjectively free. The defense of inter-subjective freedom being the kind of freedom we want, the kind worth having is that it is necessary for our existence as practical beings that pursue happiness. This defense however is not its reality. Inter-subjective freedom is a real phenomenon (part of what takes place in accord with the nature of things).

On our account originality or ultimacy and hence freedom exists only within a phenomenological perspective. By a phenomenological perspective I don't mean how our own mental goings-on introspectively seem or are to us, but rather how the world seems or is to us as we are engaged with it. We are free in relation to how it is for us in dealing with our lives in relation to one another. It is phenomenological in the Heideggerian (1962) sense of being relative to our being with others in being in the world. We are in the world as living our lives in a pursuit of happiness that involves each of us being a member of the enterprise who, so far as the availability of knowing goes, originally make available contributions to this enterprise by our deliberative actions. This constitutes a social and existential phenomenological perspective not, as Husserl's transcendental phenomenology seems to be, a perspective of stepping back and bracketing our being. The pursuit of happiness is always immersed in the ongoing unfolding of nature. Following Merleau-Ponty (1962) what makes it a phenomenological perspective is that it is descriptive of how we live, not explanatory. In the continental tradition the phenomenological perspective is fundamental to the true nature of reality—that all Being is fundamentally Being-for-us encompassing within it the theoretical explanation of our being as itself a further way of our being. Because this perspective is all-encompassing as to what-it-is-to-be-real any freedom that exists within this perspective is *fundamentally* part of the nature of things.

The reality of inter-subjective freedom does not depend on this last claim that all that is has reality only in relation to our being in the world. I believe this claim is a mistake about the phenomenological perspective and a mistake even from that perspective. The way it is to us in being in the world is that our being in the world is not fundamental to what it is to be, but that it, like everything else, is part of an intrinsic reality from which, and on the basis of which, it (our being in the world) has any reality or being. Further this intrinsic reality is grasped by us theoretically in attempting to explain the causal unfolding of things including explaining our being in the world. Although grasped by us, it is grasped as being in its intrinsic nature fundamental to our being, including our theoretical grasping being. The pertinent point for our purposes is that the reality of inter-subjective freedom doesn't depend on this last claim of the phenomenologists which would make the inter-subjective freedom that exists within the phenomenological perspective not only real but more fundamental than the explanatory order of things. All that the reality of inter-subjective freedom requires is that going beyond the phenomenological perspective to the explanatory order of things is not a matter of having a "transcendent-observer-status" that predicts the intrinsic unfolding of reality; a status which would enable us in thought to shift back and forth along each other's biographies and so estrange ourselves from our engagement with the world and each other. Even if the nature of things, ourselves included, as theoretically grasped is more fundamental than how it is to us in being in the world with others, inter-subjective freedom remains real so long as that explanation is consistent with explaining our being in the world with others with such freedom. The conception of inter-subjective freedom substantially overlaps with Merleau-Ponty and Sartre in implying, for example, that we choose our own character including whether it is changeable or not and that this deliberative choice is from nothing other than the choice itself. Nevertheless there is almost nothing of the debate over free-will and determinism in this continental tradition, since the explanatory order of how things unfold cannot possibly undercut the more fundamental reality of the non-explanatory perspective within which freedom exists. Once we abandon this claim of fundamentality the issue of the compatibility of freedom with the explanatory order cannot be side-stepped.

In sum we have set out a conception of ultimacy and so freedom according to which freedom is a power *in regard to* availability for knowing, and so availability for entering into the enterprise of the pursuit of happiness rather than a power in regard to existence. Such freedom, unlike existence freedom, is relative to "ignorance" (the incapacity to know occurrences in any other way than by their occurring), is a freedom in regard to our existence as practical beings, and is a freedom within the phenomenological perspective of how it is for us in living our lives. The claim is that none of these facts about inter-subjective freedom make it something less than fully ontologically real, because none of these facts by themselves take it out of the true order of things— the order according to the theoretical-causal explanation of the unfolding of things. Since its being real doesn't depend on any doctrines such as the primacy of the practical reason or the pre-eminence of the phenomenological perspective, the conception of inter-subjective freedom cannot be criticized as having, unlike "real" intrinsic-existence freedom only an ersatz reality. This leaves the issue of what sort of explanatory order of things is or isn't consistent with inter-subjective freedom.

Determinism per se is consistent with an ultimate power by our deliberatively acting to make that action available for the pursuit of happiness. As per van Inwagen's consequence argument (1983) it may not be consistent with an ultimate power to deliberatively act (existence-freedom), but that argument doesn't hold against availability-freedom. Even if I have no power over the laws of nature and the past I have ultimate power over their implying my deliberative actions *being* available, since it isn't until I deliberatively act that it becomes available. Even if, following Pereboom (2001), there is manipulation of my brain-processing by a neuroscientist pushing buttons which determines my deliberative actions I still have the ultimate power of availability-freedom so far as that determination is not predictable to the neuroscientist or anyone else. In this case the explanation of my deliberative actions is a "larger brain" that partly extends outside my skull to include a machine with a person pushing buttons. It is true as Pereboom contends that this explanation seems incompatible with freedom and responsibility since I am being manipulated even if blindly. However the reason is that in this case it seems improbable that my deliberative action has, say, the biographical continuity necessary for freedom (for deliberative actions to be reasonable in the sense required for the pursuit of happiness). It is unlikely that such blind fidgeting with brain-processing would leave intact the relevance of past reasoning and experience to my deliberative actions. If it does, however, then contra Pereboom there is no semblance of this explanatory order being incompatible with freedom. What difference does it make how scattered my brain is? Of course even without manipulation the natural course of things might sever or damage this biographical component, among others, of freedom, but so long as it isn't damaged availability-freedom is not jeopardized.

There is a certain kind of determinism that is incompatible with availability-freedom. If my deliberative actions are determined independent of inputs of considerations by others, including when they hold me responsible, then even if my deliberative actions aren't predictable I have no power to determine my behavior to be in accord with *reasonable* deliberation which is deliberation open to or sensitive to others' reasons. Hence I have no power to make them available for the pursuit of happiness. What Wallace (2006) calls psychological determinism is just this kind of determinism. An example would be motivational psychologies that explain our reasoning and decisions as determined by a motivational make up that is fixed in the sense of not variable according to input of reasons. If the explanatory order of things conformed to psychoanalytic determination of my deliberative action that would be incompatible with any freedom. The only difference from cases of ongoing compulsions would be that I wasn't aware of the reason-destroying forces and everyone would be under this hidden compulsion. There could as well be sociological and biological versions of this kind of determinism. It may also be that it is not an all or nothing affair – that determinism leaves us to some extent open to reason and in other ways not. Our freedom would then be limited to this extent.

Finally if the explanatory order of things is in-deterministic in the sense that the laws governing things are probabilistic ones, this would mean that I have at best a capacity to probably determine my behavior to be in accord with reasonable deliberation. This would be a modified or lessened version of availability-freedom, although as far as existence-freedom goes this would first give us any ultimate power in our deliberative actions. To see what in-deterministic unfolding implies, suppose that a copy machine produces copies by a process that includes an in-deterministic component at a particular stage, but that it most often produces good copies because of the component being very likely to go one way rather than another. The machine then has no power to determine that a good copy is produced. There is nothing in the machine's workings that guarantees a good copy and so in this sense the machine has no capacity to determine that a good copy will emerge. We would still hold the machine responsible (jimmy it up) for a bad copy even if all the deterministic components are working well if so holding it responsible increased the likelihood of the in-deterministic component working well. The person whose deliberative process isn't working optimally would likewise be held fully responsible for doing wrong if so holding him responsible increased the likelihood of avoiding the further wrong of failing to repair the damage his wrong action has done. Presuming that with determinism the repair is determined by being held responsible, our holding each other responsible would proceed just as it does when determinism is true, although it would be less effective in repairing damage. In such an in-deterministic world the modified or lessened version of availability freedom and the lessened effectiveness of holding each other responsible that goes with it would all be necessary and sufficient for a somewhat less effective enterprise of pursuing happiness. In a more random world where in-deterministic processes are not likely to yield good copies over bad ones and are not subject to improvement by being jimmied with there would be no enterprise of pursuing happiness. Hence there would be no making one's deliberative actions available for such a pursuit, hence no ultimate power to do so and so no availability-freedom.

In sum some kinds of deterministic unfoldings of reality are consistent with availability-freedom and some are not. Likewise, some kinds of in-deterministic unfolding are consistent with it and some not. It is not surprising that when the issue is a kind of freedom necessary and sufficient for the pursuit of happiness that reality might so unfold that freedom is impossible. It is neither determinism nor in-determinism per se that would make the explanatory order of things inconsistent with the reality of availability-freedom though when it is consistent, as we have seen, it is a perfectly real phenomenon even if not explanatorily deep.

Despite the reality of availability-freedom as an *ultimate* power *by* our deliberative actions to make those actions available for the pursuit of happiness, it may seem that we have secured ultimacy simply by changing the subject. Truly significant ultimacy, it may be objected, pertains to having an ultimate power over our deliberative actions themselves. The question is what is meant by "truly significant" in this objection? Why is of ultimacy over our deliberative actions themselves the truly significant ultimacy? The significance clearly pertains to deserving responsibility. The objection is that unless we have ultimate power over our deliberative actions themselves, unless existence-freedom as such an ultimate power is real, we don't really or truly deserve to be held responsible and take up responsibility for wrong-doing and for our defective moral character.

Suppose that the course of reality determined that I deliberatively acted in a faulty manner. I am not then ultimately causally responsible for having done so. It is still the case that so far as the pursuit of happiness is concerned I am the ultimate locus of being held responsible and I deserve to be held responsible (it is to my good), and I deserve it to the full and ultimate extent (because it is to my good to that extent). Since being held responsible is not being harmed any complaint that I am being held responsible is confusion on my part of what is my true good. Similarly, as far as the pursuit of happiness is concerned I fully deserve to take up responsibility. I owe it to myself as well as others to repair the damage of my action and the defect in my deliberative character. Once the exchange of being-held-responsible-and-taking-up-responsibility is seen to be something for my ultimate good, it isn't clear what is added by ultimate causal responsibility as far as what my ultimate due is or what I ultimately deserve. There is a connection of course between being causally responsible for one's faulty deliberative action and deserving to be held responsible. The connection is that if I am not the cause of the faulty deliberative action then I don't deserve to be held responsible because there is no defect in my commitment to the pursuit of happiness and so no defect that it is all to my good to repair. What my being the cause means is exactly that it is an exercise of my capacity to determine my actions in accord with reasonable deliberation. Since determinism being true is consistent with my faulty deliberative action being an exercise of that capacity, my failing to be ultimately causally responsible for my faulty deliberative action still leaves there to be a defect in my commitment to the pursuit of happiness; a defect that, for all anyone knows whether determinism is true or not might get repaired by being held responsible It remains then all to my good (to my ultimate good) to be held responsible and so it is still what I ultimately deserve in that sense. In other words from the fact that if I am not the cause of my deliberative action then I don't deserve to be held responsible, it doesn't follow that if I am not the *ultimate* cause then I don't *ultimately* (for my ultimate good) deserve to be held responsible unless being the ultimate cause makes the desert deeper. But it is only in the availability sense of being the ultimate cause by my deliberative action of its availability that my desert is made deeper by avoiding estrangement. Similar thoughts apply to deserving to take responsibility. If I am not a cause for repairing the defect in my commitment then I do not owe it to myself or others, it does me and others no good, to take the responsibility. What my being a cause for repairing it means is that the repair is an exercise of my capacity to develop better resources for controlling my deliberative actions. Since determinism being true is consistent with the repair thus being such an exercise, failing to be an ultimate cause for repairing the faulty deliberative action leaves it that I still ultimately owe it to myself and others (it is for my and their ultimate good as to the pursuit of happiness) to take the responsibility. Again, from the fact that if I am not a cause for repairing the defect then I don't deserve (it isn't due to me or others) to take up the responsibility, it doesn't follow that if I am not an *ultimate* cause for repairing then I don't *ultimately* deserve (owe it to my ultimate good) to take up the responsibility.

Once there is no connection between ultimate causal responsibility (an ultimate causal power over our deliberative actions) and ultimately (finally, to the core) deserving to be-held-responsible-and-take-up-responsibility as regards the pursuit of happiness, it is the latter as opposed to the former that is truly significant. Hence it is the demand for ultimate causal power over our deliberative actions (existence-freedom) that changes the subject from what is significant in the unfolding of our lives to what is significant in the causal-explanatory unfolding of reality. It changes the subject from being that of who and what we each most deeply and ultimately are in the unfolding of our lives as a pursuit of happiness to being that of what we each are in the causal unfolding of things. That we may not be anything ultimately deep and significant in the latter regard is simply beside the point.

That we are conscious subjects or selves who pursue happiness as self-fulfillment of our nature, including our nature as reasoning beings that set standards, is who and what we most deeply are as persons. This implies as in Part One that giving ourselves over to open-mindedness as the norm of reason in regard to setting standards is part of what we are most deeply as persons. But then as in Part Two giving ourselves over to determining our actions in accord with morality as care and respect for the pursuit of happiness of others is likewise part of what and who we most deeply are. This implies as in Part Three that so long as we have availability freedom and independent of whether we have existence-freedom, holding each other to the core fully responsible and accepting or taking up to the core full responsibility for our moral failures is also part of who and what we are as persons; as conscious subjects who seek self-fulfillment to the core of ourselves. Not only then is a fundamental principle of morality justified, but so long as we have availability freedom, moral responsibility is real and justified.

Bibliography

Adams, R.M. (2006). *A Theory of Virtue: Excellence in Being for the Good*. Oxford: Clarendon Press.

Annas, Julia. (1995). *The Morality of Happiness*. New York: Oxford University Press.

Bloomfield, Paul. (2008). Why is it Bad to be Bad? In Bloomfield (ed.) *The Oxford Handbook of Ethical Theory*.

—— (ed.). (2008). *The Oxford Handbook of Ethical Theory*. New York: Oxford University Press.

Bok, Sissela. (2010). *Exploring Happiness*. New Haven, Conn.: Yale University Press.

Brink, David O. (2007). Forms and Limits of Consequentialism in Copp (ed.). In *The Oxford Handbook Of Ethical Theory*.

Brock, Dan W. (1977). The Justification of Morality. *American Philosophical Quarterly Vol. 14, Number 1.*

Chang, Ruth. (2004). Can Desires Provide Reasons for Action? In Wallace (ed.) *Reason and Value: Themes from the Moral Philosophy of Joseph Raz*.

Cohen, G.A. (1993). Equality of What? In Nussbaum (ed.) *The Quality of Life*.

Copp, David (ed.). (2007). *The Oxford Handbook of Ethical Theory*. New York: Oxford University Press.

Crisp, Roger. (2006). *Reasons and the Good*. New York: Oxford University Press.

Darwall, Stephen. (2007). Morality and Practical Reason: A Kantian Approach. In Copp (ed.) *The Oxford Handbook of Ethical Theory*.

Dreier, James (ed.). (2006). *Contemporary Debates in Moral Theory*. Malden, Mass.: Blackwell.

Feldman, Richard. (2010). *What is this Thing Called Happiness?* New York: Oxford University Press.

Fischer, John Martin. (1995). *The Metaphysics of Free Will: An Essay on Control*. Oxford, UK: Blackwell.

——. (2006). *My Way: Essays on Moral Responsibility*. New York: Oxford University Press.

Flanagan, Owen. (2007). *The Really Hard Problem: Meaning in a Material World*. Cambridge, Mass.: MIT Press.

Frankfurt, Harry. (1969). Alternate Possibilities and Moral Responsibility. *Journal of Philosophy* 1969, Vol. 66, No. 23.

——. (1982). Freedom of the Will and the Concept of a Person. In Watson (ed.). *Free Will*.

Freeman, Samuel. (2006). Moral Contractarianism as a Foundation of Interpersonal Morality. In Dreier (ed.). *Contemporary Debates in Moral Theory*.

Griffin, James. (1986). *Well-Being: Its Measurement and Moral Importance*. Oxford: Clarendon Press.

Hare, R.M. (1963). *Freedom and Reason*. Oxford: Clarendon Press.

Haybron, Dan. (2008). *The Pursuit of Unhappiness: The Elusive Psychology of Well-Being*. New York: Oxford University Press.

Joyce, Richard. (2008). Morality, Schmorality. In Bloomfield (ed.). *The Oxford Handbook of Ethical Theory*.

Kagan, Shelley. (1989). *The Limits of Morality*. New York: Oxford University Press.

———. (2009). Well-Being as Enjoying the Good. *Philosophical Perspectives*, 23.

Kane, Robert. (1996). *The Significance of Free Will*. New York: Oxford University Press.

——— (ed.). (2002). *The Oxford Handbook of Free Will*. Oxford: Oxford University Press.

Kekes, John. (1982). Happiness. *Mind*, vol. 91.

Korsgaard, C.M. (1996). *Creating the Kingdom of Ends*. Cambridge: Cambridge University Press.

———. (1996). *The Sources of Normativity*. O'Neill (ed.). Cambridge: Cambridge University Press.

Kraut, Richard. (2007). *What is Good and Why: The Ethics of Well-Being*. Cambridge, Mass.: Harvard University Press.

Mele, Alfred. (1995). *Autonomous Agents: From Self-Control to Autonomy*. New York: Oxford University Press.

Melnick, Arthur. (2011). *Phenomenology and the Physical Reality of Consciousness*. Philadelphia: John Benjamins.

Noddings, N. (1984). *Caring: A Feminine Approach to Ethics and Moral Education*. Berkeley: University of California Press.

Nozick, Robert. (1974). *Anarchy, State, and Utopia*. Oxford: Basil Blackwell.

Nussbaum, Martha and Sen, Amartya (eds.). (1993). *The Quality of Life*. Oxford: Clarendon Press.

Nussbaum, Martha. (2011). *Creating Capabilities: The Human Development Approach*. Cambridge, Mass.: Harvard University.

Parfit, Derek. (1987). *Reasons and Persons*. Oxford; Clarendon Press.

Pereboom, Derek. (2001). *Living Without Free Will*. Cambridge: Cambridge University Press.

Rawls, John. (1971). *A Theory of Justice*. Cambridge, Mass.: Harvard University Press.

Raz, Joseph. (2004). The Role of Well-Being. *Philosophical Perspectives*.

Rousseau, Jean-Jacques. (1968). Maurice Cranston (tr.). *The Social Contract*. Middlesex, England: Penguin Books.

Russell, Daniel C. (2009). *Practical Intelligence and the Virtues*. New York: Oxford University Press.

Scanlon, T.M. (1998). *What We Owe to Each Other*. Cambridge, Mass.: Harvard University Press.

Sceffler, Samuel. (2011). Valuing. In Wallace (ed.). *Reasons and Recognition: Essays on the Philosophy Of T.M. Scanlon.*

Scheler, Max. (1961). Hans Meyerhoff (tr.). *Man's Place in Nature.* Boston: Beacon Press.

Sen, Amartya. (1993). Capability and Well Being. In Nussbaum (ed.). *The Quality of Life.*

Sizer, Laura. (2010). Good and Good For You: An Affect Theory of Happiness. *Philosophy and Phenomenological Research.* Vol. 80.

Skinner, B.F. (1971). *Beyond Freedom and Dignity.* New York: Knopf.

Slote, Michael. (2001). *Morals from Motives.* Oxford: Oxford University Press.

Smilansky, Saul. (2002). Free Will, Fundamental Dualism, and the Centrality of Illusion. In Kane (ed.). *The Oxford Handbook of Free Will.*

Strawson, Galen. (1994). *Freedom and Belief.* New York: Oxford University Press.

Strawson, Peter. (1959). *Individuals: An Essay in Descriptive Metaphysics.* London: Methuen.

Sumner, L.W. (1996). *Welfare, Happiness, and Ethics.* New York: Oxford University Press.

Tiberius, Valerie. (2008). *The Reflective Life: Living Wisely Within our Limits.* Oxford: Oxford University Press.

Van Inwagen, Peter. (1983). *An Essay on Free Will.* Oxford: Clarendon.

Velleman, J.D. (1991). Well-Being and Time. *Pacific Philosophical Quarterly,* 72(1).

Wallace, R. Jay, Petit, Philip, Scheffler, Samuel and Smith, Michael (eds.). (2004). *Reason and Value: Themes from the Moral Philosophy of Joseph Raz.* Oxford: Clarendon Press.

Wallace, R. Jay. (2004). The Rightness of Acts and the Goodness of Lives. in Wallace (ed.). *Reason and Value: Themes from the Moral Philosophy of Joseph Raz.*

——. (2006). *Normativity and the Will: Selected Papers on Moral Psychology and Practical Reason.* Oxford: Clarendon Press.

——. (2011). *Reasons and Recognition: Essays on the Philosophy of T.M. Scanlon.* New York: Oxford University Press.

Watson, Gary (ed.). (1982). *Free Will.* Oxford: Oxford University Press.

——. (1982). Free Agency. in Watson (ed.). *Free Will.*

——. (2004). *Agency and Answerability: Selected Essays.* Oxford: Oxford University Press.

White, Nicholas. (2006). *A Brief History of Happiness.* Malden, Mass.: Blackwell.

Wiggins, David. (2006). *Ethics: Twelve Lectures on the Philosophy of Morality.* Cambridge, Mass.: Harvard University Press.

Williams, Bernard. (1985). *Ethics and the Limits of Philosophy.* Cambridge, Mass.; Harvard University Press.

Wolf, Susan. (1990). *Freedom Within Reason.* Oxford: Oxford University Press.

Index